THE BRICKS AND STICKS OF LIFE

Lillian Corrigan

Four Paw Prints Press

www.fourpawprintspress.com

Published in USA

ISBN: 978-0-9908470-0-7

DEDICATION

This book is dedicated to my wonderful husband
who is strong, wise, and honorable
and who amazes me every day.

This novel pays tribute to
an ordinary man who lived an extraordinary life.
With it, I honor him.
I celebrate this admirable individual and his journey
by intertwining present events with savored memories.

The story has been a work of love, practice, and growth.

This is a work of fiction based on a true story. Places and events have been altered to protect all associated parties. Foundational characteristics have been merged, skewed, and exaggerated for the sake of the story. Character personalities do not embody any one real individual.

ACKNOWLEDGMENTS

I would like to thank my family and friends who encouraged
this writing, as well as those special people
who notably assisted in making it happen.
You inspired; you advised; you guided; you criticized.
You were a blessing of insight and support.
As a result,
I learned; I struggled; I hoped; I grew.

My pre-readers and editors were nothing short of amazing.
I admire their wisdom and advice. I am eternally grateful.

TESTIMONIALS

"As I savored every turn of the page, I was moved and inspired. It changed the way I think about life, love, health, and loss. I've never so immersed in a book where I lost all perception of time. If I were only able to read a few books in my lifetime, The Bricks and Sticks of Life would be at the top of my list."

~ Bonnie, West Union, SC

"Move over Nicholas Sparks! Lillian Corrigan's novel of faith, family and life is a compassionate tale that makes one appreciate life's blessings."

~ Susan, Homdel, NJ

"This is one of those books that was hard to put down. When I couldn't be reading, it consumed my thoughts. It brought forth raw emotion in all forms as I completely identified with the characters throughout the book."

~ Holly, Jim Thorpe, PA

"You will find yourself captivated by this heartwarming story, and by characters written with such tenderness and care that they feel truly real. This kind of novel is not my usual fare, but once I started reading, I was hooked!"

~ Desi, Lawrence, NJ

The Joyful Mysteries of Life

Chapter 1

"Another beautiful day and the only thing missing is you, my love." Mitch Conner gazed beyond his reflection to see her face materialize in the cloudy bathroom mirror. Their love had thrived through four decades, blossoming the first time he laid eyes on her. Then, after years of struggling with illness, Mandy joined the saints in heaven. Ten years had passed while he continued loving her from afar.

"I miss that beautiful smile of yours." Standing on the cool tile in bare feet, he clicked on his electric razor. It hummed. "I think about you every day." His hazel eyes absorbed her radiant image framed in fog as he pressed the razor to his cheek. She returned his gaze, studying his high cheekbones and thinning hair. "Mandy, I remember how you loved campfires and feared grasshoppers." He chuckled. "You moaned through the daily crossword, yet never missed a puzzle... until...," Mitch's mind wandered back to that unforgettable morning thirty-four years ago.

"Uh, Mitch... I think... my water broke." Mandy's soft voice cracked.

"Wha...?" He spun to face her, dropping his tape measure on the nursery's newly carpeted floor. "The baby? Now? Wait... you *think*?"

Mandy leaned over the cardboard crib box with her right arm over her round belly. "W-well... my clothes are damp... A watery pink is leaking... and there's a lot... of pain in my... my abdomen. O-o-oow," she stuttered as a contraction thundered through her body.

"But you're not due for three months!" Mitch snatched the phone off his toolbox. "Is the baby okay?" He fumbled with the numbers.

Mandy reached for him. "Mitch, here are your keys. Take me to the hospital. Something's wrong."

He took a deep breath, the keys, and his wife's hand. Leading her out the front door at a steady pace, he escorted her into the old blue Ford. Mitch sprinted to the other side, jumped in and started the engine.

He turned, backing down the driveway. *St. Joseph, take care of Mandy and my baby. Please. Keep them safe.*

"I think it's a boy," she said, clutching the armrest.

"I hope it's one of each." Mitch sped through an amber traffic light. "I want both; we'll just have to have a whole house full." He tittered, striving to maintain his composure.

"We'll see how this one goes." Mandy looked at her husband, drinking in his nervous but happy chuckle, noticing his determined grip on the wheel. Trusting him, she tried to deny her instinct to panic.

Mitch pulled up to the emergency entrance and hurried inside. Within seconds, an orderly wheeled Mandy out of sight. Two nurses lifted her onto a gurney, plugged in monitors and started an IV line.

"What's your name, hun?" the dark haired one asked.

"Amanda Conner. My husband..."

"Let's get you settled first." The nurse checked the monitors.

Pacing, staring at the door, Mitch waited. His sneakers squeaked on the vinyl floor as he repeated his sentry walk—back, turn, forth.

After what seemed like eons, the dark-haired nurse led him to his wife. He walked in wearing a smile to hide his distress, but Mandy saw the anguish in his eyes.

"Mr. and Mrs. Conner, I just got off the phone with your obstetrician's office. They're getting a message to him right away." The nurse smiled and shut the door.

Mitch sat down. Mandy reached to touch his hand. "The baby will be okay. I'm praying we'll be fine."

He closed his eyes...

Mitch wanted to take the hurt away and do the hard work for her. Seeing her in labor was brutal; his heart wrenched. He caressed her temple, wiping a lock of sandy hair from her fair face. His emotions bounced up and down like a child on a pogo stick: desperate to help, yet amazed by her faith and courage. *I should be the strong one.*

"We didn't bring anything for a hospital stay." She glanced up at him.

He gazed into her almond-shaped eyes. "Mandy, my love, we've been without *things* before. There is no *thing* we need that we can't figure out how to get. Now, how's my little one?"

Mandy winced.

"Coming," she said in a hoarse voice, squeezing his hand.

The doctor entered the room. The next thing Mitch saw was his baby boy, smeared with birth, crying, alive, tiny and fragile. He stared in awe.

When the nurse offered him the petite bundle, tears welled in his eyes. "Mandy, I didn't think I could love you any more than I already did, but I do. Thank you for our son." He swallowed. "Just look at him."

The three cuddled for a few moments. Yet danger still lurked, as the nurse drew the premature babe from Mandy's arms. "The doctor needs to run some tests." Tears dripped down Mandy's cheeks.

"Already? No, not yet." Mitch's voice trailed off, his eyes following their angelic gift. Mother and father sat in the pale, quiet room, emotions exploding like fireworks of every color: joy, fear, hope, exhaustion... They held hands and recited a Hail Mary.

"Our little tiger will be fine," Mitch whispered.

"Mitch." Mandy leaned her head toward his shoulder. He scooched closer. "We didn't have time to decide on a middle name. I've been thinking... I like my grandpa's name, Timothy."

"Mitchell Timothy Conner." He listened to the name echo in his ears, and then glanced at his watch, twice. "Geez, what's taking so long?"

At last, the nurse came to help Mandy to the nursery. "Mr. and Mrs. Conner, your son is doing very well for a preemie. He's going to be fine with a little extra TLC, which I can see abounds in this family."

Family... Yes! No longer just a couple—a family. Mitch looked at his boy sleeping in an incubator with tubes and wires connected to his miniature body. He wrapped his arm around Mandy's shoulder. "Mitchell Timothy it is, but he's gonna prove to be a tiger—our strong, brave little Tiger."

Mandy smiled warmly. "Can't argue with that."

The nurse recorded the birth certificate: June 10, 1984, 9:05 a.m., Mitchell T. Conner, son of Mitchell and Amanda Conner. The "T" stood for Timothy according to Mandy, Tiger according to the senior Mitch.

As their boy grew, the nickname Tiger stuck.

◆ ◆ ◆ ◆

Mitch finished shaving. "Mandy, even if we have to stay here all week, I'm glad to live and work with our son. He's an amazing man. I hope he finds someone special, to know happiness like we did." He blew her a kiss and stepped out into the family room.

Tiger stood in the kitchen drinking a glass of orange juice.

Mitch scanned the shape before him—six foot one, two hundred twenty pounds, with broad shoulders—a remarkable sight considering Ti's docile entry to the world. "Morning, Ti."

"Hey, Dad. I'm just about to head out. I have to change a few lights in the cafeteria."

"Okay." Mitch nodded, stroking Daisy's chocolate fur.

Father and son were similar, yet different. Ti boasted a larger build and lighter hair. Although their hands and voices were nearly identical, the two were more alike on the inside. Astonishingly close, as if one soul in two bodies, they lived—laughing, arguing, hoping, and longing their way through life.

Ti set his glass in the sink. "Champ's been staring at the bathroom door. His belly's telling him you took two minutes longer than usual today."

"I bet." Mitch scratched Chip's chin, and gave Chase a pat.

"Were you daydreaming in there again, old man?" Ti teased.

"Hey, sixty-five's not old." Champ nudged Mitch's arm, insisting he notice both him and his appetite. Mitch's four pampered Labrador retrievers stood at attention when he turned toward the pantry. Champ pranced as Mitch presented the bowls: Chase, Champ, Daisy, and Chip.

The two men shared a small rented guesthouse, located in a quiet suburban neighborhood. With an open floor plan, the living area included a worn sofa, treadmill, large television and a perpetual layer of dog hair to cushion the thin rug. The small kitchen with light oak cabinets contained a dark wooden table and three mismatched chairs.

Mitch gathered the empty bowls and unlocked the side door. The dogs scurried down the concrete steps. After a few words and one last glance at the weather report, Ti saluted his father and walked out.

Through two overlapping shifts, Mitch and Ti maintained The Good Shepherd Pastoral Center in a partnership they'd grown to love and rely on.

Mitch continued his morning routine. "C'mon doggies, let's get ready." All four followed him to the closet. He reached for a button-down shirt, slipped it over his shoulders, and tucked it into his blue jeans. Inhaling a lingering scent of drizzle in the air, he lowered the window and gazed into the distance where promise of the sun's victory shone beyond the wet treetops. Listening to the news, Mitch emptied the dishwasher.

Meanwhile, Ti drove the short distance to work and opened the building. He pulled a wrench from his tool belt and tightened the faucet in the ladies' room. Balanced on a ladder like a pro, he replaced the burned-out cafeteria lights. In the Bishop's office, he drilled two holes and ran lines for a new ceiling fan. Ti accomplished a lot before the staff arrived.

A purebred American, Ti represented a melting pot of ancestry, including Russian and Irish, with a thick stubborn streak to prove it. Genetics left him a strong, purposeful man. Although his parents had doted on him, he'd learned hard lessons too. Amid any challenge, he'd hear Mitch's voice say, "Things don't always go your way, but if you have your family, you can manage." Ti enjoyed many adventures from amusement parks to white-water rafting, yet deep down, he was a homebody like his father. Their tiny family, their special routines, their favorite place to just be, motivated him happily through each week.

Getting a jump on a job he and Mitch would finish before the Bishop's meeting, Ti measured and marked where the new banner would hang. He swung his hammer, hitting his left thumb. "Ouch!"

◆ ◆ ◆ ◆

The orange orb climbed further above the horizon, infusing a glow into the atmosphere. Mitch escorted his canines through the side door. They spent some time in their outdoor playpen, chasing a squirrel up a tall ash tree before saying "goodbye" to their master.

"Only one more day after today before we head back to the mountains, guys." Mitch liked his work, but loved his home. As a top-notch maintenance man, Mitch could fix, rig, mount, or mend whatever the office needed. Although due at 9:00, Mitch went in early for breakfast. "Later doggies." He grabbed his newspaper and closed the door.

He sauntered into his office, sat down, scanned the headlines, and turned to the sports page. After a few minutes with his nose in the newspaper, he reached into the right-hand drawer, grabbed his screwdriver, and stuck it in his back pocket.

Joining the group in the cafeteria, Mitch sat next to Betty. Married and mother of two grown sons, Betty wanted her boys to find meaningful careers. “Last night Brad applied for a sales position at Best Gadgets.”

Cassie held her teacup in both hands. “Ah, Betty, he’s so bright; electronics is a perfect place for him. I hope he gets the job.”

Ti walked in as Rick took a swig of juice and chuckled. “Matt will be lucky to make it to twelve without another visit to the ER. Yesterday he rode his skateboard down the slide, into the pool!” Rick had two adult daughters and custody of his young nephew. With more curiosity and lives than a feline, Matt’s antics often amused them. They called him “Matt the Cat” while enjoying another “cat tale.”

Mitch snickered. “Ha! As a youngster, Ti was just as feisty. I remember him jumping off the garage roof, flying into the pool, and scaring the daylights out of Mandy.”

Ti grinned, “Yup.”

After breakfast, Mitch rode the elevator to the first floor. At exactly 8:59 a.m., just like every other morning, he sat at the reception desk in the main foyer and waited for Claire. At 9:02 she dawdled through the front door and set her purse down under the desk.

“Mitch, have you seen that sunshine?” the expert greeter smiled.

“Yeah, the sky’s really blue after all that rain.” With two fingertips, he pushed a cup an inch in her direction. “Your coffee. Light and sweet.”

Claire’s grin widened as she unlocked the top drawer where she kept her two favorite bracelets. She held up her wrist.

A year ago, Claire had suffered a stroke, leaving her without full use of her right arm. When she returned to work, Mitch had overheard her coming in. Coworkers Rick and Cassie had been talking in the foyer.

Rick grabbed the door. “Here, let me help you.”

“Oh, thank you! I feel so… disabled. I have trouble carrying things or opening a car door. It’s impossible to clasp jewelry.”

"That's a shame. I can't imagine being without my locket." Cassie touched the pendant that hung around her neck.

"Yeah, with no one home to hook them, I can't wear my favorite charm bracelet or the string of hearts my daughter gave me. I always wore them before... all this," Claire said.

Mitch turned from the elevator's open door where he'd been running a system diagnostic. "Nonsense. You bring those keepsakes here and lock them in the drawer." Every morning since, Mitch greeted Claire to fasten the bracelets that completed her outfit.

"Mitch," Claire said as he finished and guided the arm back to her, "what would I do without you?"

He patted her shoulder and sauntered down the hall to the Chapel. He went in and knelt down. *Lord, I still feel empty since You took Mandy to heaven.* He sighed. *Help Ti. I don't want him alone; I want him to find love, the deep kind. One that delights in the good and supports in the bad. He might be a handful, and that'd be my doing, but he's a fine man.*

While he prayed, Rose entered and knelt behind him. "You need a little extra guidance today too?" she whispered.

"Uh huh."

"My sister's husband passed away, leaving her with three kids. I know you've been there, Mitch. How do you cope?" Tears puddled in her eyes.

"I'm sorry, Rose." He shook his head. "When I was eleven, my dad died. Worse, my uncle took over the family business, leaving my mother and four kids with nothing to live on. It was tough."

"You were the only boy too, right?"

"Yup. Grew up quick. Being man of the house was a big responsibility."

She smiled. "I still see a lot of boy in you. But that must have been hard. I'm impressed."

"Don't be. I just did what needed to be done. Working on the farm, repairing stuff, all that was easy. But I never could quite manage the budget; still can't." Mitch glanced over to an empty pew.

"Maybe you could talk to my nephew. He's ten."

"Of course. It's cool when I get to be the angel."

"Huh?" Rose sat back, her forehead furrowed.

“When I get to make a difference for someone else. Thinking back, I wonder if all that tough stuff was somehow prepping me for later.”

“You think hardships lead you somewhere?”

“I do. Don’t get me wrong, I doubted everything when Mandy died. I was downright angry with God. But I’ve come to know that going through adversities can include gifts for our future—wrapped in old brown paper. There’s something more inside. If you’re willing to open it, you can find strength or discover your purpose.”

“You lived through losing your father, and later your wife, your home, and your business. You miss Mandy and you’ve wanted to get back to construction for years. Still, you take care of us day in and day out. And you’re pleasant, even playful.”

“Ah, that’s just to hide my longing. I’m a stubborn old guy who believes you give your best to whatever you’re doing. That’s all. Still a bit of a rebel, and kinda brazen, don’t you think?”

She chuckled. “Half charming, half wayward. No wonder you’re popular with everyone from secretary to director. We all fall for your charm.”

“I wouldn’t care much otherwise. I’ve been strong willed since I was born. You’ve heard me. When I disagree, if I can’t persuade you, it’s your problem.” He grunted proudly.

“I know!” Rose laughed. “Thanks for the talk, Mitch. I feel better.”

“Me too.” He touched her hand, stood, and left.

“Howdy.” Mitch ambled into Sister Judy’s office, holding up his favorite green and yellow screwdriver. “Brought my handy-dandy helper. We’ll have that chair fixed in a jiffy.”

“Good.” Sister Judy welcomed him, swaying her arm back.

“Nice day. How ‘bout that blue sky with those puffy white clouds? I saw one that looked like a bear cub,” he said.

“Lovely weather. But it’s not such a good day. My chair is broken, my report is overdue, and I forgot my watch.” She groaned.

“Well, you’ll be able to finish that report soon. Your chair’s just…,” Mitch tightened the screw, “about….” another twist, “perfect.” He stood. “How’s your niece?”

Her demeanor shifted. “Graduation was wonderful. Nell got an award in science! Did I show you her prom picture? Doesn’t she look like a fairy princess?" With a glowing expression, Sister Judy held the silver frame toward him. Mitch took the photograph. *Absurd. Proms are so outrageous these days. Although I understand being proud to show off family. I wonder how Ti and his bride might look in a frame like this.*

He handed the photo back. "If I was fifty years younger, I just may have been in that picture with her. Nell is a beauty."

"Thank you." She sat down. "More sturdy than ever."

Mitch entered Jackson's office. Rick and Jackson were debating the call by a new umpire in the eighth inning of last night's game. Jackson motioned for Mitch to join them.

With no concern for who could hear, or who was on which side of the debate, Mitch interjected, "That young umpire better get glasses if he intends to stay an ump for long." Jackson concurred with a nod. Mitch went to the window and fastened the latch. Mimicking the tipping of an invisible hat, Mitch left them with wishes for a good afternoon.

Later, Mitch arranged the conference room for the Bishop's meeting. He tightened the leg on the last table and glanced at his wrist—3:54. Knowing the exact time was a small dependency, but a strict one.

The door creaked open slowly, as if being peeled from its frame. Mitch peered up at a young lady with a bewildered expression on her face.

"Can I help you?"

"You must be the janitor. Point me to Youth Ministry, won't you?"

Mitch looked at her thin frame, noticing her bleached hair and bright red lipstick. "Sure. Down the hall—that way, third door on the left."

"Thanks." She turned on a pointed heel, and a waft of perfume tickled his nose. Mitch shrugged, finishing his job and his workday.

As he entered the guesthouse, the dogs greeted him with wagging tails. He escorted them to the yard, then back to the family room where he sat in front of the television. His pals nuzzled him, each vying for the two hands that stroked the velvety fur of all eight ears.

◆ ◆ ◆ ◆

Ti reached and pulled. *Forty-eight, forty-nine, fifty. Ah.* He took a deep breath and put the barbell down. Working the early shift, Ti spent Monday through Thursday afternoons at the gym. The only thing better than a long, hard workout, was a Friday trip home to the mountains.

"Here, let me help you." Ti reached for the thirty-pound weight that a young woman was trying to fit back in the rack.

"Thanks. That's not heavy for you, is it?" she said.

He shook his head. Visibly muscular, Ti had wide shoulders that tapered down to a trim waist. With light hair shaved close to his head, he resembled the good guy in a high-action movie.

"It's tough to stay in shape with my appetite," he chuckled.

"Is that why you're here every day?" she asked.

"I like my routines," he shrugged. Ti enjoyed pushing his muscles to their limits and found a sense of stability in keeping to a schedule.

◆ ◆ ◆ ◆

At 10:00 p.m., after a quiet evening at home, the two men performed their nighttime rituals. Ti walked into the sparsely decorated bedroom and checked the alarm clock. Mitch opened the window inviting the night air to join his slumber, pulled out the sofa bed, and fluffed his blue blanket. Laying his head on a firm, worn pillow, he prayed.

Dear Lord,
Thank you for this day, with all I got to do and see,
  Experiencing each event, that you generously gave to me.
Watch over those I love
  as you guide me and Ti from above.
And, please, no more catastrophe
  for our little family.

He turned his attention to St. Francis, adding to his homemade recitals.

To you my favorite saint I ask,
  find Ti a love that will last,
with all my desire to you I pray,
  just in case I ever go away.

Finally, he whispered, "I miss you, Mandy."

CHAPTER 2

Mitch started the engine and checked his mirrors before putting the car in gear. "Mandy, seeing your pretty face appear in my mirror always makes my heart leap," he said. "I wish I didn't have to leave our favorite place." She looked back at him with sympathetic eyes, as if she knew he longed to stay at the cabin. "I wish I could afford to stay here." He sighed. "If only I hadn't lost you, then our house and our business." Left behind to rebuild it all, his heart ached. Mandy smiled, sending solace. "I guess going back isn't so bad. It's not the life I envisioned, but I do like working at The Good Shepherd." He straightened his shoulders, turned the wheel, and drove south to prepare for another workweek.

With a mix of clergy and lay people, the Pastoral Center was an interesting place. Mitch had memorized every inch around and between the brick walls. He knew every occupant and most of their families as well.

The campus included the main building, a convent, a retreat house, and a Catholic school behind the large parking lot. Together the Mitches maintained all but the school. Everyone called them the M-&-m duo.

◆ ◆ ◆ ◆

As Monday dawned, Mitch dressed and fed the pups. After pouring his coffee, he checked the mail and realized he'd forgotten to pay the Visa bill—again. Despite his rigorous routines, somehow bill-paying eluded him. He wrote out a check including the late fee, stamped the envelope, and stuck it in his shirt pocket. Mitch shook his head.

"Ti keeps telling me to set reminders," he told Chase. The dog cocked his ears. "This is just between us, okay, buddy?" He rubbed his eldest pup's neck and left for work.

At the office, he checked voicemail. Sister Katarina had left a long message. “Mitch, the sink in my room is leaking. Large drops of water are making a loud plunking noise that kept me awake all night. And the water is frigid. When I brushed my teeth, it chilled me to the bone. What a waste of an important resource. Mitch, I need your help.”

Those sisters are sweet, but they sure can talk... Mitch pulled out the plumbing catalog before heading off to breakfast.

As usual, Betty, Cassie, and Rick joined the Mitches. Entering the cafeteria with her lanky gait, Betty’s flat shoes clacked on the speckled tile. Sunlight shone through long windows on the east wall.

Mitch followed. He pulled out a gray plastic chair and sat down. “Hey, Ernesto, how are you?”

“*Excellente!*” The stocky chef began concocting the day’s feast well before the workers came in, starting just after Ti opened the building.

Ti entered the room sniffing the scent of bacon and syrup.

“Hey Ti, thanks for trying the sauce earlier,” Ernesto said. “I added basil. Come. Tell me if it tastes *perfecto*.”

“Hey, you.” Cassie stepped in his way. Her black hair swished behind her shoulders. “So you want to join us for drinks on Friday?”

“Nah, I don’t do the bar scene.” Ti stepped toward the kitchen.

Cassie touched his forearm. “C’mon. There’s a new girl helping in Youth Ministry for a couple of weeks. I could invite her... introduce you?”

“The tall one with the bright red lipstick?”

“Yeah, the pretty one.”

“Lot of makeup,” he mumbled. *Not sure how much of her is real. But it might make my father happy*. “Maybe.”

“I say go,” Mitch butted in.

“Dad, please.” Ti glared at him through narrowed eyelids, and then turned to meet Ernesto in the kitchen.

“You know who I was thinking about?” Betty said, pulling out a muffin. “Millie.” Millie had been a regular breakfast attendee who’d retired last year. “And the rhyming card Mitch made for her sixtieth birthday.”

“Delicious.” Ti returned to the group, smacking his lips.

“Dad loves to rhyme. I remember that card and the line, ‘*A bit of a nudge and always teasing, still your friendship is quite pleasing!*’”

"Mitch, you're such a prankster." Rick laughed, removed his glasses, and chomped into his bagel.

"Yeah, you two have us all fooled. Everyone respects Big M like a royal and Little m as the dashing, though distracted, prince." Betty giggled.

"I think Mitch is more like the court jester," Ti said.

"Yeah, but somehow his charisma distinguishes him," Cassie added.

"Well, yeah. Who do you think taught me everything I know?" Ti pulled back his fingers. "Relying on routines, operating power tools, keeping a sense of humor, respecting good sportsmanship, standing up for what you believe, appreciating the small things, and spoiling the ones you love."

"Good boy," Mitch said, pleased with the ideals that had stuck in his son's head over the years. "So why was Millie on your mind?"

"I was thinking how jealous I am, having another four years till retirement. Millie must love Monday morning." Betty sighed.

"I sort of miss her." Mitch glanced sideways with a devilish grin. "Not sure I'll miss you though."

Playfully, Betty pouted and shook a slender fist in his direction.

Often Monday's conversation recapped the M-&-m duo's weekend away. Mitch told anyone who'd listen about the spectacular log home, the views of deep green treetops and grey stone hills, the smell of pine, and the sound of the coyotes amidst the brightest stars he'd ever seen.

"You see..." Mitch had told the tale a hundred times. "The autumn Ti turned fourteen, Mandy and I purchased a little vacation trailer in a community near Walleycito Lake. We looked forward to our Friday getaway, heading to those shores lined with colorful flycatchers, warblers resting in cottonwoods, hawks soaring overhead..."

"Their own little paradise," Ti interjected.

"Paradise?" Deirdre entered the room; her long paisley skirt swayed over flat open sandals. "The only paradise on this earth is sitting right here." Deirdre flung her head back. Her mousy brown hair swayed as she put her hands on Mitch's shoulders, persistent in her perpetual chase for his affection. "When are you going to whisk me away to your special place?" A full set of white teeth showed behind her sly smile.

"Not today," Mitch told her, as he had many times before.

"Tsk." With a grimace, Deirdre took a step back. She moved to the counter, poured coffee and walked to the door. "See you soon, darling."

"You bet." Mitch continued his conversation where he left off. "Mandy and I enjoyed the outdoors from when we were young; we used to play in the fields and swim in the creeks."

"We know, we know, you'd swing out the farthest on the Tarzan rope." Betty rolled her eyes.

"Back then, there was no such thing as watching television or playing video games. We used our imagination and made our own fun," Mitch said.

Rick nodded. "I try to get Matt outside for an hour every day."

"Good for you." Mitch put a thumb up and sipped his tea.

"Saturday was gorgeous. We took the boat out," Ti said.

"The sun rose on our right and set on the left." Mitch motioned an arc with his right arm. "You know, we get out there before the tourists to avoid traffic at docks. Timing is important," he said in a teaching tone.

"We know." Betty grinned. "I wonder if Millie misses your stories. Probably as much as having to get up for work on a Monday."

"Oooh, she got you back, Dad." Ti smirked.

Ignoring them both, Mitch continued. "We pulled the boat on shore, putting old tires under the tip of each pontoon. Ti dragged a rope from the port side to a birch tree and tied it off. I did the starboard side. We always go to the same place."

"What? You two? Hold to a routine?" Cassie laughed.

"Dad still insists on tying his end. He tripped and a branch whacked him there." Ti pointed to the inch-long red stripe on Mitch's forehead.

"That's our clumsy Mitch." Betty squinted to see his scrape.

"Yeah, yeah," Mitch moved on. "The dogs couldn't wait to swim."

"After playing, I got to fishing," Ti said.

"You catch anything this time?" Betty asked as Rick chuckled.

"I caught my one bluegill. There must be a hundred hook marks in his mouth." Ti smiled, knowing there were thousands of bluegills in the lake. "I still can't figure out how those fishermen pull ten-pound trout and walleye out of the same lake."

"Makes no sense," Mitch said.

Ti turned up his palms. "I've tried every lure they make."

"Well, maybe if you had a lady friend to take along, it might bring you some luck. If not, it could...," Betty finished with a slow singsong voice, "still be quite entertaining."

Cassie grinned with a snort. Ti's face flushed. Scooping a spoonful of granola from her bowl, her eyes met Ti's and she shrugged.

"Well, you know," Mitch said, embarrassing his son further, "I pray to St. Francis every night, hoping my son here...," he poked Ti's shoulder, "...will find the right woman to share his wacky life." Mitch lowered his eyes. "If something ever happened to me, he'd be alone."

"You're healthy as a horse," Rick said.

"Yeah, thank God." Mitch rapped his knuckles on the table. "No more than a backache now and then. Still, Ti's missing out."

Ti swallowed. "I've dated, just haven't connected with anyone." He flashed back to a conversation with their pastor a few years ago.

"Pastor, I'm lost. First Mom passes away, then my best friend moves to Ireland, and now the girl I hoped to build a life with just... leaves. I stood there like a fool; her taillights faded as she headed south with a surfer."

"I know it hurts, Ti." The pastor motioned toward the crucifix. "We all suffer. It's important to bear our crosses with faith: to accept them, pray about them, and when we're ready, move on."

"I'm jinxed." Ti sighed.

"Don't feel forsaken by women you've loved. God has a plan."

Ti looked up. The pain stung his chest. "My father says family's everything. I'm starting to feel that relationships aren't worth it."

"You don't believe that, Ti. You'll know when it's authentic. If it's God's will, there's a Ms. Right out there for you. Let's pray together."

Although Ti liked the idea of finding Ms. Right, he wasn't in any hurry. *I'm not just guarding my heart. Life's fine at the moment. Besides, how could I find someone with our crazy schedule? Monday through half of Friday, I live in a tiny guesthouse where I work early and exercise all afternoon. On Friday, I dash home for the weekend the instant my shift is over. Who could fit into that? There's no room for change, and no need.*

The ladies' giggling returned Ti to the present.

"Mitch, you should try praying to St. Anthony," Betty suggested.

Cassie nodded. "St. Anthony is the patron for finding important things."

"But St. Francis is Dad's favorite—the patron saint of animals."

Betty smiled at their predictable friends, knowing both men loved four legged critters, almost preferring other mammals to humans.

"Still," Betty reminded Mitch, "you can consider other saints who are patrons of different things. You never know..."

Mitch shrugged. *Well, why not?*

When they broke from breakfast, Rick grabbed Ti's arm. "Why don't you ask the new temp girl out?"

Ti contemplated the high-heeled girl, and pictured the aloof oval face overdone with lavender eye shadow and bright red lipstick.

"She's not my type," Ti said. "But I'll think about it. Cassie's group might invite her out with them; could be a good way to get to know her. My father seems desperate for me to date again, although he wasn't fond of the last girl. Still, maybe a date or two would satisfy him for a while."

"Can't hurt," Rick said.

"We'll see." Ti's form deflated. The idea would please his father, but something about her didn't feel right.

Rick motioned as if to elbow his ribs. "You'll have to take her out for lobster. She comes from a wealthy family on the west coast."

"You mean no burgers?" Ti laughed, concealing a slight wave of nausea.

◆ ◆ ◆ ◆

Mitch strolled to the convent. After greeting two nuns in the living room, he walked up a flight of stairs, and continued down a cream-colored hallway. He tapped on the door. Relieved, Sister Katarina opened it and reached for his arm as if to help him into her room.

If only all life's troubles could be so easy to solve. "Nice day," he said.

Katarina huffed with a hand on her hip. "Well, it will be nicer when that dripping stops." Realizing how melodramatic that sounded, she relaxed her arm and changed the subject. "How's the younger half of your duo?"

"My son's fine. We had a nice weekend at home." Mitch entered the bathroom and crawled under the sink with his wrench, bumping his head. "Ouch! So, how's your sister?"

"She's doing much better. Those spots on the x-ray were not what they'd feared. The car door was so heavy it broke her arm and caused some splintering. It will take longer to heal and reduces her movement, but it's still a much better prognosis in the long run."

"Wonderful," Mitch said.

"Thank God." She clasped her hands near her chest.

"See Sister, there's plenty to feel good about, and less to be anxious over when you stop to think." He rotated his wrench. "I'm happy your sister will be okay. Do you want to hear a story?"

"Sure, I love your stories."

"Sink's all set." He wriggled out from beneath the marble counter.

Heading into the living room, she settled into an antique leather lounge next to her mother's old lamp. Mitch followed and sat on a wooden chair.

"The summer Ti turned fourteen, he and five of his friends began working maintenance at St. John's. The boys were mischievous, or should I say, they had a 'healthy curiosity?' I had to steer them through the consequences of their shenanigans all the time." Mitch shifted his feet.

"I was working at the school. One of the boys, Tony, got caught on a fence and tore the right pant-leg off his old jeans. He was worried the other boys would make fun of him. I sat him down and told him this story over a cold soda: When Ti was about seven, he fiddled with a clogged can of spray paint. The tip cracked and royal-blue paint squirted everywhere, all over his face, hair, and clothes. He screamed '*Dad!*' I ran in, saw him, and yelled, '*Don't move!*' then hurried to get my camera. I must have snapped a dozen shots before helping him clean up. What a mess, but I had to laugh. From that, my son learned to appreciate the lighter side of prickly situations."

Enthralled in his tale, Katarina twirled her rosary beads.

"Tony started to understand how some things that seem awful might not be so bad. Then we ripped the left leg off his jeans and he had some sharp looking shorts. See sister? Sometimes how we look at a situation can make all the difference."

Mitch took Katarina's hand and squeezed as he gazed into her eyes. "It's wonderful your sister's healthy." He paused. "And your drippy sink is fixed." Mitch stood up.

"Thank you Mitch, for the repair... and the story," Katarina said.

He turned toward the window and noticed two figurines standing on the sill. She saw his gaze linger. "Those statues belonged to my grandmother. One is St. Joseph. The other is St. Anthony. I need his intercession frequently—for things I'm desperate to find."

Mitch smiled while a mystical energy flushed through him. Her final words reverberated inside his mind—*for things I'm desperate to find.*

St. Anthony again, eh? Okay my friend, will you help Ti find love?

CHAPTER 3

Jennifer rubbed her face with her favorite scented soap and splashed her olive skin with cool water. As she looked in the mirror at her blue eyes and wild wisps of curly brown hair, memories of the last few months clouded her mind. *I'm almost thirty-two. How can I still misinterpret men?*

Through the opened doorway, she could see the photo of her family hanging in the hall. *Perhaps that's why I don't get men—growing up with four crazy sisters. Mom always said I was the naïve one... Which of Sienna's boyfriends used to set me up, call me gullible, and have a good laugh at my expense every time he got the chance?*

Jen's Italian ancestry came with passionate goals, thick traditions, and good cooking skills. She recalled the movie she'd seen the previous evening, about a girl trying to find a nice guy who'd tolerate her large, zany family. *Good movie*. She grinned. Although since this recent break-up, few things caused her to smile. Over four months ago, it still hurt like last week. Her grin faded. *Shame on him; shame on me... After ten months, I thought he could be the one. What girl wouldn't fall for his charms? He knew exactly what to say, and exactly how to say it.*

She pictured the day they sat on the park bench. "Jen, you make me happy," he had said, mustering up a look of sincerity as he gazed into her eyes and stroked her fingers. "We're going to build a life together. We should plan our future." *I never liked that slimy black leather jacket that crackled when he moved.* "I'm going to be the best man I know how to be." Enamored by his suave style, she remained unaware of his intentions. *If only I'd seen the cracks in his charade, his omission of the word commitment, or the way he averted his eyes when he said 'best.'*

Jen moved in closer to the mirror, studied the kaleidoscope in her eyes, and remembered one of many heart-to-hearts with her friend, Allie.

"Gosh Al, how could I have been so fooled? I really thought he cared."

"There are people with no morals, who spend their lives manipulating others." Allie touched Jen's shoulder. "I'm telling you, this guy was a pro. He fooled me too, using his three-year-old kid! Poor little guy. Can you imagine growing up as a hook for your father to meet, swindle, and exploit women? He was a real con artist."

"I thought con men only exist in movies...fake... conjured up in a cynical writer's imagination. Ugh! He always responded to any question with just the right answer. Oh Allie, he wound up having the worst traits a man can have: lying, cheating, *and* stealing." Tears poured out from her red eyes.

Allie let her cry before responding. "I know. He broke your heart, which was already bruised enough by your ex-husband."

"I thought I'd learned to be careful with my affection. Nope. I trusted him. This guy got in, and got in good."

"Stop being so hard on yourself. Both of them hid their true colors. Jen, you take life at face value, and that's not a bad thing."

"People who complicate life with lies and deceit confuse me. I loathe those who take advantage, use, and bully," Jen sobbed.

"Give it time. We both know, deep down, you hold hope in that tender heart of yours like no one else. Find that strength, Jen. Remember how you overcame the abuse, you left, you got the annulment. You're strong. You've been strong since we met in second grade."

The residue from her failed marriage had saturated her mind like a wet blanket. But, after doubting her self-worth, Jen had worked hard to uncover herself from its smothering effects. She wrung that blanket out until it was dry, fluffy, and colorful—forming her into this Jen, now wrapped in a cloak of sanguinity.

"You would think I'd know better."

"No, my friend, I don't. I envy your bravery and your ability to see the good in everything. You're special, and there's someone out there for you. I know it." Allie's reassurances helped remedy her wounded spirit.

I'll grow from this too. Jen blinked, exhaled, and brought herself back to her morning routine. *I just have to figure people out... someday.*

The worn carpet tickled her toes as she walked to the bedroom and turned on her exercise video. *Ready, set, go!*

The instructor stood in a room with four tall glass panes that looked out over a pretty garden. *That's the kind of garden I'm going to have someday. Ha! It'll be easier to get than that family I always wanted—an amazing husband and four kids, two boys and two girls!* She tried not to think about her age or the time it would take to get to the crest of that mountain. Until then, Jen would wade through the mud and the muck of people who might not be so altruistic.

"One, two, three. One, two, three." The instructor led the workout with a loud voice that sounded a lot like Jen's older sister's. *What a loud screechy voice. I'll do my soft-sounding yoga DVD tomorrow.*

"C'mon, keep up. Left kick..." The instructor led the choreography. Jen switched feet to get back in sync. Even when familiar with the routine, she had no sense of rhythm.

After her workout, she hopped in the shower. The warm water caressed her taxed muscles. Jen breathed in the steam.

Refreshed with a cleansed body and mind, Jen walked to her room. She raised each arm into a purple T-shirt and pulled on her blue jeans.

Time to get Nate up.

Jen and her son Nathaniel lived in a quaint two-bedroom cottage. She tiptoed across the tiny landing to his room.

She gazed upon him sleeping on his stomach, half covered in racecar sheets, with his stuffed toy, Benji, leaning up against the wall as if watching over him. *God, please help me give Nate the kind of life he deserves, including a male role model with faith and integrity.*

She touched his shoulder. "Nate, time to get up."

"Already?" he grumbled.

"Yup, you've got a great day just waiting for you."

Nate blinked. He saw the sun peeking through the shades. He reached to hug her, and then hopped out of bed. "Oh yeah, I forgot! I'm going to Scott's today! I want to pack my dinosaurs, okay Mom?"

"Sure. Don't forget to brush your teeth."

Jen strived to give her son a secure, happy environment. Sacrificing conveniences like a smartphone and cable television, for swim lessons, bicycles, and books, Jen preferred doing things with Nate. She sighed every evening as she adjusted her bunny-ear antennas.

Back in her room, Jen tied her sneakers and bundled up her long curls.

"Hey Mom." Nate bounded in, full of energy. "When are you going to fix this doorknob?" He rattled the loose knob on her closet door.

"I don't know. I have to call Poppa."

"He helps us fix everything."

"I know. He helped me fix the house before we moved in. We painted all these walls." Jen pointed around the room, tinted with a soft hint-of-lavender color. "See that spot? I always stare at it."

"Hey, there's a weird smudge in the ceiling."

"Yeah, we missed it somehow." They both giggled.

"Isn't it great to be able to fix things with your bare hands? Poppa has to teach me more. All I can fix is a good meal."

"And dessert!" Nate licked his upper lip.

She tussled his hair. "See these nightstands? We rescued them from the curb. Just a little sanding and varnishing, and they still look awesome."

"Wow. I want Poppa to teach me too!"

Jen and her dad had been close until she was eight, and his employer called him away to England. Not wanting to move the girls, he insisted they stay behind with their mother. Her dad was gone for three years, with only a half dozen visits home. Jen had tried not to feel abandoned by the only family member who understood and accepted her for who she was.

Jen's father lived by a simple "this is me" doctrine, which is where she figured she got her "what you see is what you get" mentality. Jen acquired her work ethic from her mother, as well as her love of children and nervous high energy.

"Let's invite our handyman Poppa over on Saturday. Nana and your aunts are going to the city museum."

Nate chuckled. "You hate the city, Mom."

"I know. All that traffic, noise, and crowds." She inhaled with her arms stretched up. "Give me fresh air and trees swaying on a breeze!"

They both laughed.

"They're city mice, and Poppa calls you his country mouse."

"Yup. There's nothing like strolling on a gravel path along the creek, smelling the sweet scent of wildflowers, listening for deer footsteps, and watching a sunset. How about we spend Sunday out by the creek?"

"Great! Can we have a picnic?"

"Good idea. I'd better make something for Poppa if he comes over."

"We have dinosaur cake left. I'll share it with him." Nate grinned. "You make the best birthday cakes ever, Mom. Everyone said it was cool, like last year's train cake!" Nate had just turned seven.

"Maybe we should offer him food too, like dinner... then cake. Especially with Nana out for the day." She reached to tickle him. "Let's go have breakfast. Waffles today."

They headed downstairs to the tiny kitchen.

"Would you take some napkins out to the table, please?"

"Okay, Mom." Nate walked through the archway and sat at the table in the family room. Well-lit with many windows, it overlooked a small yard. "Mom, look, our cardinal's in the evergreen near the fence again."

"Oh yeah. Gosh, he's stunning."

"There goes a bunny." Nate pointed.

"How cute. I love our yard." *I'm so glad Nate has a yard to play in and can grow up in a nice neighborhood.*

"Is it gonna stay sunny today, Mom? I want us to ride bikes later."

"I know my little cyclist. Ever since I taught you to ride, you want to go every day. I woooonder if that was a mistake." She stuck out her tongue.

"Mo-om, we've been riding since I was four. It's so fun!"

"After three years, I'd think you'd be tired of it." She winked.

"You love it too." He put his hand on his hip.

Jen nodded with a smile.

The phone rang. "Hello."

"Hi Jen," Kay said. "Just checking what time you're dropping Nate off. My mom's looking forward to having the boys today."

Jen had two friends with whom she could share not only time and energy, but also her real essence. They supported each other through ups and downs, managing to laugh at themselves and grow from their experiences. Kay and Allie were a blessing. Jen hoped to find a soul mate with the same authenticity and compassion she found in her two friends.

"In about a half hour," Jen answered. "Nate's counting on it. Oh, and I want to return your movie. I watched it last night."

"Wasn't it funny?"

"Yeah, I have a lot in common with the lead girl!"

"Oh, stop. Lots of us want to meet a nice guy. I'm single too."

"But your family is normal." Jen laughed.

"Funny, Jen. Hey, are we still on for the park tomorrow after work?"

"Yup. I'll have to run past Nate's father's house to get his ball and glove. He left it there last week." Jen sighed. "I know Nate should have a relationship with his father. But I sure miss him when he's there."

"I feel the same when Scott goes to his dad's. Saturday I'm taking Scott to the dinosaur park again, wanna come?"

"Nah, we're going to cook for my dad. Besides, we went last time, so we'll hold off. Gotta watch our pennies."

"Jen, you're so good at budgeting expenses."

"Leftovers for lunch and limited shopping excursions rule!" Jen snickered then cleared her throat. "Hey, we live modestly but happily."

"How you manage with no child support, I don't know."

"Do you think I'm going to regret forfeiting child support for his college fund? I'm concerned. He's not put much in Nate's account since the divorce. It's been four years." Jen wanted Nate to have options for his future, and somehow that was going to happen.

"Nope, that's his legal responsibility. And it'll be just like Disneyland; somehow the good Lord will find a way." Kay spoke with confidence.

"Yeah, once on my own, I didn't see how I'd be able to keep my promise to take Nate to see Mickey before kindergarten. I still swear that's when it's most magical." Jen nodded, remembering.

"Who knew? One day we began chatting about the new Disney movie... one thing led to another, and there we were, sharing expenses and taking the boys together." Kay's voice encouraged Jen.

"Nate and Scott had a great time. We even enjoyed some fun and sun, despite the activity of two five-year-olds," Jen said.

"Yup, see? Just one example of something that worked out."

"Even better than we expected." Jen knew it. *Yeah, more will work out for us.* "Okay, see ya' in a bit."

Jen packed lunch, dropped Nate off, and drove to work. Her mind wandered again. *Why don't people say and do what they mean? Wouldn't that be easier? Then again, what if I'm the one with the wrong idea? It's true; I don't always seem to fit in.*

Halfway through the movie last night, Jen's mother had called. "We're going to the theater on the twenty-third. Why don't I get you a ticket?"

Jen had checked the calendar on the fridge. *Whew.* "No thanks, Mom. I have plans for a bike trip. We're going early, hoping to see some wildlife along the riverbank."

She could hear her sister in the background. "Jen's so weird." *That's me, always the odd man out.* Three sisters were outgoing; Jen was shy. They vacationed in exotic, faraway places; Jen camped. Four sisters danced; Jen preferred aerobics. They played instruments; she read.

After the phone had hit the base, Jen said, "Black sheep, signing off." *They never get me. If I didn't see my mom's smile and dad's eyes stare back from the mirror, I'd be convinced of a switch at birth.*

An optimist at heart, Jen repeated her "triumph-philosophy" as she drove down the street. *I can learn from challenges I face. Adversities can inspire growth, motivate, and fortify my faith. This recent boyfriend mess is awful, but only a setback in the overall plan. I will be strong and well again. I've got a son to take care of.*

Jen was proud of Nate, who had walked before he was nine months old, counted past twenty by age three, and started subtracting the French fries on his plate soon after. Nate's eyes were blue and his hair was light but wavy. His personality and inclinations were cloned from his mother. *Yes, he belongs to me—no possible baby switch in his case.*

After her short but pensive drive, Jen parked her faded green Chevy and walked inside. Classes had completed for the summer, so the building was quiet. She vowed to catch up on her growing to-do list. Despite her outstanding tasks, Jen accomplished much. Over the last decade, as the Computer Coordinator in a large Catholic high school, she'd grown two small labs into a campus-wide network.

She opened her office, turned on the computer, and checked her voicemail. The message dictated, "Jen, it's Sam. Our printer's not working." Jen cocked her head. *An unexpected call, but it's nice to have a little mystery in my day. I can't believe no one called about the system update again. That caused all kinds of havoc last week.*

Jen forged ahead with her day. She might malfunction when it came to relationships, but she was confident in her vocation.

About mid-morning, her phone rang. "Computer department."

"Hi Jen, it's Cassie." The Office of Education at The Good Shepherd Pastoral Center oversaw many schools, and hers was right next door. "I was hoping I could have a copy of your technology plan. I'm working with the assistant principal from St. Augustine, who's trying to meet the new regulations. I want to take sections from plans like yours to use as examples during our meeting."

"Of course. How about I stop over in ten minutes?"

"Great! See you then."

Jen opened a folder and surveyed the blue cover with pride. After the committee established the objectives, Jen had composed the twenty-three page document. She stuffed one into a manila envelope and walked out.

The office secretary pulled off her thin gold-framed glasses. "Where are you going? Over to that place?"

"Yeah, delivering a report." Jen held up the envelope.

"They are nasty over there. You know, before they built that Center, we held writing and photography classes outside, and used the stream for science experiments." She pointed out the window to the tree line.

"I know. Our nemesis." Jen raised her right shoulder, offered half a grin, and then continued across the parking lot toward the new building that almost matched the burnt-orange brick of her old school behind it. Jen observed the manicured shrubbery, which grew in contrast to those on her side of the lot. The school's bushes were unkempt with haphazard limbs, mimicking the personality of its inhabitants: young and wild.

Walking through the front door, Jen noticed that the entrance seemed brighter than its dark reputation implied. *I wonder if anyone here realizes they work in a wicked place.*

"Good morning!" Bubbling with enthusiasm, Claire greeted her at the front desk. Jen signed the visitor log. Claire directed her toward the elevator... where fate beckoned from behind the silver doors.

CHAPTER 4

The elevator doors opened, revealing two passengers. Big M held a hammer, while Little m stood behind an aluminum stepladder, leaning over it on his elbows. “Good morning,” they greeted Jen in unison.

“Going up?” Mitch asked.

“Hello, uh, yes,” Jen replied with a shy smile.

Gee, more cheerful faces, and cute too. Jen took note, and entered the tall tin box. *Why didn’t I take the stairs?*

Jen hated elevators. Trekking up and down flights of stairs kept her in good shape and away from boxes that dropped her belly to the basement. Her stomach would lag behind as she traveled in the unsteady compartment, catching back up about thirty seconds after she escaped again onto solid ground.

Oh well, I’m stuck in here now. The steely doors closed.

“Nice day,” Mitch said.

“Yes, it’s beautiful.” She felt oddly safe inside the tin box, as if their presence emitted a sense of security. Six seconds later, the doors opened and all three stepped out.

“Where you headed?” Mitch asked the guest in his building. Just as Jen opened her mouth to speak, Cassie exited from a door on the left. The light reflected off the gold clip that tethered her black hair. She carried an air of intellect, wearing black slacks and a paisley-print blue and gold blouse.

“Hi,” Cassie said. “Lucky you, getting to ride the elevator with the Mitches. They’re our maintenance guys. They take good care of us.”

Turning to Ti, Cassie asked, “Where are you guys off to?”

“Parish Life,” Ti replied. “Gotta hang a new set of portraits.”

“Have fun, you two.” Cassie turned the office suite doorknob.

Realizing her gaze lingered on the younger man’s jeans as they walked away, Jen quickly turned to see if Cassie had noticed. *Whew.* She followed Cassie through the doorway and presented the envelope. Hoping her familiarity with the forms could be of assistance, she explained, “Section two requires an outline, section five...”

Back in her own territory, Jen thought about the young man in the elevator. *I wonder who that was... with his tan face and dimpled smile, not to mention those paint-splattered jeans and tan work boots. Gotta love an attractive handyman!*

“I see you made it back from the evil building.” Jen’s coworker snarled. “Have you been inside it before? Those large glass doors and that atrium make me think they’re all, like, authoritarian in there.”

“No worse for wear. The people I met were friendly.”

“Good actors. Do you know they took not only our land, but two holidays from the school calendar last year?”

“Oh.” Jen shrugged. *There’s got to be more to it. What’s the real deal?* She went to work, spreading out her data reports, but her mind remained distracted. *Actually, I bet their people wonder about us, and we aren’t dark. These guys just miss the open space out front, and no one likes anyone telling them what to do. I bet there isn’t any truth to the prattle about the “dark side.”*

She stretched, stopped her wondering, and went back to her paperwork. *Argh, yellow is out again.* She peeked out the doorway.

“I need a highlighter.” Jen gave the department assistant her best puppy-dog face. “Pleeease.”

“You go through highlighters faster than ice melts in the desert.”

“Color keeps me organized. How else do you think I keep track of all this equipment?” Jen lifted her palms and grinned.

“Yeah, yeah. You’re lucky I like you. Here, we just got a new box.”

“You just keep me happy in case that printer jams again,” Jen chuckled. “Seriously, thanks!”

Jen laughed at herself. She was lost without color-coding. Back in school, she had deliberately chosen her notebooks: bright blue for math, her favorite subject; green, symbolic of nature, for science; and yellow, sunny and inspiring, for theology. Color helped Jen maintain harmony in her often-hectic world.

She completed her report and walked down the hall. “Hi Sam. Where’re you heading?”

“Upstairs, to work on a few windows and an outlet.”

“How do you know how to fix so much? I’m jealous.”

Sam swatted the air. “Pffwah, don’t be silly. I don’t know that much.”

“Hey, without you, none of this would work.” Jen circled her arm around the open hallway, gesturing to the lights, heaters, and utility room.

“You keep the computers working; imagine being without them.”

Jen’s eyes widened, as she considered the school having no internet access. “Ha! Yeah, that would not be fun.”

“So I guess you can say between the two of us we keep the entire operation, well... operating,” Sam said with a grin.

◆ ◆ ◆ ◆

“No way,” Mitch said, standing in the lobby waving his right hand. “You have to let the man go with dignity.”

“But, Mitch, we don’t want to lose my baby brother,” Claire cried.

“Claire, men don’t want to feel reliant; they have pride.”

“I can’t bear to give him up. Maybe if he tried a new treatment, we could have him one more year.”

“It’s a fine line, honey, between what is best for you and what is best for your brother.” Mitch touched her shoulder.

“Yes, dear, but God is calling.” Deirdre approached, adding her opinion in a sanctimonious voice.

“How do you know?” Claire said.

“Because dying is a journey to new life.” Deirdre crossed her arms.

“Are you sure?”

“Of course. Don’t you have faith?” Deirdre leaned forward with too much confidence. “You should *believe*. Heaven is our true home.”

“Oh, don’t be so insensitive.” Mitch moved between them.

“Everyone knows that paradise waits on the other side,” Deirdre said.

“It’s not that simple. Illness is complicated: there is the individual, the family, and the faith. They *all* matter,” Mitch said.

"It's all about heaven." Deirdre glared at Mitch.

"Seriously? The man has to be ready. But, if he wants to go, that's when the family should support him."

"They should advise him to go now." Deirdre put a hand on her hip.

"Dei... Oh, sometimes you can be so arrogant!" Mitch exhaled and stomped down the hallway.

Deirdre eyed Claire, and walked in the opposite direction.

◆ ◆ ◆ ◆

Ti entered the guesthouse to the enticing aroma of fried onions, kielbasa, and sauerkraut. "Can't wait for supper. After that workout, I might be hungrier than Champ."

Mitch glanced at his yellow Lab. "Not sure anything rivals his appetite."

Ti breathed in the scent. "Smells good." He looked over the pan to the golden pierogies swimming in a bath of browned onions.

"You're lucky I like to cook."

"Ha. Dad, you even like to shop."

Each Sunday Mitch attended the early Mass at St. Mark's Church in their scenic mountain town, followed just as religiously by a trip to the Walleycito supermarket. The week's menu was determined by the time he crossed the entryway. His list always started with dog biscuits and ended with a chocolate candy bar that never made it all the way home.

Ti dropped his gym bag. "C'mon doggies. It's not seventeen acres like we have at the cabin, but let's play." He herded his welcoming party into the yard. The dogs dashed after the ball, despite the confined space. After a few minutes, he brushed their coats, and then led them back inside.

Like soldiers, all four marched behind Ti to the family room where the anchor announced the evening news. Listening to the highlights, Ti called each dog, one by one, for teeth brushing, ear cleaning, and some hearty back scratches.

Mitch recapped his afternoon. "Rose needed help getting boxes of seminar materials to her trunk. There were five of them, not too heavy. Jackson called me to fix a noise in the air vent. Oh, and Cassie stopped in with news from the pound. Someone dropped off a young Shepherd."

Cassie volunteered once a week at the animal shelter and knew the Mitches were good ears for her pet-rescue tales.

"Cassie's a sweetheart," Ti said. He mumbled under his breath, "Wonder if she has a pet-loving friend."

Mitch raised his eyebrows. Acting nonchalant, he said, "There's a pretty temp in Youth Ministry, you know."

Ti noticed the twinkle in Mitch's eye. He visualized the temp's overdone makeup and couldn't shake an air of arrogance about her. His mind flashed to the scene of Jen entering the elevator. *I wonder where the girl visiting Cassie came from.* "So what else happened after I left?"

"I had to tighten Claire's keyboard tray. Poor thing is devastated. Her brother took a turn for the worse."

"That's horrible." Ti shook his head.

"And Deirdre knows how to make my blood boil! She interrupted our conversation, insisting Claire coax him to give up."

"Geez. She should know that it has to be up to him," Ti said.

"Right! She's determined that wanting heaven proves your faith is strong. Crazy." Mitch stirred the sauerkraut. "Enough of that. Later on Jackson left a message about painting the Missions office."

Ti sighed. "What? When am I going to fit in painting? Jackson knows we paint in the winter, when there's less outside work."

"They hired a new director. As usual, we have to steady the furniture, spackle holes, paint..." Mitch stopped explaining what Ti already knew.

"Well, not in my business. I'd paint rooms in a rotation... one that'd refresh every five years."

"I know." Mitch admired Ti's strong will. "You rarely agree with requests that don't follow Ti logic."

'Ti logic' was uniquely his. Ti amused himself with sharing his vision of the world. He and Mitch had no name for this pretend game, but it always started with "Not in my *blank*." Whenever something came up at work, on the news, or in conversation, Ti would offer the way he'd handle that particular thing in his office, his restaurant, his store, his town, his country, his planet, his *whatever*.

But Ti respected his supervisors. "Of course I'll make it work."

"I told Jackson we may need to bring Jimmy in," Mitch said. The two-man team managed a lot on their own, but had a solid relationship with an electrician, a plumber, and a Jimmy.

A jack-of-all-trades, Jimmy contracted tree trimming, snow plowing, and painting work. The Mitches liked Jimmy. Disheveled with day-old whiskers, unruly hair, and dark calloused hands, not everyone knew how to read him. Mitch, however, saw past his surly appearance and treated him like a well-loved nephew. "I'll give him a call in the morning."

Mitch turned as the phone rang. "Hello."

"Hey you old bugger. How's Little m, the dogs, the house, the office?" Millie asked in a vibrant voice. Mitch loved Millie like an extended relative who he wasn't sure he wanted to speak to at the moment, but was always glad to have chatted with after the conversation concluded.

"Hey yourself, you old biddy. Things are good. Ti and I are busy. Rose is leading a seminar tomorrow and Cassie's shelter has a new pup. Betty asked about you yesterday."

"Yeah? How is she?"

"Same," Mitch said. "Jealous you retired first."

"Well, you can tell her I spent the last two days helping my daughter with the baby, who's running a fever. She's a delight, but exhausting. When's that son of yours going to give you a grandchild?"

Mitch moved toward the sink and lowered his voice to a whisper. "I don't know. In his own time, I guess. Hopefully while I'm still young enough to enjoy it. First, he has to find a wife."

Millie cackled. "You give him my best, now. Mmmwah." She smooched at the phone and hung up.

"Dinner's ready," Mitch announced. Their taste buds appreciated what their noses had anticipated. The dogs stared with dangling bits of drool, waiting for clean-up time when Mitch would award them a taste before washing the cookware. He spoiled his pups as much as his son.

CHAPTER 5

Aside from a few cottony clouds, the morning sky was wide in a vivid blue. Jen drove her Chevy past the Pastoral building, toward the school. As she rounded the bend, she recognized the handsome man edging the lawn with a weed whacker.

Before looking up, Ti waved as he normally did when a vehicle drove through his lot. He stood, wiping sweat from his brow. *Hey, that's the girl from the elevator.*

With a twinge of exhilaration, Jen returned his gesture. She noted the neat landscape as she studied the man responsible. *Huh, a quality job. Not like my garden. I prefer a more natural look. Then again, there's elegance in those smooth edges too... or maybe it's just the cute guy that makes them look so good.*

Gathering her bags, Jen got out of the car and entered the school. A cool shiver ran over her skin, unlike the warm welcome she'd felt at "the dark side" yesterday. *Such friendly people over there. Then again, I was a guest. That probably deserves... Why am I so interested in that place?*

She let the computer boot-up and signed in. *C'mon Jen, don't let yourself get interested... Sure, he's attractive, but you can't risk getting hurt again... or more important, Nate getting hurt.*

Settling in, she checked voicemail first, then glanced through the summary lines of email messages. Her stomach dropped. There, in black and white, was a message from the cheating, lying, conniving fraud!

Jen, I miss you. Maybe I'm not as good a person as you deserve, but you should forgive me and learn to live with my weakne...

"Why would he email me at work?" Jen asked aloud, as her stomach flip-flopped again. "He has no class." She'd seen enough. Jen punched DELETE. Then, with lingering nausea, she bowed her head to recite a Hail Mary and calm her nerves.

◆ ◆ ◆ ◆

"Hey, there's my dreamboat." Deirdre approached Mitch and Ti, who were replacing a ceiling tile in the Youth Ministry office. "Have you met our new temp? She's helping us till the end of the month."

"Hello, nice to meet you... formally." Mitch held out his hand.

With crisscrossed arms, the white-haired girl clutched a clipboard; her brightly painted talons tapped the stiff plastic.

"I met the janitor a few days ago." She stared at his outstretched hand. Her gaze traveled down to his boots and then back up to his striped shirt.

"Oh, honey, Mitch isn't the janitor. He's the Facilities Manager, and the most eligible bachelor in the state."

The girl pursed her lips, "Oh?"

"Maybe we can double date!" Deirdre nudged Mitch with her elbow.

"We'll see," Ti replied, before his father said something he might regret. Finishing their job, they gathered their tools. "See ya' later."

The girl spun on a pointed heel, turning to Deirdre, "Bet I can get him to ask me out."

"You think so? Neither of them are pushovers. Trust me, honey." Deirdre wagged a finger through the air in front of her.

"C'mon, they're janitors... oh, I mean... facilities workers. I've got a way with men, Deirdre. A hundred bucks, in the next two weeks. You'll see."

◆ ◆ ◆ ◆

For the rest of the day, Jen capered through her tasks, taking inventory and fixing a printer. Afternoon arrived before she knew it. Jen headed outside, looking forward to her afternoon with Nate, Kay, and Scott. *Ah, the weather is great for a playdate*. The radio came on as she started the car. She began to hum.

After a sewer grate slipped out of Mitch's grasp and fell on Ti's foot, Ti was off schedule. He'd stayed late with Mitch and Jackson to fill out paperwork in case any injury hid beneath the surface. *If I guard my sore foot, I can still get in a good upper body workout. Don't want to be too far off schedule though, especially not on Chinese night.*

Jen pulled around the bend with the windows down and "Porch Meetings" playing on the radio. Spotting Ti as he walked toward his truck, she observed the sun on his bronze skin. She slowed. Ti looked as if he'd like to approach. She stopped and smiled. "Hi again."

"Hello." He peered into the Chevy's open window. "You know, they're going to be at the fair next week."

Jen cocked her head, "Huh?"

"Texas Star... on your radio," he said. "They're playing at the Tulleytown Fair next week. They're headlining Thursday night. It's nice to meet another country music fan."

"Oh yes," Jen said. "Their greatest hits album is so good!"

The attractive man nodded.

Noting his interest, Jen continued, "I love country music; it's the best. Well, at least to me. I love the lyrics." Country songs had touched her soul during both good and difficult times. Her father was the only other family member to appreciate the simple tunes and sentimental statements. "My dad's a fan too. You should hear us try to sing along to this one..." She blushed, attempting to rewind. "Uh, I mean, we're big fans. Music's something we bond over."

"Yeah," Ti said. "I like them too."

Delighted to find a fellow fan, not to mention one so handsome, Jen studied the man peering through the car window. His blue eyes shone amidst his tan face and sandy hair. He smelled earthy and masculine, like fresh-cut cedar.

"Tulleytown, huh? I'd love to see them," she said before she could think better of it. "I bet they're even more amazing in person."

"Well, it's a nice venue. Tons of vendors: subs, games, crafts... the subs are my favorite though." He rested his arm on the window edge. "The concerts are usually good. I've been to four others there."

"Really?" she said. "Lucky you!"

"I haven't seen Texas Star yet. Eve McDermott is the opening act."

Jen's eyes lit up. "Oh, she's amazing! I love her!"

"Yeah, me too," Ti said with a chuckle.

"Sounds great... outdoors, at a fair. Um, I have her CD. If you're thinking of seeing her, you could borrow it to learn the songs. It's so much better when you know the words and can bebop along," Jen rambled.

Bebop... heh, cute. He tried not to show his amusement with her. He observed her hair—pulled up along the sides, with light brown curls flowing down her back—and tried not to stare. "Tomorrow I'm going to look up more information. I can let you know what I find out." As their eyes met, he felt a jolt of electricity and decided he might like to go to this concert.

Jen attempted to sound casual. "Okay. I'd be interested in more details." *Why not?*

◆ ◆ ◆ ◆

Ti's workout energized his body and readied his appetite for supper. He arrived home to the typical barrage of dogs and began his evening routine.

"How's your foot?" Mitch said.

"Actually, not bad. Feels like a deep bruise."

"Jackson's sister is going in for knee surgery for the third time."

"It's too bad they can't fix that for her." Ti shook his head.

"That new temp came by. She wanted some packing tape." Glancing away, Mitch threw the idea out there. "I think she was looking for you."

"Dad, stop imagining things." Ti turned toward the television.

Mitch frowned and changed the subject. "Rick's daughter from Alabama is coming to visit. He's looking forward to it."

"Good. He's been hoping to see her in person ever since her accident."

Mitch was a busybody, a friendly, curious, esteemed busybody, but a huge busybody nonetheless. After his recounting of the day's sagas, he pulled out the menu from the local Chinese restaurant.

"Hey, this is Mitch. I want to order. Yeah, the usual."

The man on the other end anticipated Mitch's well-known order as he checked off the list to a cadence of clanking dishes in the background.

"Ten minutes? I'll be there. Don't forget my crispy noodles." Mitch hung up. He walked to the couch. "C'mon doggies, lets watch four minutes of news, before I go. Just four though."

Ti snorted. "There are two things I can put money on, Dad. You'll never wear a T-shirt, and you'll never be late, even to pick up takeout."

Mitch chuckled, proud of his predictable nature. He sat with Champ and stroked Daisy until the clock showed four minutes had passed. Grabbing his keys, he started toward the door and checked his pocket. He'd already retrieved the weekly cash allowance from the bank, which he got every Friday at the drive-up window from the lady with hot-pink nail polish.

"All set?" Ti asked.

The takeout cost twenty dollars and forty-five cents. *Five, ten, twenty, one*—Mitch counted the bills. He never paid with anything but paper. He'd slip the change into his left pocket and later empty it into his coffee can savings plan.

"Yup, all set," Mitch said, half distracted.

"By the way," Ti called behind him, "I forgot to mention... I'm probably going to the Texas Star concert next week. I'm going to check the information online in the morning."

"Okay."

"I'm gonna invite that girl from the school we met the other day."

"Sounds good. She seems nice. Cassie likes her." Mitch acted casual.

"Yeah, she's into country music. I get the feeling she's athletic too." Ti recalled Jen's toned arms, not realizing until now that he'd noticed.

Ti obsessed over physical fitness. His voracious appetite challenged his ability to maintain the physique he desired. He could easily devour an entire pizza followed by a pint of Brownie Supreme ice cream. Working out kept him in shape. He kept to a regimented diet, insisting on a full glass of orange or grape juice every morning and one of skim milk every evening. Suppers were always well balanced; he could skimp on breakfast or lunch, but never on dinner.

Ti was an extremist in his own stubborn way. He threw himself into every project with unique intensity. This attitude applied to his work, pet care, workouts, and construction projects, even to the washing and waxing of his spotless car. He never did half of anything—if he couldn't finish, it wasn't worth starting. He never let his tools stay dirty, never ate mushrooms or any food over two days old, and he never missed a before-bed flossing.

Despite his meandering thoughts, the elder Mitch was aware enough to realize the clever timing of that casually discarded tidbit of information.

Concert.

Girl?

Huh, St. Anthony!

Happy and almost feeling a sense of relief, Mitch started the car and headed out of the driveway with a silly grin.

CHAPTER 6

"C'mon, Nate, time to go. Got your backpack?" Jen grabbed her keys. "Might have to mow the lawn after work today."

"You're the only mom I know who likes cutting grass."

"It's more about stretching my legs in the fresh outdoors," she said.

"Yeah, I know. We both love the outdoors. Me and Nana are going to feed the ducks at the pond today while you're at work."

"Lucky you! Wish I could go." Jen drove as they chatted.

"Do you think Poppa will like the picture I drew?"

"Who wouldn't love a knight and his pet dragon? I'm sure Nana will have it on the fridge before I get back. Here we are, good sir."

Nate leaned between the two front car seats and kissed her cheek. "Love you, Mom. Bye."

"Love you back. Have a good day." Jen watched his baseball cap bob up and down as he walked through the side door.

She drove down the street. *I wonder if the cute handyman was just being polite, or if he'll really let me know more about the concert.*

The workday was busy and time passed quickly. Jen left an hour later than expected. Approaching her car, she found a piece of yellow-lined paper folded and tucked under the windshield.

Hi,
Thursday, June 29 in Tulleytown
Games, food, and craft booths open at noon
Concert first act starts at 7:30 p.m.
m

That's all it said.

Cool. He actually got back to me... He even bothered to find my car...

Thrilled with the idea of the concert and the potential to see Ti, Jen decided to go. *He's easy going. I like that.* On her way to get Nate, she hummed along to an Eve McDermott song playing on the radio.

"Mom, it's a great day! Let's go for our bike ride."

"Okay, the lawn can wait. Let me start the laundry, and we have to practice a few pages from your summer workbook afterward."

Once home, Jen met Nate at the garage to help with the bikes. As they started down the driveway, she recognized the familiar grille of a small black pickup truck. *Oh no!* Her nerves quivered; sheer panic loomed. *It's the creep! Breathe. Stay strong. Be polite to the cheating weasel. Nate's here.* The pickup slowed alongside them.

"Hi Nate. Jen." The voice sounded sour in her ears.

"Oh, hello," Jen called over her shoulder, avoiding eye contact.

"You haven't returned my calls. C'mon, I'm not so bad. *No one* is faithful anymore. And I didn't borrow *that* much."

"Oh?" Jen continued to walk with her bike, allowing Nate to get ahead.

"You won't find a saint, you know," he said defensively.

Pulling strength up from her toes, she hopped up and steadied herself on the bicycle. Fortunately, the self-conscious con man didn't like to make a scene. "I don't think you want to get into it out here. Besides, I'm on a tight schedule."

His shifty eyes surveyed the neighbors sitting on porches, walking dogs, and playing with children. "Maybe later." He drove ahead.

Relieved, Jen turned left down the familiar side street. The exercise and fresh air helped her refocus for her evening.

After the bike ride and two pages of math practice problems, Jen supervised bath time, prepared dinner, and finally flopped on the couch. She'd been working hard. Thinking about why she seemed to choose self-centered, emotionally detached men still exhausted much of her energy. After reading the third chapter of a book on loan from Kay, she fell asleep.

◆ ◆ ◆ ◆

Sam greeted Jen as she entered the building. "Good morning."

"Hi Sam. Happy Friday."

"Hey, how's Nate? Still bike riding?"

"Almost every day. Good for me too," she said, patting her tummy.

Sam chuckled.

"He can't stand anything that interrupts our afternoon ride; he's a bit of a fanatic." Jen smiled.

"Just wait until he's in control of four wheels."

Jen took a step back. "Oh my gosh. I'm not ready for that!"

Sam laughed. "Have a great day."

"Thanks, you too."

Her untidy desk greeted her. She vowed to restack the piles and sort through the mess by the day's end. It was hot: one hundred two degrees. A red elastic held her hair in a ponytail to keep her neck cool. Turning on her computer, she sat down to investigate the Pastoral Center.

"Perfect." The website included a directory of names, extensions, and email addresses. Finding the only Mitchell listings didn't take long. There were two, identical except for the T in the second one.

She opened her email and wrote, *Hi*. She paused. *What should I call him? The directory lists Mitchell. Cassie called him "Little m." Well, I'll just leave a name out for now.*

Hi,

Thank you for the information on the concert. I'm considering going. Do you have directions or advice on the best way to get to the fairgrounds? How long does it take to get there?

Thanks!

Jennifer

She clicked SEND.

Jen walked down the hall. "Hi. I came to talk about a new program for tracking the student volunteer time."

"Wonderful. Here are the paper forms I use." The white-haired teacher walked to the filing cabinet.

"You guys make a difference for a lot of families. This program will make the record keeping easier and let you focus on the events," Jen said.

Back at her desk, Jen noticed the red light on her phone. *More messages—already*. She dialed up the voicemail. "Jen, the repair you're waiting for is delayed..." She scribbled down the number.

The second message surprised her. Her heart skipped a beat as the strong male voice began. "Hey, thanks for your email—great way to get in touch. Uh, so listen... I'm definitely going next week. The drive takes about an hour. Umm, you probably want to go with your own friends. But we can go together... if you want... S-so, do you want me to order you a ticket when I get mine? I'd be happy to. Call me... or email, yeah... either one works. I'll only be here until two o'clock today, then I'm away for the weekend. If you need time to make plans, we can catch up Monday too... Umm, so, yeah, let me know..."

Hmmm, if Kay can't go, a travel partner might be nice—no fear driving home late from somewhere unfamiliar. A tingle ran up her spine. *Breathe, Jen. Don't even consider... Ugh, my sister will kill me if I don't wait long enough to date after a breakup.* She wrinkled her nose. Jen knew it was important to protect not only her heart, but Nate's. "Nine month's gestation is required to give birth to a new relationship after heartache," Sienna would insist. Her older sister wrote relationship articles for *Living as Family* magazine. Avoiding the wrath that would come from her critical siblings if she expressed interest in a man too soon was a huge consideration. It had only been four months.

On her way down the hall, Jen ran into Sam again.

"Hey, I was thinking of going to see Texas Star at the fair. Do you know anything about Tulley...? " she started.

"Oh, yeah. We go most years, but this year we have a graduation party for Alicia's nephew. Tulleytown is a great time."

"So, I've heard," Jen mumbled, thinking about Ti's description of the fair, and the attractive way his eyes crinkled when he smiled.

"You should go. It's fun. The concerts are fantastic, and affordable."

"Thanks. See ya' Monday."

Back at her desk, Jen scrolled through her email.

Hey, Jen, it sounds like fun, but Scott and I have granny's birthday dinner. I'd love to see Texas Star, but my family's counting on us. We had a blast seeing Rudy Hall last year. You better let me know how it is!

Kay ended her message with a smiley face.

Jen wondered how she could go with Ti and not break the no-dating-for-nine-months rule. *Sienna will make me miserable if I go against her decree. She's right; I should take time to know myself.* Jen walked to Allie's classroom and found her typing up a sports flyer.

"So, Al, I met this nice guy across the street... I mean the parking lot out front... a few days ago. We had a couple of short conversations."

"Oh?" Allie's eyebrows rose.

"He's going to the concert in Tulleytown and suggested I tag along. What do you think?" Jen intertwined her fingers.

"Great. What's the problem?" Allie asked.

"Well, I continue to misread people, especially guys, so I wonder if it'd be a mistake although it's not, like, a date. It was nice; he just invited me casually, no pressure." Jen shrugged. "I don't want to be stupid either; you can't be too careful these days."

"I say, go. Have a great time."

"Really?" Her white knuckles relaxed; she tapped her thumbs together.

"Sure. This guy works in our district office. Although... they *are* evil over there," Allie snickered.

"Very funny," Jen chuckled.

"No, seriously, Jen, it's not like you met in a saloon. So... how did you meet and how'd the concert come up?"

"Well," Jen said, "I took a report over to a friend in the education office. She introduced us, since we were on the elevator together."

"*You* took an elevator?" Allie laughed.

"Yeah! Whatever possessed me to do that?"

"Destiny," Allie blurted out. "And...?"

"And... I waved to him when passing the building. Later I saw him from my car. I slowed to say hello. The radio was on... it just kinda came up."

"So, what do you think of him?" Allie pushed.

"My gut says he's not the psycho kidnapping type." Jen smiled.

Allie giggled. "Good. What else?"

"He's cute."

Allie rotated her hand requesting more information.

"Okay, okay... *more* than cute in his handyman jeans and work boots," Jen confessed dreamily.

"Even better!" Allie said, "Just your type! You're going."

"I am?"

"Yes. I'll know where you are and who you're with. Be sure to give me the details. I'll check in with you that night after my game."

"What about Nate?"

"What about him? He's with his dad Thursday nights, right? It's a casual outing, no more." With a big Cheshire-cat grin, Allie added "for now" under her breath and patted her friend's arm as they parted.

After almost an hour, Jen called Cassie. "Hey, how'd the meeting go the other day?"

"Very well," Cassie replied. "They got enough information and by following the examples will be able to get a plan in place on time."

"That's good news." Jen closed her eyes and took a deep breath. "So, Cassie, those guys you introduced me to, how well do you know them?"

"Oh, the Mitches? They've been here almost ten years, I'd say. Everybody knows them. They keep things running around here... nice guys too... got a quirky, sorta charming sense of humor."

Jen felt better. Cassie might have a notion she was interested in Little m, but Jen didn't care. She glanced at the clock. 11:30 a.m. She decided to ask Ti to get her a ticket. Then, she remembered the Eve McDermott CD she'd stuffed in her knapsack. *Why not bring it over around lunchtime? I did offer to loan it to him so he could learn the words. It's just so much better if you can sing along.*

◆ ◆ ◆ ◆

"Hi, Cassie," Ti said, approaching her in the cafeteria.

"Oh, hey."

"You getting a refresh before lunch too?"

"Yeah, it's a double java type of morning." Cassie decided to toy with Ti. "So, what'd you think of that girl in the elevator the other day?"

The conservative Ti replied, "Uh, seemed friendly. You know her well?"

"Jen's great, super nice; always eager to help out. We do favors for each other once in a while."

"Oh, uh, that's good." Ti turned back to the coffee pot, feigning a lack of interest.

Cassie leaned in and whispered. “Though, I suggest you act casual. Jen’s had two lousy relationships. Not that you’re interested, but tread lightly.”

“Uh, thanks.” Ti offered a bashful grin. “I thought you were trying to set me up with blondie what’s-her-name.”

“Yeah, but my intuition’s telling me this might fit you better.”

“Really?” The memory of Jen sitting in her green Chevy, with those long curls cascading over her shoulder, flashed through Ti’s mind. He realized he was more interested than he’d admitted. Looking up from the coffee counter, he said, “Well... See you later, Cass.”

“Okay. Have a great day.” Amused, Cassie walked out, not mentioning she’d had a similar conversation with Jen.

“Ti, can you check the dishwasher? Something’s not right,” Ernesto called. Ti entered the back of the kitchen.

“Yeah, looks like a busted pump. I’ll get one on order.” Walking toward the door, Ti heard the click of pointed heels on the shiny floor.

“Oh, hello, Mr. Fixit man.” Two bright red lips curled upward.

Ti stopped. “Hi.” He stood still.

“So, Deirdre says I should let you take me out. I’m free tomorrow night. I’ll send you the address. Don’t worry, I never disappoint.” She ran a long pointed finger down the center of his chest.

“Ah, I’m tied up tomorrow.”

“I don’t take rejection well,” she said with a sly smile.

Ti forced a laugh. “Seriously, maybe another time.” He slinked back toward the kitchen. “Oh, Ernesto, I forgot to tell you...”

◆ ◆ ◆ ◆

At noon, Jen walked outside and strolled across the lot.

“Good afternoon,” Claire greeted her.

“Hello. I’m here to see Mitchell, the younger one.” Jen signed in.

“Sure. Down one flight, make a left, straight down the hall.”

“Thanks. I’ll use the staircase.” Jen entered the stairwell. Exiting the large door at the bottom, she ran into Mitch, who was returning from the hardware store.

“Hi there.” Mitch shifted the brown sack to his other hand.

"Hi. I'm looking for your son. I brought this CD for him." She held up the thin square.

"He should be in the office. I'll show you." He walked her down a long hallway with speckled carpeting and a painted chair rail.

"Nice day," Mitch said.

"Yes, I love warm weather." Jen flipped the CD case in her hands.

"We're due for rain this evening."

"Good for my flowers," she said.

"You like baseball?"

"Sure."

"What team?" he asked.

"The Mustangs are my favorite."

"Good! So you work at the school?" Mitch led her to the last door on the right. The maintenance office contained two wide desks and a wall of cabinets filled with parts and tools. Ti was at the computer reviewing directions to the fair grounds.

"Hey, look who I found," Mitch said.

"Hello," Jen said, wanting to be friendly and hating to be anxious.

"Hi." Ti turned around. An electrified pulse ran through him.

"I thought I'd drop off the CD I mentioned." She cleared her throat to steady her voice. "Like I said, it's better when you know the songs. Oh, and I would like to go, so could you count me in your ticket order?"

"No problem." Ti wanted to suggest he take her as his date, but remembered Cassie's cautioning advice. "Consider it done."

On the wall, she noticed a photograph of a stunning log home surrounded by pine trees and a blanket of white snow. "Gorgeous picture. Where's that?"

"That's our house in the mountains," Ti said.

"Yeah," Mitch explained. "We stay here during the week for work. We live there on the weekends."

"Wow. It's beautiful," she sighed.

"We love it," Ti said. "It's our real home. We used to live up there full time, and then life led us down here for a while. Someday we'll get back."

"Yeah, everything in life leads us someplace. Not all good is good, not all bad is bad, but it all leads us down the path we're supposed to follow."

After expounding one of his philosophies, Mitch sat back in his chair. "So..." He put his feet on the desk and folded his hands over his belt buckle. "You like dogs by any chance?"

"Yeah." Jen fidgeted with her fingertips. "I love pets. My sister was allergic, so we had a non-shedding schnauzer growing up. I had goldfish in college. Now I have a cat; his name is Toby."

"Cat!" Mitch exclaimed, plunking his feet onto the floor as he jet forward. "Cat? Huh. My cousin used to shoot at them when I was a kid."

Jen took a step back.

Ti laughed. "He grew up on a farm with lots of barn-bred strays. BB guns and 'cat-hunting' were considered less barbaric in those days and in *them thar parts.*" Ti smirked.

Jen put her hand on her hip, "Well, Toby's great, and you'd like him if you met him."

"Doubt it," Mitch joked. With a wink and a devilish grin, he added, "I'm a dog man through and through now; haven't had a cat in years. We have four Labs, you know."

"Four? Wow, that's a pretty big family," she said.

"It works for us," they said in unison.

She looked at them. They didn't look too much alike at first glance, but they were surely related: similar mannerisms, similar voices, and the same large rugged hands. Mitch was slimmer than Ti, with hazel eyes and thin dark hair, which was turning gray. Ti's hair was light and beginning to bald. Unlike his father, he refused to use the old comb-over-to-hide-the-bald-spot trick and just let it be, wearing the style well. With those beautiful blue eyes and that triangular shape from his broad shoulders to his tapered waist, it was hard to notice anything else.

After their visit, a peppy Jen bopped back across the parking lot.

◆ ◆ ◆ ◆

With only ten more minutes of work on a Friday, his favorite day of the week, Ti's spirits were high. When the clock struck two, he jumped in his big red truck, ready for the drive north to the log cabin and the lake.

Ti pushed Jen's CD into the player. He listened to it twice on the drive, wondering how Eve would sound in person. He never mentioned that he already owned that CD, along with hundreds of others. A huge music fan, he played tunes with whatever he was doing. His vast collection included mostly country artists. He had several CDs by the famed island musician Jake Kenny. He also had a handful of oldies and odd albums—what Ti referred to as "all over the place."

"Everyone must have variety, with a few odd albums to make a collection complete," Lenny, a fellow enthusiast of good music, had taught him. Lenny was like a favorite uncle; the same age as Mitch, with the same old-fashioned style and stubborn beliefs and an ear for quality sound. Lenny was the one who'd persuaded Ti to install a high-tech surround sound system in their family room.

"There's some stuff you can do without and some stuff you can do cheap, but there's some stuff you just have to do right," Lenny would say. Sound was in the "you-have-to-do-right" category. He loved old movies. Lenny had mounted a sound system at his place so he could hear each and every special effect, as if he were once again a teenager sneaking into the back of the movie theater.

The Mitches had met Lenny and his wife Camille when they worked construction full-time. The Mitches had built their house and, over the years, grew as close as kin.

Ti drove contentedly, his thoughts alternating between the music, the concert, Jen, and what to put on tonight's pizza: pepperoni or onions and peppers. He was in an exceptional mood, so perhaps all three...

Meanwhile, after Jen's visit and a bit of paperwork, Mitch set up the conference room. Once finished, he also hit the road, eager to get to his plush couches, full bed, large soaking tub, big oven, acres of yard space, and feel *just right*. The guesthouse was fine, but home was *home*.

◆ ◆ ◆ ◆

"How come weekend time flies like a hummingbird instead of gliding like a hawk?" Mitch wondered as he stood on the back deck, observing an eagle soar beyond the treetops in an overcast sky. He had enjoyed his weekend. They'd boated on the lake, worked the grounds, attended Mass, shopped, and cooked on the grill. Mitch preferred grilling on the back deck to going out for a five-star gourmet meal. The appetizer when grilling was two rounds of drippy, margarine-smothered corn on the cob. Fresh-husked corn on a summer weekend was as necessary as wonton soup on a Wednesday.

The boating and grilling relaxed their spirits and satisfied all of their senses. Before they knew it, it was time to return south.

Mitch went to bed Sunday night thinking about his son. *Ti is such a fine man. I can't wait for him to find the right person to create a life with, just as I did with Mandy.* Remembering their courtship, his cheeks flushed.

"Oh, Mandy, I hope Ti can have what we shared." He sensed her presence. Mitch imagined that once Ti found someone, the changes would be tough. Ever since Mandy had passed away, and Tiger had moved back into the log home so they could afford to keep it, they'd grown accustomed to sharing much of their lives with one another.

Mitch wondered how that might play out. *If Ti finds a life of his own, how would I fit in? Who would stay where?*

Thoughts for Ti's future were always with him, but more so in the last few years. He knew that the person Ti married would need to enjoy physical activity and the outdoors, have patience to laugh off his quirks, and desire to dote on Ti as Mitch himself had done. *Ti's an honorable man, a little rigid in his routines and definitely stubborn, but he'll be a great companion to the right woman.*

The dream was always with Mitch, in the back of his mind and the front of his heart, almost haunting him.

As father and son, they'd shared great times. There was nothing they hadn't done that he wished they had, and nothing they'd done that he wished they hadn't. The only thing missing now was the right spouse. He needed to know that Ti would be well taken care of, as he himself grew older. Mitch recited his prayer, addressing both saints.

"And, to you, Anthony, special patron, I ask,
find for Ti a love that will last,
with all my desire to you I now pray
just in case I should ever go away."

Before making the sign of the cross, Mitch asked St. Francis to watch over his dogs. Then he spoke to Mandy, who was always in his heart.

Mitch enjoyed a restful sleep. Before he knew it, four slobbering tongues welcomed him to the morning before the alarm sounded.

"Chip, that's enough. Okay, okay, I know... time to get up." Mitch stood, wiping his cheeks. "C'mon doggies, time to open the gift of a new week."

◆ ◆ ◆ ◆

When Jen walked into her office at 7:02 a.m., that darn light was blinking. The machine had recorded a voice message at 6:15 a.m. *6:15?* Her ears perked up when she heard Ti's voice.

"Hi Jen, we're all set. I got an email this morning confirming the ticket order." A tingle ran up one arm and down the other. *Guess we're going!*

She settled in and returned his call. To her surprise, he answered. "Hi."

They spoke for a while, although later neither could recall what about. Their conversation started with the tickets, concerts, bands, and country music, and then continued for what seemed like five minutes, but had been sixteen minutes, twenty-two seconds according to the phone's clock.

Nice way to start the day. Humming a favorite tune, she went about her tasks as if gliding along on a magic carpet.

CHAPTER 7

Standing in the closet, Jen slid the hangers to the left, with the cordless phone tucked against her shoulder.

"Are you looking forward to your 'non-date' concert?" Kay giggled.

"Yeah. Can't believe it's the end of June already. And the keyword there is '*non*'. I'm not getting worked up about it."

"Yeah right. What are you wearing?"

"My spiffy new sneakers. I expect a lot of walking," Jen said.

"Wear those nice fitting jeans. You know, the light ones," Kay said.

"Already on. I'm just looking for my green shirt."

"The scoop-neck? Oh that's a great color on you."

"Thanks. I'd better go. I'm glad Nate can play with Scott till his dad gets him. You're the best. Okay, I'll text you later."

"Sure thing, bye. Oh, and Jen, have a great time."

"Yup." Not wanting to admit it, Jen felt like she was standing on the edge of a scenic rock cliff with crystal blue water inviting her from below. Considering the plunge, she felt energy, thrill, and trepidation.

She finished dressing. Wearing her curls long, she tucked a hair tie into her pocket in case the wild swirls required taming later. *I need a sweatshirt, of course.* Jen never went anywhere without a plan for layering, often with multiple options. *Okay, all set.*

Elated, as if his team had just won the playoffs, Ti hardly thought about clothes. He quickly pulled on a sleeveless T-shirt and denim shorts. *Time to gas up the car and check the oil. Gotta take my transportation responsibility seriously.* Attire-shmire, but washed, gassed and ready to roll he would be.

I wonder what we'll talk about, together in the truck for an hour. Here we go. I'll pop in Jen's CD and my Texas Star one. He pushed each disk into the player. *That'll set the mood... for the concert, of course.*

Ti pulled into Jen's driveway around 3:30 and found her ready and waiting on the porch. He smiled as he opened the truck door. "Let me help you with that." He reached to hold her knapsack while she climbed up.

With anticipation soaring like hang gliders through a clear sky, they set out, leaving plenty of time to walk around before the show.

"Want some pretzels? I brought some travel snacks."

"No thanks. I had a big lunch—leftover lasagna."

"Homemade?"

"Yeah, I love to cook. My grandma was the best Italian cook ever."

"I don't cook much, but I love to eat." Ti grinned.

"I even like cooking on a campfire."

"You like to camp, do you?" *Chalk up another plus.*

"Yeah," Jen said. "No idea where I get it from. I used to go on overnight canoe trips back in college. They were so much fun."

"I love being at the lake. Nothing like a day on the water," Ti sighed.

Jen admired his tan arms. "I should take Nate camping again soon. He loves being outside. We ride bikes almost every afternoon."

"That's great. Kids need to spend time outdoors. Many of my fondest memories are from playing in the woods near my house."

Gosh, I really like talking with him... it's so easy, comfortable. Jen appreciated his openness in sharing his experiences, both good and bad.

"Walleycito is amazing. The views can take your breath away. Great sunsets too. I still enjoy seeing deer in our yard."

"My aunt and uncle thrive on city life. But even they needed an escape. They have a house on Eagle Lake. My sisters and cousins call it Lake Cranberry because the shore is full of cranberry bushes. My aunt made jam and pies... and cranberry tea for the adults in the winter."

"Adults?" He wondered why the tea was exclusive.

"We kids preferred hot chocolate!" she giggled.

"Ah." Ti raised and dropped his chin in a slow nod.

"I love it there. The house is small but charming. The family room arches into a porch that overlooks the lake with windows on three sides."

"Sounds nice." Ti imagined Jen standing in the sunlit room, wearing shorts and a tank top, looking out at the lake.

"We had fun in summer splashing around in old black inner-tubes, and gliding on our ice skates all winter. It's my favorite place to spend time." She was happy to share her most prized sanctuary with him. "I've often dreamt of living in the country, on a lake like that, even though I know it's not at all practical—not with my school paycheck."

They pulled through a guarded entrance. Jen sent a quick text to Kay: *Hope Nate and Scott are enjoying the afternoon*, followed by another to Allie: *I'm fine, all is well.*

After Ti parked the truck and helped her out, the two wandered around the fairgrounds on a tepid afternoon. They passed the craft booths first. Jen picked up a wooden duck carving. "I love wood work. I tried to whittle once; cut my thumb pretty bad."

"Carpentry is my favorite part of construction. Still, I've seen my share of injuries. I've nailed myself to beams, and got whacked with a hammer countless times. I even had a screwdriver go in my eye once."

"Oh my gosh!" Jen put her hand to her mouth.

"I was lucky; it missed all the important parts and healed fine."

She looked at him. *And you'd never know, those eyes are so blue.*

"I wasn't so fortunate with a strain I got last year. I was building an addition for a neighbor. Their three-year-old wandered underneath a leaning wall frame. I pushed the whole thing up to get him out from under it and pulled something. Still bothers me. I've had every possible test, but haven't found any relief that lasts."

"Wow, that's a shame. I don't know what to say."

"Oh, don't feel bad. I just hope it stays manageable. It bothers my right leg the most." Ti had no trouble sharing with her.

They stopped at a concession stand. A longhaired little girl with chubby, dimpled cheeks stood at the counter. With her sister and parents, she was selling homemade tapioca pudding in large crispy waffle cones.

"I'll take one with cinnamon. Would you like one, Jen?" He touched her elbow, guiding her to see the menu taped on the gray-painted counter.

Distracted by the feel of his hand, she looked up at him. "Uh, no thanks. Too much for me."

Ti dipped the plastic spoon into his cone. "How 'bout a spoonful?" He leaned in. "The girl's smile made a part of me melt. I love that they're working together as a family. Family is the most important thing in life."

His sentiment warmed Jen's heart. At that moment, she not only wanted their non-date to continue, but she hoped it could turn into a real date someday. *Ti's handsome, sincere, and devoted to whatever he's doing. My instincts say he's trustworthy too. His construction stories fascinate me. I can't wait to see something he's built.*

Ti hiked beside Jen, making mental notes of his own. *I enjoy her laugh, her enthusiasm, and how she tosses her hair back when a curl falls onto her face. And I like that she's so interested in our conversation.*

Eager for each discovery as they meandered about, the two walked through the fields for a second time. "Can you smell the cotton candy?"

"Yup, can't be a fair without that smell, huh?" Ti sighed. *She's a perfect companion for a fair.*

Floating on their private cloud, they walked through the displays.

"Here you go," Ti plunked a quarter down. "Pick a number." The man spun the wheel. It buzzed and then slowed.

"Not even close!" They both laughed.

"Let's stop here and have something to eat."

"Okay, those cheese steaks smell amazing."

"Just what I was thinking. Be right back." Ti stood in line.

He returned with two long sandwiches, wrapped in foil. "Here we go." Ti took a large bite. "Mmmm. Fair food has its own taste, doesn't it?"

They made their way past the ticking sounds of the game wheels and shouts from the participants, back to the truck. Ti slung two camp chair sacks over his shoulder. Jen carried her vital knapsack, which contained an array of useful items, including a cap, water bottle, and her bulky hooded sweatshirt that she was just about ready to put on.

Ti found a good spot close to the stadium's gated area. As they set up their chairs for the concert, it began to drizzle.

"I'd hoped the forecast was wrong, but we...," Jen pulled a rain poncho out of her knapsack and held it out, "...are prepared." As the sky darkened, Ti debated the impending rain and her thoughtful offer, versus his determination to look and act like a tough guy. Since plastic rain ponchos were spreading through the crowd like wildfire, he accepted and put it on. She shook open a second poncho with a cheerful Mickey Mouse figure on the back, and pulled it over her head.

He watched her. *She's cute.*

As she smoothed out the plastic with both hands and tucked her curls into the hood, the heavens let go. Raindrops plunked on their shoulders.

"Good evening!" The man from the local radio station's voice boomed. "Are you ready to see Eve McDermott?" The audience exploded.

Eve began playing along with the cloudburst. Singing like an angel, she entertained the cheering crowd. Eve's rapport with her fans amused them. They enjoyed her show, soaking up the sounds rather than the rain.

◆ ◆ ◆ ◆

Mitch mulled around the hardware store and stopped at Colossal Burger for takeout. He arrived home with the usual burger, large fries, chocolate shake, plus a small order of fries for the dogs. Whenever he ate alone, he took the occasion to satisfy his craving for a fast food fix.

Contemplating his son at the concert, he hoped Ti and Jen were enjoying their evening and at least the music, if not each other. "Well, doggies, do you think Ti is having fun?" He patted Chip's head, and then dumped his takeout onto a pan and put it in the oven.

After a good soak in a bubbly bath, and with a jaunty feeling, he devoured his burger and fries, allotting the dogs their share.

The phone rang. *This better not be Ti with car trouble.* "Hello."

Millie's perky voice greeted him. "Hi-ya' old man."

Whew. "Hey, what do you want?" Already knowing it was nothing in particular, he chuckled. "Ti's out at a concert."

"You should have told me. I would have made a real dinner for you."

"I'm just fine."

"I bet you're eating a Colossal burger. We both know you need to mind your cholesterol. How much of that junk did you feed those beasts?"

"That's what the meds are for, so I can cheat now and then."

Their conversation was brief and they hung up after a few minutes of playful banter.

Mitch dozed by the TV until bedtime. The ceremony was the same. He looked to the windows, already open, let the dogs out, brushed his teeth, and unfolded the sofa bed. The five of them settled for the night.

Dear Lord,
Thank you for this day,
with all I got to do and see
Experiencing each person and event
That you generously gave to me.

He turned his attention to St. Anthony.

To you, Anthony, special patron, I ask,
find for Ti a love that will last,
with all my desire to you, I pray,
just in case I should ever go away.
Francis, don't forget my four legged kids.

And lastly, "I miss you, Mandy."

Thinking happy thoughts, Mitch fell into a pleasant slumber.

◆ ◆ ◆ ◆

Texas Star performed like a perfectly synchronized choir. The band members captivated the audience with personal stories, entertained with upbeat songs, and harmonized with slow ballads. Jen sang along as loudly as she could, since no one could hear anything in or out of tune over the booming speakers. She didn't care. She was swept away in a tide of music and gleeful emotion. The rain poured down the back of their ponchos; they stayed dry except for the bottom of her jeans and their soaked feet.

The concert ended late. In sloshing sneakers, amid a large crowd of exiting fans, Ti and Jen made their way down the long path toward the parking lot. They trudged through low spots in the road where the rainwater ran four inches deep.

Ti grabbed Jen's hand to lead her through the crowd and around a deep ditch. With care, he instinctively shepherded his lamb through the treacherous valley.

Warmed by his touch, Jen felt no chill, no dampness, only the marvelous mood in the air between them.

Chapter 8

Friday morning the sun triumphed again. Jen had taken the day off to enjoy time with Nate while he was out of school. Kay had done the same. Allie and the kids were expecting them. Excited to tell her friends about the concert, Jen hurried through her chores. She noticed the light on the answering machine. *Hmm, must be from last night*. She pressed PLAY.

"Jen, I found a new job. Let's talk about getting back together. I can chip in some and we can have an open relationship. You'll see."

She felt a dank sensation wash over her as his words flooded her ears, drowning her equilibrium. She swayed, then steadied herself with a slow, calming breath and hit ERASE.

"C'mon Nate, time to go. Do you have your backpack?"

"All ready, Mom."

Welcoming them at the door, the kids tugged Nate inside and ran through to the backyard. The grownups gathered in the kitchen.

"Yeah, it was... pleasant... relaxed... We talked a lot and neither of us seemed uncomfortable or awkward. I like that he's so open. We walked all over the place... had a great time!"

"So, he was good company?" Kay nudged.

"Yeah, real good," Jen said. "He was fun to be with. It's as simple as that." *Huh, yeah, simple. Simple is nice.*

"Ha-ha," Allie snickered, "Soooo... do you like him?"

"Well, I knew he was handsome, and you know I love a handyman." She paused. Kay and Allie hung on her words, waiting for her to continue. "Sure, now I know he's also nice to be around. But it wasn't a date. I don't know if he's interested, or available."

"Of course he is. If he had a girlfriend, why wouldn't she have gone?"

"Could be a thousand reasons." Jen changed the subject. "The event was huge. Music was fantastic. Food, scrumptious..." Her voice trailed off as she recalled Ti's sentiment about the family at the pudding stand.

"How was the weather?"

"Interesting. Gorgeous in the afternoon, gray later, then it poured. Everyone got drenched, but no one seemed to mind."

The three women enjoyed their day of visiting. Nate and the kids climbed all over each other, amused themselves on the swing set, played hide-and-seek, and threw the ball around.

Ah, what a beautiful day. Content, Jen relaxed in a cushioned patio chair, catching up with her friends and soaking in the sun.

Later, Jen and Nate enjoyed their Friday game night and home-baked pizza. They both got a scoop of vanilla ice cream after declaring a winner.

Jen woke Saturday and began her cleaning ritual. She pulled on a pink tank top and ripped jean shorts. She washed a load of laundry and tidied up the clutter that seemed to scatter around the house on its own. By 9:00, she was ready for outside work. A few soothing hours spent tending to the yard satisfied her craving for nature's serenity.

Jen called to Nate, who was circling on his bike. Together they stacked the fallen branches. *The concert was so amazing. I wonder what it meant when he said, 'I had a good time. See you later.' Was that a good thing or a bad thing? Well, it doesn't matter. It wasn't a date—just a good show with two of my favorite artists. No need to consider anything else. I have to move forward with my life, take care of Nate, and not upset my family; they'll definitely disapprove if I date now.*

◆ ◆ ◆ ◆

Mitch opened his newspaper. "So if you enjoyed her company, maybe you should ask her to dinner one night next week." He brought the idea up without prying and dropped it just as easily. While he spoke, his head remained down. Holding his glasses in his left hand, he stared at the paper.

All he knew was that the evening had gone well. Ti kept emotions to himself. But Mitch had a burning desire to hold Ti by the shoulders and demand his boy tell the truth, as if he were eight and in trouble for throwing snowballs at cars with his friends.

Mitch acted cool, but his curiosity was boiling hot. *Perhaps if I grab Ti by the throat.* Mitch snorted. *No, I can't coax anything out of him anymore, particularly with something like this.*

"I can't wait for our long holiday weekend, Dad."

"Yeah, I'm looking forward to visiting at Lenny and Camille's—one of my favorite Conner-built houses." Mitch sat back.

"I love how the yard slopes up from the shoreline. They've got the best view of the lake and fireworks."

"We'll get to enjoy that new patio we helped put in last fall."

"The town's having the show on Sunday, right?"

"Yeah, Ti. Best part is we'll still have two more days off at home."

◆ ◆ ◆ ◆

Sunday afternoon, the group of friends moseyed out to the deck. Lenny and Ti arranged the chairs and organized the coolers.

Camille called Ti back to the kitchen. "Can you reach that dish?"

"You'll never guess who I saw play at the Tulleytown Fair last week."

"Rudy Hall?

He handed the ceramic bowl to her. "Nope, Texas Star."

"No way! I've always wanted to see them."

"I know." Ti flashed a grin. "I also had a lovely companion, which made it even better. And..."

Mitch listened in on their conversation. He was able to confirm that it had been a good experience—nothing more, at least not within earshot.

The scent of charcoal filled the deck and patio. Mitch placed the drumsticks across the grates. Lenny uncovered the salads.

Camille emerged from the kitchen. "Made my taco dip just for you Mitch—not too hot, not too mild."

"Ha! I'll never forget that time at the Chinese buffet when you tried to prove how solid-as-steel you were, asking for extra hot sauce." Lenny patted Mitch's back with a wily smile.

"I could hear Dad's thoughts when the waitress brought that small dish with only about a tablespoon of dark liquid."

"But when he dipped his finger in and licked it, his eyes watered. Then his face and bald head turned red as a tomato!" Lenny laughed.

"All four water glasses couldn't extinguish the heat in my mouth and throat." Mitch put his chin up and rubbed his neck.

Lenny bent over in stitches recalling Mitch's red-hot expression.

Camille ripped open a bag of chips. The grill sizzled and conversations flourished. Later they witnessed a fantastic fireworks display over the lake. Bright, glowing sparks flashed in green, red, and gold. Ti found himself wondering if Jen was picnicking and enjoying loud bursts of light too.

◆ ◆ ◆ ◆

Jen and Nate spent two days with her family at her sister Sienna's house. The kids jumped and splashed like performing dolphins in the large pool. The new basketball court fascinated Nate. Although the net seemed a mile high, he squatted down and threw, extending his arms all the way up. He made several baskets. Later, Sienna brought out the karaoke machine.

Due to the long weekend, almost a week passed before Ti called Jen. She smiled as he spoke. "I'm glad you went to the fair with me. Thank goodness for your ponchos!"

"My pleasure."

"I had a great time."

"Me too." She blushed.

He told her about his weekend. She told him how Nate had played basketball and managed a few clean shots.

"I'll call you again soon," Ti said.

"I'd like that." Jen twirled a curl with her fingertip.

The following weekend Ti thought a lot about Jen. Although happy to be in the mountains, his mind was elsewhere. He and Mitch took a ride to Lenny's to discuss screening in a section of the back porch. Although he didn't say anything, Mitch noticed Ti was distracted.

Monday morning Ti called Jen. "How've you been?"

"Good. You?"

"Fine. Um, so would you be interested in having dinner this week?"

"Sure, how about Wednesday?" she replied, before thinking about it.

"That's great." Ti felt a quiver dance up his spine. Now the pressure would be a little greater than when they went on the "non-date."

Jen's heart swooned, intensifying her excitement for their dinner date, and winning the argument over her cautious mind. *It's okay, Nate will be with his father. I wonder what I should wear...*

Ti arrived to pick her up. He took her hand to help her into the truck. There was that quiver again, waltzing straight up his arm. "Where would you like to go?"

"I don't know. What do you like?" Jen hesitated to presume his taste.

"I'm pretty open." Ti hoped she didn't suggest the new seafood place with the huge chandelier and marble tile floors.

"Well, I prefer something simple, kinda laidback."

"Whew, me too! How about the diner? It's got a great reputation."

"Awesome," Jen said, happy to be with another down-to-earth person.

Over the next hour, they spoke about enjoying things like a day on the lake and vivid sunsets. They agreed that a long hike in the woods was gratifying, and that witnessing wildlife was a bonus.

Jen recognized the connection between them. *We have a lot in common. Ti's different from other guys who put on pretense. Tonight's relaxed, and more real. Ah, so refreshing!*

Dinner was excellent. Jen basked in the harmony of homemade pasta and handsome company. Ti savored the food and conversation. He brought Jen home, walked her to the door, and gave her a kiss on the cheek. "I really enjoyed our evening."

◆ ◆ ◆ ◆

Mitch sat in front of the television as Ti walked through the door with a bounce in his step. Inside Mitch smiled so big it almost hurt. Even though he had no idea what his role might be, should Ti and Jen's friendship blossom into something more, he didn't care. Mitch went to bed feeling euphoric, as if he'd had his own successful second date... well, first date, but second encounter.

The following Monday, Ti left Jen a message hoping to return her CD and reciprocate by loaning her two of his favorites: Mississippi Mongrels and Sugarloaf Mountaineers.

"How about I stop over around noon?" Jen suggested.

Her morning crawled at a snail's pace. Finally, at 12:00 Jen crossed the parking lot and entered the bright atrium. A cheerful Claire greeted her as she signed the visitor log. "Hello there."

Jen entered the office doorway to find Ti tinkering with some loose castors on a rolling chair. Mitch was reviewing a lumber order. The three CDs were stacked on the edge of Ti's desk.

"How was your morning?" busybody Mitch asked.

"Oh, fine. I'm working with student health records today."

"So," he said, "You eat lunch?"

"Not yet."

"Perfect," Mitch said. "Ernesto's got some mighty fine chicken parmesan subs on the menu, and I insist you join us."

Ti gave his father a look. *Join us? Since when do we plan an office lunch?* Realizing what his father was up to, Ti figured Jen would not know how to respond without some indication from him as well. "Yes, stay. I'd like you to have lunch with us."

Jen, who had been looking at the cover of the Mississippi Mongrels CD, looked up. "Well, okay. Would one of you split a sub with me?"

The two rugged men snickered. "We don't split meals," Mitch said grinning, yet quite serious.

"But we'd be happy to help with whatever you can't finish," Ti added.

"My treat. Be right back." Mitch held up a finger and sauntered out the doorway. Excited his date had accepted his offer, Mitch glided into the cafeteria. "Ernesto, the room smells divine."

"Speaking of deeevine," Deirdre said, "how's my favorite bachelor?"

"Good, but running late. I'll catch you later. Promise." Mitch packed the sandwiches—one pre-cut, grabbed napkins, and selected three large chocolate chip cookies at the cash register. Then he returned.

The three ate their sandwiches—or half—in the office with light conversation. Mitch looked up Jen's horoscope, after reciting his and Ti's. Ti observed them interact, happy his father had asked her to stay. He realized that her liking his father was important to him.

Over the next month, Jen and Ti had several conversations, two office lunches, a date at an ice cream shop, another at the diner, a bike ride, and a walk in the park where they gazed upon a slow, orange sunset.

As the end of August approached, Ti wanted to invite Jen to his mountain home for fishing, swimming, and rafting on the lake while the sun was still warm. Autumn approached swiftly in the mountains. Jen was receptive to the idea once before, so he hoped she might accept an invitation. The thought of sharing his special place with her thrilled him, like lightening splintering across his every nerve ending.

Normally, Ti loved Wednesday, which meant Chinese for dinner—except once, which was his date with Jen. *Wow, it's Wednesday already. Whoa, is that possible? Weekends never come quick enough. But weekends mean less contact with Jen. I hope she can visit soon, or else the summer season will be gone.*

Ti called her. "It's going to be a nice day."

"Yes, and rain tonight."

"Did you hear the news report on the lost school bus from Valley Summer Camp? How bizarre for an experienced driver." Ti felt like his father, making small talk about the news.

"Nate's been playing more basketball and avoiding his summer reading," Jen chuckled. "I need to stop on the way home to buy jeans in the next size; he seems to spike a growth spurt every time I turn around."

Ti coughed. "Jen, I'd like you and Nate to come to Walleycito. It's so much fun. We can go out on the boat, rent wave-runners, fish, swim, hike, and anything else you might like. You'd both have a blast."

Wow, a trip to the mountains. She took a breath. "That sounds fun. I'll look at my schedule and let you know."

They wished each other a good day and hung up.

Jen knew she was committed for a few weekends, including a family shore trip and Labor Day picnic. Then, a birthday party for Nate's buddy Travis the Saturday after that.

Since when am I so popular? Most weekends, Jen spent the morning cleaning the house and yard, and the afternoon at the park climbing up the slide and spinning the merry-go-round. She summed up the details for Ti in an email and sent it. *Guess it'll have to wait till mid-September.*

Ti slumped in his chair when he read her message. Focused on warm weather and the dwindling opportunity for a day on the lake, he replied:

Well, I got your message and looked over your schedule. I can't believe it's almost the end of summer. Looks like you have a lot going on. Hey, you didn't mention this coming weekend. I know there is not much notice, but if it's open for you, it may be our last chance to swim this year. It will be out of the question next month. So, what do you think?

Write soon, m

Jen thought and thought, and thought some more. *Can I drop everything and go? Better yet, should I? Not that there's anything but chores to drop. But should I accept his invitation... to include Nate? Is it too soon to introduce them? Is there anything wrong with this?* She had no doubt Nate would have fun. Ti said swimming, boating, and wave-runners. After a few hours of debate in her mind, she wrote back:

Okay. Send me the details. It might work. Nate and I will be at the park with friends on Friday until about 4:00. We are free after that!

Ti's spirits soared. He turned to his father, who was sitting across the office. Absorbed in the building inspector's report, Mitch held his glasses in his left hand, which also held up his lowered brow.

Good thing Ti had an easy boss.

"Dad," he said, trying to conceal the enthusiasm in his voice, "I'm taking tomorrow off. Jen is coming to the house this weekend, and I'm going to clean and get the upstairs bedroom ready for guests. I'll stay in your room; you get the small bed in the spare room. Okay?"

Mitch acted casual, staring at the page, even though he no longer had any idea what he'd been reading. "Umm-hmm. Okay with me."

Mitch wanted to jump out of his skin with excitement for Ti. With adrenaline glands working overtime, they both felt the same rush of excitement but for different reasons.

CHAPTER 9

Jen rummaged around the house, packing provisions for their outing with Allie and the kids. She made lunch, packed paper plates, napkins, and a tablecloth, checking each item off her list. She stuffed the Frisbee and baseball gloves into a canvas sack and topped it off with her book, just in case she found a few quiet moments. Thinking about the weekend, Jen scribbled a second list. Upstairs sat a duffle bag containing two changes of clothes with multiple layers for each of them, bathing suits, toothbrushes, and Nate's favorite stuffed animal.

We'll need sun lotion, bug spray, sunglasses, and a hat would be good... flip-flops, shoes for hiking... Oh, and the fishing poles—our prize purchase from that garage sale... the orange raft...

The phone rang, interrupting her thoughts.

"Hi, Al." Jen's mind returned to the present.

"Travis has a fever," Allie sighed. "It doesn't look like we can go today. I guess that's that for our last trip before school starts. Sorry."

"Oh, poor thing. Don't worry about us. We'll hang here, maybe roller blade. Tell Travis we hope he feels better."

Around midday, the phone rang again. Jen and Nate were batting the pink and blue badminton birdie around the back yard.

"Hello," she gasped, grabbing the portable from the side stoop.

"Hi," Ti said. "I was calling to leave a message. I'm on my way back. I left yesterday to get the house ready. You guys have the second floor to yourselves, big bedroom, full bathroom..." He paused, realizing something was amiss. "So, what are you doing home?"

"Our plans got canceled due to illness." Jen caught her breath, as Nate continued to bat the birdie on his racket, moving in slow circles.

Ti's stomach dropped. He swallowed. "Not either of you..."

"Nope, we're good. We're running around in the yard enjoying our day off. We're all packed, and ready anytime."

"Great! We'll get an early start. Be there in an hour to get you. Bye!"

"We're getting chauffer service too?" she mumbled.

Ti called his father. "Hey, what's up?"

"Nothing much. I'm getting psyched to get home and settled for our company." Mitch sounded casual, but as he spoke, he felt effervescent, as if champagne had been poured into his veins and tiny, light bubbles were carrying joy through his whole body.

"Yeah, Dad. Jen's schedule changed; we might be a little earlier than we thought. I'll call when we leave. No telling how long it will take if we hit traffic at the bridge."

"Okay." Mitch smiled, understanding Ti's enthusiasm to share their place with guests, especially these guests.

The Mitches frequently had company. First, it was a beautiful place. Second, there was a lot to do—no need to search for entertainment. In fact, there was never enough time to do it all. Third, they liked to be home, especially since they weren't able to be there every day. Except for going to Lenny and Camille's, they preferred to be the hosts. And finally, they were darn proud of that house.

So, with a little pep in his step, Mitch snuck out fifteen minutes early. "Okay doggies, in the truck you go. Can't wait to get home. We are having company this weekend." He put the car in gear.

His brain turned on autopilot, getting lost in thoughts of building the cabin. The first time it evolved as their lives took new direction, like a river diverted when a tree falls in its path. After a decade of mountain life at the trailer, the Conner family sought a bigger, more permanent place. They found a perfect plot of land but couldn't locate a decent builder. During their research, Mandy fell in love with log cabins.

"We know as much about construction as anyone," Mitch said.

"Yeah, Dad, we can build it. We'll be the general contractors and hire experts as we need 'em. We've got a long list of contacts from work."

They made the commitment, purchased a log kit, and employed workers for different parts. A year later, an incredible log home stood on their once empty plot of land: a seventeen-acre parcel, semi-private with the house up the hill, in the rear half of the lot.

One day, when the house had been almost finished, a car drove up the driveway and a man stepped out.

"Hello!" The man yelled to the two workers. Mitch was closer, since Ti preferred the high jobs and was up on the roof.

"Can I help you?"

"I've seen this house go up. I was hoping you'd refer me to your builder. My lot's just up the road. I'm doing a log home, but I'm not having any success with construction. I've let two contractors go already."

"Well... actually, we're doing it." Mitch put his hands in his pockets.

"Great, when will you be ready to start your next job?"

"Uh, well, we're not official builders. We have other jobs. We built our house without a deadline. I don't think we could do yours."

"Are you sure? You guys are the best I've seen, and I've seen a lot of builders. I'm serious. I'd like to hire you."

"Yeah, we're sure. Good luck!"

The man drove away. Mitch told Ti about the conversation, and they joked about building homes as careers. Their jesting turned into dreaming.

"I see that look in your eye, Dad. You're really considering this, huh?"

"I don't know. I wonder about expenses and insurance and whatever else we'd need. Can we make a living at it?" Mitch paced as he spoke.

"Seriously, Dad. You're no spring chicken." Ti poked fun to conceal his hesitation. *It would mean big changes. But I trust this man with my life.*

"Hey, you're just about twenty. I'm barely past fifty—a perfect combination of muscle and wisdom."

Two weeks later the man had returned. He approached with his hands on his hips. "Okay, listen. I want you to build my log home. What can I say to get you guys to reconsider?"

That appeal began a decade of building custom log homes. Mitch and Ti worked well together. Ti observed carpenters and electricians; Mitch paid close attention to plumbers. They learned all components of construction. Soon they had contracted several jobs and hired a crew. Their relationship evolved from parent-child to partner and friend. Mitch smiled. *We were so blessed to build together*.

Mitch also remembered how it all fell apart. His beautiful wife became sick, remaining so for years. She had six surgeries and eight rounds of treatments. Seeing her suffer seared his soul. The stress drained him both emotionally and financially. Even his faith unraveled. After she passed, Mitch and Ti decided to sell Ti's cabin, a half-mile up the road, in favor of keeping the original and more sentimental house together.

Four months after Mandy's death, they experienced another disaster. Their log home caught fire and burned to the ground.

January.

Saturday.

A faulty appliance in the basement sparked; that's all it took.

"Ti! Ti! Get the dogs!" Mitch had called.

What's that awful noise? Ti rolled over, dazed. Coming into consciousness, he'd scrambled for the staircase. "C'mon doggies, c'mon. Dad, what's going on?"

"I don't know. Get the dogs in the car, drive it down the driveway."

Ti got the dogs settled and ran back up.

"What are you doing?" Mitch yelled from the front, as the orange glow in the rear grew brighter.

"I'm getting your thirtieth anniversary grandfather clock. The porch is safe." Ti also snatched his mother's statues from the nearby china cabinet. That was all they could save—no photos, no certificates, no furniture, no clothes. Lenny gave them clothes, shampoo, and the cash he had on hand to purchase shoes and a toothbrush. Camille insisted that the Mitches stay with them at least until they rebuilt the exterior.

What a mess. Mitch's form wilted. *It's hard to imagine possessing absolutely nothing in a matter of minutes, but…*

Driving with little traffic on the road, Mitch recalled how they'd gone back to the rubble and sifted in search of one thing he'd hoped to find, knowing it was next to impossible. There was nothing but deep ash, a sink, a tub, and a couple of crunched pipes. The insurance adjuster walked them over the debris, explaining how to detect the fire's cause.

That was a rough time, but somehow we managed. When things get tough, that's when we learn the most about our strengths and our purpose in God's plan. They were lucky then, and they were lucky now. Mitch's frown vanished; his dark memory brightened.

◆ ◆ ◆ ◆

Ti pulled into Jen's driveway. She walked outside just in time to hear a car screech down the street. For a split second, she thought she recognized the small black pickup. She turned her attention to Ti getting out of his oversized red truck with the huge tires.

Nate's eyes lit up. "Cool!"

"Nate, this is my friend Ti, who I told you about."

"Hi, I'm Nate." Nate stared at the truck.

"Nice to meet you, Nate. Let me show you inside," Ti said.

"Uh, I have all the gear loaded into my car. I just need the fruit out of the refrigerator. I'll follow..."

"No way," Ti interrupted. "The mountain roads have sharp turns and hazardous hills. I'm not comfortable with you in the small car; the truck's much more stable." He noticed her hesitation. "I won't kidnap you, I promise. If you aren't having a good time—either of you—I can bring you back at any moment."

Jen paused, seeing his sincerity.

"Really, I insist. It's much safer."

He unloaded her trunk, transferring their gear to the truck. Jen put the snacks from the refrigerator into a cooler. She checked Toby's food and water, rubbed his ears, locked the door, and they were off.

"It'll be nice to get away for a few days, huh Nate?"

"Yeah Mom. Do you have a basketball hoop?"

"No, but I think you'll like the stuff we do have." Ti smiled.

The ride was easy. They spoke about work, school, biking, and topics on the radio with open and pleasant dialogue from all three. Jen noticed the curvy roads and the array of wildlife as they drove by several deer, two turkeys, and a skunk near the roadside. *Now I understand Ti's concerns.*

They reached their destination safe and sound. As they pulled up to the house, Jen admired how beautiful the property looked.

"The picture doesn't do it justice," she half whispered, her eyes sweeping the front of the house and the charming woods surrounding it.

Jen helped Nate out of the truck while the dogs barked at the window.

"You hear the dogs? They're excited to meet you," she said.

"Yeah," he muttered.

"You're not afraid, are you?"

"Gee, it sounds like there are ten of them!"

"Nope, just four," Ti told him.

"Four! Gosh, when mom said dogs, I figured two!" Nate blurted out.

"Don't worry; they'll love you," Ti scooped the little guy up. He carried him upstairs, holding him high on his shoulder.

He placed Nate on the kitchen counter.

"Hello young man, I'm Mitch." Mitch reached to shake the boy's hand. "Don't worry about them. They're just big teddy bears."

Nate nodded and slowly shook Mitch's much larger hand.

"When you're ready, you can give them a biscuit. They'd never bite, but especially not the guy that gives them treats." Mitch pointed to the cookie jar, and Nate laughed. *Oh, I remember Ti's seven-year-old chuckle.*

"He'll come around; Nate loves animals. This place is beautiful." Jen moved her head from side to side, looking around the picturesque cabin.

Ti gave her a quick tour.

Within five minutes, the prancing, snorting, and sniffing subsided. Still, Nate chose to stay put for a while.

"How was the drive?" Mitch asked.

"Not too bad." Ti reached for a glass. "Want something to drink?"

Nate shook his head. Jen rubbed his shoulder. "No, thanks. The ride was nice, very scenic. We saw lots of wildlife."

"Ah, did you see any bears? I love the bear." Mitch's eyes shone.

"Bear?" Nate looked at Mitch.

"Yeah, they're amazing. Seeing a bear is a bonus."

"How do you ride bikes with bears around?" Nate asked.

They all chuckled and the conversation continued.

After a while, Mitch said, "I'm hungry."

"Me too!" Nate rubbed his belly.

"You just had a snack," Jen said.

"I'm with Nate." Mitch winked at the boy, who smiled in return. "It's almost dinnertime. The pizza place will be busy; let's order." Almost an hour passed before Mitch returned with the piping hot boxes.

They enjoyed the meal, even though Nate ate his share from his strategic position on the kitchen counter, just a few feet from the table.

"Mom, look how the dogs circle near Mitch." Nate laughed and pointed. After his belly was full, he decided the dogs weren't so scary.

"Nate, why don't you bring your bag upstairs? You can unpack and show Ti and Mitch some of your cars."

"Hey, yeah, wanna see?" Nate ran to his backpack.

Mitch followed, keeping the dogs behind him. "You like cars, huh?"

"Gosh, yes," Jen said.

As Nate pulled out a yellow Mustang, Mitch smiled. "Ti, look at this. Bring back any memories? May I?" Nate handed it to Mitch, who held it up.

"Oh." Ti exhaled, and turned to Nate. "That looks a lot like my very first car. When I was fifteen, Dad bought a Mustang just like that."

Nate's eyes widened. Jen sat back in her chair.

"We worked on that thing for two years before Ti got his license. Lot of work, lot of fun. It was a beauty." Mitch took a deep breath.

"Yeah, until Mitch here..." Ti bumped his shoulder. "We finished working one night. The car was perfect. We'd just replaced the air filter. I was vacuuming the seats. Then... Dad slammed the hood."

Mitch winced. "My coffee cup was sitting on the engine block."

"No!" Jen sat straight.

"What?" Nate jumped.

"It left a perfect round dent in our newly polished hood."

"What'd you do?" Jen asked.

"We tried to bang it out but only messed up the paint. We had to replace the whole hood." Mitch shrugged, secretly delighted to share a family story. *That would be nice to do again... with a grandson.*

Ti shook his head. They all moved to the family room. Nate sat on the couch next to his mother and Ti, who continued to keep the curious Labs at bay while they watched a movie together.

The weekend weather cooperated. They parked the boat along the shore. Jen soaked in the scene of birch and pine trees. Nate swam and threw toys for the dogs. They spent hours basking in the sun. Mitch took Nate for three rides on the wave runner, going faster each time. He was in his glory having a youngster to share his favorite pastimes with again.

"Weeee-heee!" Nate shouted, wedged between Mitch's forearms.

Ti took Jen out twice. The second time, as he showed off hopping over waves, one got the better of them and they tipped. Laughing, Jen didn't mind the unplanned soaking.

Later, Ti pulled the old ATV out from the back of the garage.

"Some fresh gas and new spark plug should do it." Ti pulled the starter cord three times.

"Hey, Muscles. Move aside," Mitch said. He stroked the handle. "C'mon old gal, you've got more rides left in you. Start up for us." He yanked. The rusty machine coughed and sputtered, then hummed as the engine caught.

"Wow!" Nate climbed up. Mitch taught him all the basics. "This is the throttle, turn it this way... Here's how you shift, but you'll stay in second gear on the driveway... see, this one..." Mitch's paternal instinct clicked on without a thought.

Nate grinned from ear to ear, circling slowly around the large stone driveway. Jen pulled on a sweatshirt, watching Nate ride back and forth with glee. Ti threw his flannel over her shoulders, not so much because she needed another layer, but more because he felt chivalrous and hoped it might remind him of her when he wore it later. She smiled up at him, as Nate called out, "Mom. Watch me, watch me!"

Thrilled, Jen observed Nate having fun. *He deserves it.*

As Jen tucked him in that night, he said, "Mom, this has to be the coolest place anyone's ever lived in."

Ti and Jen reveled in their activities. They connected, learning more about each other. A foundation of trust and friendship formed.

Mitch, too, relished his contact with both Jen and Nate, wondering how it might be to have them around more often. Watching Ti and Jen, his mid-section filled with butterflies, like it had when he took Mandy out the first few times. Mitch went to bed in the spare room, praying, drifting into a peaceful sleep with doggies lying all around him.

On Sunday, nobody wanted to leave. All four attended early Mass together. Mitch led the others through the Church entrance. *Thank you,*

Lord. This weekend is great... and Mandy, my angel, I know you're watching us. St. Anthony, did you have a hand in any of this?

After bonding through an uplifting Sunday worship, followed by a pancake breakfast, they enjoyed a few more hours of fun and sun.

"C'mon Nate, I'll teach you how to cast." Ti waved for him to follow.

"Don't you mean fish?" Nate ran behind him.

"Ha! Nope. Ti doesn't quite *fish.* He never catches anything!" Mitch chuckled, waved at them, and sat back. "Good luck!"

Jen told Mitch about her book. "I brought it along, thinking I might have time to read, but I've only read a few pages. I like it. It's a love story set in medieval times..."

"Ah, you're a romantic."

"Oh, yeah... can't help it." Jen blushed.

Mitch chuckled, "Yeah, me too. Don't tell Ti I admitted it though."

After about twenty minutes, Mitch and Jen joined them at the dock. Ti caught a small bass. Nate marveled at the scaly creature before Mitch unhooked and tossed it back mumbling, "Darned Betty and her premonitions. St. Anthony... a young lady... more luck... Can't believe it..."

As Jen and Nate left, Mitch said, "Come back anytime, now. Okay?" He wanted her to feel welcome by him too. *They make a good pair... compatible in interests, music, taste, and especially values.*

Ti drove them home and helped Jen carry her bags inside. "Bye, Nate."

"Bye, Ti! Thank you. I have to go put this in my room!" Nate ran to his bedroom with his new treasure.

Mitch had given Nate a miniature ATV with four oversized wheels and camo-colored paint. "How about you hang onto this until you come back?"

The boy leapt up. "Oh, yes. Could I?"

Nate placed the ATV on his dresser, right in the middle where it was sure to be seen from anywhere in the room.

Jen gave Ti a big hug and thanked him for a wonderful time—time that felt good, easy, relaxing.

He gave her a gentle kiss goodnight and moseyed to the driveway.

Wow. Jen watched him start the truck.

Wow. Ti backed out.

◆ ◆ ◆ ◆

The following week, the two spoke every night and had each other over for dinner once apiece. Jen was having mixed feelings about the weekend at the shore with her family. But Nate was excited for the anticipated fun, not to mention the spoiling. They arrived after her sisters.

Jen stood on the deck listening to the seagulls. *Gee, I miss him.*

"Yeah, we had a blast. We rode wave runners, and..." Nate bounced around, describing his weekend in the mountains.

"Oh?" Sienna looked up. Colton sat at the table and placed another piece in his puzzle. "Who was with you?"

While prodding him for details, her siblings made mental lists of reasons to be displeased. Their instincts filled with concern, wondering how Jen could put the child in a situation where he could get hurt again.

The cool stares and awkward exchanges were agonizing. Her sisters and brothers-in-law acted cordial, but uneasy. Even though she understood that they were being sensible, Jen felt like a rabbit among a pack of circling foxes. *Why do my choices always seem wrong to them? We simply had fun. There are no strings attached that could hurt Nate. He was able to experience things he's never done before.* Jen wanted to be able to expose Nate to people and things without scrutiny.

What an opposite feeling from the lighthearted time spent last week. She decided to go for a walk. The soft sand and crashing waves calmed and lifted her spirits.

◆ ◆ ◆ ◆

Mitch's weekend was normal, but seemed a bit empty. Ti mowed the lawn and cleaned the boat. After playing last weekend, he had to catch up on chores. Mitch folded laundry at the dining room table, smiling as he recalled their Friday pizza together with Nate on the counter.

Mitch made dinner with laughter on his mind and lightness in his heart.

"Dad, let's eat a few minutes early. I want to get on the road. Dad? Did you hear me?" Ti normally waited until the last possible second before leaving. They had to travel but were never eager to do so. But this Sunday after dinner, Ti scurried off hoping to see Jen.

Mitch got in his car to drive south. Consumed with blissful zeal for Ti's new relationship, the urgency he felt for his son to find someone minimized. *Hmmm. I wonder what will happen to me? What's my place in the family, if this works out? Well, whatever happens, it's a small price to pay for Ti's happiness.*

It was important to secure that future for Ti. Mitch just knew.

Mitch reached the guesthouse, unloaded the car, and carried out his bedtime rituals.

Dear Lord,
Thank you for this day,
with all I got to do and see
Experiencing each person and event
That you generously gave to me.

He turned his attention to St. Anthony.

To you, Anthony, special patron, I ask,
find for Ti a love that will last,
with all my desire to you I pray,
just in case I should ever go away.
Francis, don't forget my four legged kids.

Lastly, he said, "I miss you, Mandy."

◆ ◆ ◆ ◆

Meanwhile, Ti had called Jen, suggesting he stop by with some ice cream.

"I never turn down ice cream." With Nate in bed, Jen waited on the front porch. She heard a car approaching and turned. Her stomach dropped. A black pickup pulled into her driveway.

"Hey, Jen baby, nice to see you relaxing on the porch."

An eerie cold crawled over her skin. "What are you doing here?"

"I miss you. You were good with little Kyle. Are you ready to talk about us, about getting back together?"

"Not at all. You can't be serious."

"C'mon, Jen. No one's exclusive anymore; you're delusional."

Jen swallowed, speechless.

"I've got a new job. Let's start over; you'll see..."

She stood. "I think you should go."

A red truck pulled up along the street in front of Jen's cottage. Ti surveyed the scene as he approached. Jen stood facing a tall man with a thin nose and dark, shifty eyes. Noticing her clenched fists, he sensed the tension. "Hello, Jennifer. How are you tonight?"

"Okay," she murmured.

"And you are?" Ti looked at the man.

"Her boyfriend. We're fine, and you're not invited in this conversation."

"Oh, on the contrary, I'm quite invited, and certain you should leave. In fact, if I ever see your lousy, scrawny face on this block again, I'll beat the crap out of you."

"Who do you think you are?" The man's thin form stiffened.

"A friend, a neighbor, a cousin... doesn't matter. I'm her exterminator. She's moving on with her life. No more cockroaches."

Jen watched them standing toe to toe. Ti was not backing down. His sense of protection was like a lioness: confident, instinctive, endless.

As if a switch had flipped in her subconscious, her heart clicked and locked, connecting twice as deeply to Ti as when he'd shared his sentiment at the pudding stand.

Ti hissed, "Just go."

The insect breathed the poison and shriveled. He turned, walked away, started his black pickup, and did not look back.

Ti watched Jen's form relax. He rubbed her biceps for a moment, and then held up his index finger as if to say, "hang on." He retrieved the carton from his truck and presented two cups swirled high with cool cream.

"They're a little soft." His lips curved into a coy smile.

Jen giggled. "Let's sit."

They enjoyed the flavors and the opportunity to savor an hour in each other's company. Sitting on the porch, they gazed at the stars. The minutes flew. When it was time to go, Ti gave her a long kiss good night. Jen felt alive, like a princess freed from a dungeon.

CHAPTER 10

The following week, Jen invited Ti to Sienna's Labor Day picnic. Sienna welcomed him at the door. "Nice to meet you."

"Hey, my little country mouse." Jen's dad hugged her. "Hello." He smiled at Ti. "Glad you guys could make it."

Nate looked at Ti and pointed. "She's a mouse, his only country one. Poppa's the mouse king." He ran inside.

Sitting on the couch behind a newspaper, one brother-in-law mumbled to the other, "Ignore him. Maybe he'll leave and we can talk some sense into Jen about dating so soon."

Only her father overheard. *Having a concern is one thing; being rude is another*. He directed Ti out to the patio, putting one hand on his broad shoulder and shaking his hand in a warm gesture with the other. "So, you work construction and maintenance?"

"Yes, I've been around maintenance my whole life. My father mentored me... well, several of us. We built houses for many years." They walked outside together.

"I'm a bit of a fixer myself, but I just tinker around the house. Know anything about attic fans? Got one that's on the fritz." Her father had no trouble making conversation.

Neither Jen nor Ti was aware of the sibling exchanges, but Nate later asked his mother, "How come Uncle Colton wanted Ti to go away?"

◆ ◆ ◆ ◆

Time passed into the fall. Despite cautious resistance, Ti and Jen continued to build their relationship. They ate dinner at each other's places, chatted daily, and visited with Mitch and Nate for two outings, including one at

Walleycito Lake in October with the foliage in full splendor. All four enjoyed hiking along trails in the vibrant woods, riding bikes—despite the potential for a bear sighting—and walking along the country roads. Mitch smiled a lot that weekend. *Ti and Jen remind me of Mandy and me; they've got the real thing.*

One morning in early November, Mitch sat in the office sipping a cup of ginger tea and flipping through the last two pages of the newspaper. Ti searched the toolbox for his measuring tape.

"Hey, remember your mother's jewelry when you decide to give that girl a ring," Mitch said, his eyes set on the page.

"Okay." Ti looked up; his mind drew a blank.

"Good. It needs to be cleaned, fixed, probably sized..."

Holy Cow! Did my father just say that? Ti shook his head as if to cast off an annoying mosquito and absorbed the statement. He paused to refocus. "So what are you saying? And since when are you inside my head?"

"Well, what I'm saying," Mitch said coolly, "is that the ring went through a lot and it's been stored a while. If you want to give it to her for the holidays, you have to arrange for all that. It'll take some time."

A week prior, they'd attended Mitch's niece's wedding. The event was held outdoors on a beautiful day. Jen met Mitch's three sisters and many of Ti's cousins.

"Pleased to meet you," one said, offering her approval through a subtle wink. Another whispered to Mitch with a nod, "Nice."

"Yeah, they're good together." Mitch leaned close to her. "Won't be long before we're celebrating another wedding; I can feel it."

Mitch snapped several photos of the lovebirds laughing and goofing with each other in the field near the reception area before attaining one properly posed shot. Ti and Jen enjoyed the celebration, making mental notes about various aspects of the wedding. Noticing the beauty in the outdoors, the fields, the décor, and even some of the prayers, they considered how something similar could fulfill their own dreams.

And the senior Mitch had simply soaked it all in...

◆ ◆ ◆ ◆

Ti arrived to get Jen for dinner and sat on the couch. Jen was at her desk sorting through the mail. “What’s Mitch making for dinner?”

“Pork chops.” Ti sat up straighter. “I’ve got my mom’s diamond ring. Dad mentioned it. I’d like to show it to you. Jen, I...”

“What?!” she spun around in the chair, jaw dropped, eyes wide.

Ti rewound. “Today, my father brought up my mother’s ring.”

“What exactly did he tell you? You mean your mom’s engagement ring? Wait, please... some details...,” she blurted out.

“My father said this morning, ‘*Don’t forget your mom’s jewelry when you’re ready to give that girl a ring.*’ That’s what he said, word for word.”

“Just like that?” Her eyes twinkled.

“Yup. He saw us at Kate’s wedding. He’s no fool. He must know we spoke about an engagement and marriage, especially after attending hers. I think we should keep talking about it.”

He took a small breath. “Jen, I’m crazy about you. We’re in sync with just about everything. We get along great. It’s clear to me we have a future together. I know you feel the same.”

“Yes, Ti, I know we’re going to be together. I feel it too.”

“So, I want to talk about the first step, the ring.”

“What about it?” Jen’s whole face softened to reveal a genuine smile, bright as a ray of sunlight. “You have your mom’s diamond ring, and you want to give it to me! Really? Wow! What’s to talk about? I thought you lost everything in the fire but the clock and a few collectibles.”

“I’m concerned,” he began. “Because you need to see it... to look it over before we decide to use it. I want you to adore the ring I’m going to give you. That’s important to me.” Processing the rest of her queries, he explained, “And, yes, we did lose just about everything. I was able to get the clock and statues. Having a few things from my mother means a lot.”

Jen sat on the edge of her chair.

“But we went back to the debris in the daylight. Dad thought about mom’s engagement ring as we walked the grounds with the insurance man. The guy searched the rubble looking for clues about the fire’s origin. After he left, we figured out where Dad’s room was and how the dresser would have fallen through the floor. We started sifting.”

Jen’s jaw dropped a little.

"It took a while. Dad picked up what looked like a hunk of charcoal. He went to toss it aside but thought twice and called me over. We stared at it for a second, then pried it open. The ring was... there. We figured the old-fashioned jewelry-box foam had melted, insulated, and preserved it. We almost sold it to get by, but we're so glad we kept it now."

She floated on his every word.

"And I want to talk more seriously about this wedding stuff. I'd like us to get engaged and move toward marriage."

Her eyes overflowed with soft, light tears. "Let me make sure I understand," she began with a low voice that increased in volume as she spoke. "You come in like it's no big deal and tell me that you want to talk more about getting engaged. Your father not only gives us his blessing, but wants us to use the ring that your parents shared... with, from what I hear, was a very close and special love... You tell me the story of how it's the only thing you regained after the fire." She sucked in a breath. "You want to give it to me, and you want to know *if* I will like it? What are you, nuts? Of course, I'll love it. I already love it!"

She jumped up and hugged him, stretching her arms all the way around his thick rib cage. She squeezed as wet droplets fell onto his chest. Joy flowed from her head to her toes. Ti was excited, relieved, and pleased all at once. They felt the love they shared grow in that moment.

He pushed her shoulders back and looked into her eyes.

"Oh, come on. You might say that, but you've not seen it. What if it's so much not-your-style that it can't be everything you want? And you have to check it out because it needs to be cleaned and sized and that could take a while. It would be nice to have for the holidays, wouldn't it?"

"Oh, Ti," she whispered in an exhale. She stood straight. "Well, like I said, I already love it."

He was being practical. Jen always thought she was practical, but she had met her match. When her practical side was tinted with emotion, Ti could be more practical than she.

"I was never one for surprises. So if it's important for your peace of mind that we look it over, it's okay with me. But I already adore the idea and all it represents."

◆ ◆ ◆ ◆

Big M beamed with anticipation for the upcoming Thanksgiving holiday. The buttons on his striped shirt almost burst open despite the free air space around his middle. A fit sixty-five-year-old, Mitch felt like a proud poppa, excited for his son, but for himself too. *We're having a real family Thanksgiving. In our own home. The first holiday in over ten years, since we lost Mandy, rebuilt the house, and changed jobs.*

It was a long time coming, and they deserved it.

A week before the holiday, Jen stopped at the Pastoral Center.

"Oh, we're so happy about what you've done for those two men!" Claire exclaimed. Cassie was in the lobby too.

"Huh?" Jen reached for the visitor log pen.

"They are so excited. Big M is actually glowing!" Claire said.

"All they speak about is how they've ordered this huge Christmas tree for you guys to put up on turkey day," Cassie moved her arms out wide.

"And how you'll decorate the house all weekend." Claire clapped her hands. "They've not had a tree for Christmas since Mitch's wife died."

"Now it's different. They have you; they have Nate. Their enthusiasm rushes out of those two like water down a waterfall." Cassie grinned.

"Big M is ecstatic that you're both cooking parts of the family Thanksgiving supper," Claire continued.

"They speak about their plans for just about every hour of the holiday weekend: cooking, decorating, ballgames, fires in the fireplace... like I said, it gushes on and on." Cassie raised and twirled her hands.

"They don't talk about anything else, not sports or the weather," Betty said with a smile as she walked by.

"Well, not unless it's about how Thursday's forecast calls for flurries to make the ambiance even better," Claire added.

"Yeah," Betty said. "They are looking forward to these four days like someone who's won an all-expenses-paid trip to Hawaii!"

Jen heard something like this from everyone she spoke to who knew them. *Yikes, the pressure's on. I can't disappoint either of them.*

◆ ◆ ◆ ◆

"Hi, Mom," Jen called, entering the house. "Go find Nana, Nate."

"Hi, Mouse," her dad said, as she entered the family room.

"I just came by to give you a Thanksgiving hug, since we'll be celebrating in the mountains this year."

"C'mon in. We're just sitting down for a snack," her mother said.

"Yay, cookies!" Nate grabbed two and plopped in a chair.

After a half-hour visit, and with Nate entranced in a video game, Jen's dad said, "Come help me in the garage."

"Sure." She bopped behind him.

"Jen, uh, listen... Your siblings are concerned about your spending Thanksgiving with Ti. He seems like a nice guy, but if this doesn't work out, they're worried about Nate. I know you've had it hard, honey."

"Dad..." Jen's jaw dropped. Her hands began to shake. "I don't know what to say." She swallowed. "I thought it... was okay, at least with you."

"It was. I mean, it is. I like him. They just asked me to remind you, I'm sorry. But Colton made a good case for your being careful. You know..." He touched her shoulder.

"Dad, Ti's a wonderful man. We have a lot in common—all the important things. We were just having fun, getting to know each other..."

"Were?"

"Well, it's getting serious. I've known they didn't approve all along. But now I know Ti and I are going to have a future together."

Jen's father sucked in a deep breath and put his arm around her. "I just want you to be happy, Jen. As long as you and Nate are happy." He stepped back and looked at her. "You know, Colton's become pretty important in Nate's life. He doesn't have a son of his own. Maybe his attachment to Nate is influencing his opinion too."

"He doesn't have to lose his bond with Nate. Having more positive role models is a good thing. Since when is there a limit on the number of people a person can love?" Jen huffed.

"Let's hope he comes around. The others are warming up. I have faith." Her dad smiled and kissed the top of her head.

As she was leaving, some of her family members drove up.

Colton got out of the car. "I can't believe you're spending Thanksgiving with that guy. You and Nate belong with your family."

"Thanksgiving *is* a time for family, Jen," Sienna added. "I hope you won't regret this."

Jen waved. "I'm good. Have a nice holiday, guys." She drove home, put Nate to bed, and had a long, hard cry.

◆ ◆ ◆ ◆

Jen packed all her decorations, and she had plenty. Her family started ornament collections for each child when they were born. She also had stuffed animals wearing Santa hats, lights, and her favorite manger scene for the mantel in the log home. *It will look better there than ever before.*

With a full and heavy truck, Ti drove Jen, Nate, and the decorations north for the long-awaited weekend. Mitch and Jen cooked their delicacies in the country kitchen.

"Hand me the garlic powder," Mitch reached toward Jen.

"Here you go. What are you doing with that measuring spoon?"

"I gotta measure it."

"Measure shmeasure... I just toss in a good dash." Jen laughed.

With a bright fire roaring in the fireplace and grand smells wafting throughout the rooms, they enjoyed their first holiday. The traditional football game played on the television. Snow flurries whitened the crisp air outside. Even the best artist painting the most joyous scene could not have captured the emotion and sentiment filling the cabin that day.

Ti hugged Jen. "Oh, it smells so good. When will it be ready?"

"Yeah, me and Ti are done playing checkers. I'm hungry," Nate said.

"About ten minutes. Nate, wanna help me set the table?" Mitch handed him a stack of plates.

As they said grace, Mitch added, "Lord, thank you for bringing our little group of misfits together."

"Even Toby," Nate added as the cat watched from atop the stairs.

Jen giggled. Mitch held back a tear. *This is the best—a big dinner, at the table, on the old china, a real holiday. I may even have a daughter and grandson soon. Misfits or not, we are meant for each other.*

Enjoying their feast, bliss filled their spirits as if the air contained traces of nitrous oxide. They visited; they ate. *It's been so long since we enjoyed a real holiday*. Mitch rested his chin in folded hands, supported on his elbows.

They deserved every precious moment that the day brought to them. Mitch went to bed Thanksgiving night with the window cracked open.

Dear Lord, thank you for this day—and what a really great day it was: full of fun and love and joy.

On Thanksgiving, thank you for the good things in my life—today I had even more of Your blessings to enjoy.

St. Anthony, please let those two grow in the love that's begun. True love is all I ever wanted for my son.

"Oh Mandy, I really miss you, my love. You would be so proud of our son! We had such a wonderful holiday! After so long, we had a family again–his family."

◆ ◆ ◆ ◆

The next day, the tree almost didn't arrive for their perfectly planned weekend, sending Ti into a fury. "I can't believe it!" He paced while Jen made some turkey sandwiches for lunch.

"Look!" Nate pointed at a large, white truck climbing the driveway. Mitch moved beside him. Jen smiled. They both watched with their right hand on their hip and their weight on their left leg.

The driver unloaded the heavy box. Ti carried it inside. He measured the window to center it precisely. It took the entire afternoon to un-fluff the large branches, bringing the pine needles almost to life. While Ti and Nate put her little tree in the family room, Jen unpacked her decorations.

"Well, you were right. You do have enough ornaments to decorate both trees!" Mitch shook his head.

"Yeah, but the glitter-covered ones you got will add just the right touch in between." Jen held a silver and green glass ornament up to the light.

Nate wrapped garland along the railings. Ti sat stuffed animals on any beam or furniture top that would hold one.

One day while shopping, Ti said, "We need a Christmas bear with the date on its foot for our first holiday together."

"But which one, the girl or the boy? They're both so cute!" Jen giggled.

Ti couldn't resist and grabbed them both. Being a carpenter, he then constructed a little wooden bench. He stained it light brown and sat the bears in their green and red outfits on the seat. He stepped back. *Perfect*. Then he hung it like a swing from the rafters in the family room.

"That has to be the best gift I've ever received," Jen said softly, staring up at it. She treasured it because Ti had made it. Seeing how much she liked it, he made two small ladders with the rest of the wood and ropes. One held her stuffed snowmen and the other her three silly reindeer.

Over the weekend, Ti and Jen learned how much Mitch and Nate had in common. As town criers, one or the other announced each hour and what it meant—like lunch or taking out the dogs. They both thrived on routine, both enjoyed silly jokes, both took baths in the evening, and both liked to wear the same jeans as often as possible.

"Hey Mitch. Knock, knock." Nate bounced in front of him.

"Who's there?" Mitch played along.

"Orange."

"Orange who?"

"Orange you glad we get to stay up late?" Nate said.

"Nice try, my little weasel." Jen giggled. "Just a few more minutes."

Jen and Ti snuggled on the couch Saturday evening. They sat still, quiet, and content... taking it all in with sincere gratitude.

"Oh Ti, just look at it all: the decorations, the flurries, the fire..."

"We created our very own winter wonderland, right out of a magazine." Ti put his arm around her and pulled her closer.

Mitch had always wanted a family for Ti and for himself too. That weekend felt like they might be fulfilling their dreams. With the four of them, the family started instantly: the couple, the proud dad, the endearing child, and the five adorable pets.

CHAPTER 11

At Church on Christmas Eve, Jen's family filed into two pews. Ti sat close to Jen. Nate bubbled with anticipation for dinner and presents. He could barely sit still as they waited for the first hymn. Mitch sat proudly on the far end of the second row filled with Jen's family. He wore a pair of dress slacks and an un-striped shirt, one of the rare occasions when he altered his dress code. Instead of attending Mass with Lenny and Camille, Mitch and Ti were joining Jen's traditional Christmas Eve celebration.

Ti had reclaimed the ring almost two weeks prior, and it had been burning a hole in his pocket ever since. It took all the restraint he could muster to keep it there. Both he and his father stole several opportunities to take it out for a peek. Out of their hands for a while, their jewel returned better than expected. Its new shine stunned them.

Mitch and Ti sat in the pew like proud peacocks. Mitch looked over at Jen and then down to her hand holding his son's. He knew that soon it would carry the diamond he'd purchased for Mandy—a moment he recalled as if it were yesterday. Delighted for them, Mitch kneeled and prayed, surrounded by images of the Holy Family and filled with the splendor of Christmas. *God, give Tiger and Jennifer the gift of deep love, like Mandy and I knew. Thank You for bringing them together*. Mitch sat back and exhaled as an unconscious sense of relief flowed over him.

Back at Sienna's, each sister had prepared part of a delicious feast.

"Ti, taste this." Sienna held out a spoon.

"Mmmm, wow. Jen, can you make this?" They all laughed.

Everyone was cordial, including Colton, and the evening was pleasant. They gathered for a family prayer, sang an off-tone rendition of "Rudolf the Red-Nosed Reindeer," and exchanged gifts.

Before they knew it, Mitch, Ti, Jen, and Nate were collecting pets and driving to the woods for a mountain Christmas.

"Jingle bells, jingle bells..." They sang along with the radio.

"Mom, I can't wait to put out the milk and cookies for Santa. We won't get there too late, will we?"

"No way. I have a fresh pack of carrots and two green apples in the cooler for the reindeer." Mitch nodded toward Nate.

The roads were clear and the ride was short, but their eagerness made it seem longer. When they arrived, Mitch flicked the switch that lit the house with Christmas lights. Brightly colored dots outlined the porch and the white ones shone like stars on their special tree.

They emptied the car and got the animals settled. Somehow, all four of them wound up in the living room, staring at the tree. They held hands and wished Jesus a happy birthday as the peace and joy of Christmas and hope for their future consumed them.

I swear I saw the angel smile. Mitch watched her.

Nate broke the silence. "I'll get the cookies and apples!" After he and Jen put them out, she tucked Nate snugly into bed.

Mitch and Ti started a fire in the big stone fireplace, which had never looked so splendid. Jen's nativity scene glowed in the firelight. Mitch bit into a magnificently decorated Christmas cookie.

"See you two in the morning. Merry Christmas!" He kissed the top of Jen's head and patted Ti on the back.

Knowing Nate and the dogs would wake early, the two scurried around preparing the scene for Christmas morning. Then they sat on the couch holding hands, mesmerized by the blaze in the fireplace. "What Child Is This?" played softly on the stereo. Together they savored the harmony in the room.

Ti slid off the couch and onto one knee. He pulled a deep burgundy box from his pocket.

"Jen," he began, "I never knew I could be this happy. I didn't think feelings this deep were of this earth. You make me joyful; you make me a better man; you make me whole and alive. Will you be my wife?"

Hearts swollen with love and eyes brimming with tears of joy, they looked deep into each other's souls. Their destinies locked in that moment.

"Of course!"

Ti pulled the ring from the box. As he placed it on her finger, droplets glided down her face. His tears spilled over too. They sniffed at the same time and laughed. She pulled him up to the couch, kissed and hugged him.

"This is amazing," she said as Ti spun her around so her back was to him. He held her hand out in front of them.

"Now, it's where it was meant to be," he whispered in her ear. Jen gazed at the sentimental symbol Ti shared with her. The flames across the room enhanced the iridescent sparkle.

"Wow, it's even prettier than I remember." She cried some more.

"Yeah, what a bit of cleaning can do; not to mention that it shines because it's on you, my love." Ti held her.

She patted his bicep. "Oh, Ti. It's absolutely perfect."

He moved her hand, tilting it to examine the antique setting. The round stone was set on a high square mount with old-fashioned paw-like prongs of white gold. Even though he knew the ring well, he shared the discovery of each angle with her. They fell asleep in front of the fireplace and dreamed of their perfect Christmas.

Champ rustled at 6:00 a.m. Ti slipped out from under Jen. He opened the back door. The dogs made their way onto the snowy deck. He gazed out over the yard. Small flakes continued to fall as the pooches sniffed and sauntered around the yard. Daisy saw a squirrel dart across a stone and up a tree. It only took two barks to wake Nate. He blinked.

Realizing where he was, he scrambled out of bed and ran into Mitch's room. "Mitch, c'mon! We have to see what Santa brought!"

Mitch moaned. "I'm coming."

Nate dashed out. "Mom, did you see Santa?" With enchanted curiosity, he climbed over his mother on the couch.

"No, but I must have dozed off hoping to catch a glimpse of him."

Nate tugged, pulling Jen upright.

"Good morning you two." Mitch smiled. "Ah, I see it's official."

"Mitch, it's absolutely perfect. Thank you for sharing this with us." Jen held out her hand.

Mitch placed one hand under hers, studied it, and then placed his other hand on top. "I'm thrilled for you both, and proud this symbol of love works for you guys, like it did for me and Mandy." He sighed.

"That's really pretty, Mom," Nate said, with one eye on the tree. "Can we check out what Santa brought?"

Jen nodded.

"Yay!" Nate led the way, still in his pajamas.

Ti followed. "He better've brought me something good."

After a fun morning, courtesy of Santa and the elves, they cooked Mitch's favorite Christmas breakfast: French toast with lots of cinnamon. They cleaned up before opening the gifts they had bought for one another.

"This is awesome!" Nate held up a new ATV helmet.

"Ah, you like that?" Mitch asked, as Nate hugged him.

Ti unwrapped a red toolbox ornament with a hammer on top. "Jen, this is great." He kissed her cheek.

"Jen, this means a lot to me." Mitch opened a photo frame of the four of them standing in front of the tree after they decorated it Thanksgiving weekend. He turned away so no one would see the tear in his eye.

"Let's play my new game!" Jen put the game on the coffee table.

Their spirits soared, delighting in games, music, meals, and giving.

Later, they shared the engagement with family and friends.

Mitch's chest puffed up proudly as he saw his special gem being valued by his son and soon-to-be daughter. *I couldn't be more content with Ti's choice. Ah, Mandy, I'm so happy for them; just look...* Not only was Ti getting a wonderful wife, but she insisted Mitch remain living with them. There was never a doubt about how they'd merge the two families.

"Nate, Mommy and Ti are getting married. Ti will be your step-dad and Mitch will officially be your grandfather."

"Wow! That's great."

"We'll have a wedding, and afterward Ti and Mitch will come live with us in our cottage during the week, when we're at work and school."

"Even the doggies?" Nate asked. Mitch smiled.

◆ ◆ ◆ ◆

Almost everyone was thrilled about their announcement. Jen visited her family the following week. "Hi everyone. I'm so glad you're all here. I have news!" She held out her hand.

Her dad took it. "Oh Jennifer, how nice!"

"It's Ti's mother's ring. It's very sentimental. They—"

"Oh broooother," Colton said, sitting at the table with his newspaper.

"Don't be such a stick-in-the-mud, Colton. C'mon Jen, tell me every detail, what'd he say, how'd he do it?" Sienna led Jen to the couch.

"Are you sure it's not too soon?" her mother asked.

"She's sure," her father replied. "Look at her, it's written all over—this is the real thing. They've made a commitment."

"We want you to be happy," her mother said.

"I know. I am." Jen's thoughts spun in a whirlpool.

"When's the wedding?"

"Have you made any plans?"

"Some." Jen spoke with her sisters and parents for an hour, enjoying the conversation. They accepted her news, truly glad for her and Nate.

On Jen's way out, Colton mumbled, "Don't say I didn't warn you when this rebound of yours falls apart." He looked away. "Notice I didn't say *if*."

Jen scrambled for a response. "Seriously, Colton..."

"We're good. I just want it on record that I disapproved from the start."

"Noted. Now that's the last I'll hear of it." Jen's father stood tall.

"Yes, my kids will get along," her mother said. "Oh, I'm getting a new son-in-law. How wonderful."

◆ ◆ ◆ ◆

"My friends the saints finally answered my two-year novena. I'm so excited for this wedding!" Mitch told Claire in the lobby.

"Wedding?" Deirdre approached, touching his arm.

"Deirdre, you amuse me." Mitch laughed.

"Oh, Mitch, I know it's not your wedding, else I'd be buying a dress. Who's getting married?" she asked playfully.

"Little m." Claire reflected Mitch's glow.

"Yeah, my son is finally getting married."

"They met last summer," Claire added. "Such a romantic story!"

"This past summer? He'd better be careful." Deirdre leaned back.

"Don't be silly," Mitch said.

"How do you know it will last? It's too soon." She glared.

"No, it's not. When it's right, you know." Mitch straightened.

"That's ridiculous. Look how long it's taking for you to ask me out." She puckered her lips and blew him a kiss. "Still, I won't let my daughter get married until she's dated for a few years."

"Years?" Mitch raised his voice. *If I had waited years, I'd have missed even more time with Mandy.*

"Now-a-days, young people take their time. They don't jump in."

"Nonsense! These two are great together. And, my dear, you know I don't date. I've had my one true love."

"You'll come around. But they can't possibly be compatible already. You should slow this down." Deirdre wagged a finger.

"You don't know what you're talking about." Mitch huffed and marched down the corridor.

"Don't worry," Claire said. "You know Mitch never stays mad long."

◆ ◆ ◆ ◆

"I love my new-old ring!" Jen showed Kay and Allie.

"It's beautiful!" Kay held Jen's hand higher.

"The guys are glad they hung onto it. It's so sentimental."

"Dreamy... Jen you deserve a romance right out of the movies." Allie hugged her friend.

"Well, the engagement was perfect; even though I expected it. Christmas Eve... the fireplace... the music... oh, I can't even tell you!"

"Just after midnight on Christmas Eve... utter magic," Kay smiled.

"I'm so happy for you," Allie squealed.

"Of course, you guys will be a part of it, right? We're not sure where or how we're doing it, but you have to be there!" Jen said.

"Wouldn't miss it!" Allie crossed her heart with her fingertip.

"Ditto!" Kay followed suit. They all hugged again.

◆ ◆ ◆ ◆

Jen and Ti relished their engagement and wedding preparations as they began to plan the details.

When? Summer was their favorite season and held many special memories, including the concert and Jen and Nate's first visit to the cabin.

Where? After visiting two lovely establishments near the mountain house the last weekend in January, Ti and Jen confirmed their instinct.

They sat on stools at the island counter.

Mitch stirred the stew in the crock-pot. "Well, what did you think?"

Ti looked at Jen. She took a deep breath. "Mitch." She swallowed. "Would you mind if we had the wedding here?"

"Here?" he repeated. "No, of course not. Really?"

Ti and Jen let out a breath.

"Oh, that's good," she said. "There is no better, more beautiful place we could ever find that would be all we want it to be. This house, the logs you two stacked together, creating this home… the woods, the birds, the fresh crisp air…" Her voice trailed off.

"It's perfect." Ti took her hand.

"The best representation of our love and our family," Jen said.

"I'm all for it!" Mitch said.

How? The following night over supper, Mitch pondered the how. "There's a lot to do. We have to consider the space we have to work with."

With his finger, he drew an imaginary map of the house, garage, and yard on the table. "How'd you figure all this would unfold? I mean the layout of the grounds?"

"Well, I envision our ceremony here, on the front porch." Jen pointed.

"I want a huge barbecue, probably back this way." Ti drew a line through the pretend yard. "Music, of course. I suppose live, although we could choose a selection to play through the stereo and outside speakers."

"Nah," Mitch said. "Live is better. This is the celebration of a lifetime."

He turned back to Jen. "So, chairs and tables, tents… How about we put chairs in the front for the ceremony, and the tents in the back for the reception, here by the garage?" He indicated both on his table map.

"Exactly what I was thinking." She nodded.

"We also need potties." Mitch added.

"Huh?" Jen wondered if he was teasing her.

"Yeah," Ti answered, "the septic tank could never handle an event with so many guests."

Mitch grunted in agreement.

"How does that work?" she asked.

"You leave that to me." Mitch crossed his arms. "Remember the bathroom at my niece's wedding last fall?"

"Sure," Jen said, thinking about the wedding that started their minds toward planning their own.

"That was a mobile trailer," Mitch continued. "Really nice bathroom, but rent-a-potties nonetheless."

They all laughed.

"I really want our day to be unique," Ti said.

"One where both adults and kids can have fun, and remember for years and years," Jen added.

They worked hard, moving from planning to preparation. First, they debated how formal the event should be.

One morning with the breakfast club, Mitch said, "After a heck of a lot of research, I think these kids have figured out what they want."

"Oh, do tell." Betty looked at Ti.

"We're going to have a somewhat traditional ceremony outside on the front porch, followed by a casual reception with catered grilling, music, horseshoes, and volleyball." Ti beamed, picturing his special day.

"What?!" Deirdre chastised Ti with a scowl. "You can't have some back wood, hick barbecue. Weddings should be elaborate and formal."

"Not for me and Jen." Like a crossing guard, Ti motioned for her to stop. His mind re-heard Jen's whisper as he dropped her off Sunday night. "This day will be so perfect for who we are... natural, wholesome, genuine..." The look in her love-struck eyes had been priceless, now and forever etched in his brain.

◆ ◆ ◆ ◆

Once they decided on the ceremony, they worked on the dress. That would dictate what the men would wear. They traveled to shops near and far—all of them. Ti insisted. "Forget superstitions. It took us too long to find each other. We're going to enjoy every minute of this experience together."

"Well, it makes sense, since everything else we want isn't quite traditional either." Jen liked Ti's sentiment too much to disagree.

Of all the evening gowns she tried on, one stood out as a good candidate. It was long and flowing, light lavender with just the right amount of sequins.

Still, Ti took Jen to a bridal shop to explore, and compare the feel of a wedding dress. "But Ti, you know we can't afford a bridal gown."

He took her hand. "Let's just go see what we see."

Mitch shrugged. "Jen's right, but, who knows?"

They entered the shop with open minds and hearts. The attendant brought Jen several lovely gowns.

"That's a beauty." An elderly woman saw Jen exit the dressing room.

"Thank you." Jen smiled and headed back to try the next one.

"I like the train on that one." The attendant held up the long fabric.

Mitch strolled around the store, shuffling his feet, with one hand in the front pocket of his jeans. He found a rack in the back. He glanced through it and saw a simple gown with a tag large enough to catch his eye.

"Hmm, right size." Mitch pulled it forward. As it emerged from the crowded rack, he saw the pretty, delicate lace that trickled down from the waist so elegantly, yet simply. *Oh, this is so... Jen.*

"Jen," he called. "Come see this one."

Jen and Ti went over. Her eyes lit up.

"Oh, it's gorgeous!" she said. Mitch grinned from ear to ear. She left them for six or seven minutes to put on all the undergarments, so they could witness the dress properly. She came out. Their jaws dropped.

"Oh, Jennifer," Ti sighed.

The dress had spaghetti straps with a simple bodice. The lace that pyramided down from the waist was exquisite, light, and uncomplicated. At the bottom, the lace continued as it wrapped around to outline a small scalloped train.

"I feel like Cinderella."

The attendant saw her interest. "Jen, this dress..."

Mitch's heart sank. *Oh no. Is she going to say it is in the back because it's on hold for someone else?*

"...was discontinued last year. It's been sitting on the clearance rack at half-price for months. I think my manager would discount it another ten percent for incentive. She's eager to make room for newer designs."

Mitch gazed up toward the ceiling. "Ah, Mandy, it's so good you are here with us," he whispered. "Thank you!" He looked at Jen, who was glowing with excitement, and then back to an effervescent Ti.

◆ ◆ ◆ ◆

Working through the spring and summer, the foursome created a wonderful venue. Their first accomplishment was clearing a flat spot near the garage for a volleyball court.

"Ti, can I ride in the backhoe too?" Nate jumped up and down.

"After Ti clears the rock debris. Help me pull these out when he moves to the other side." Mitch bent to pick up a large rock slate.

"What a shame. Can't we do something with all these rocks?" Jen stood staring at the pile. "Hmm, a pathway... Yeah, what if we laid them from the garage to here, like this..."

"Good idea, Mom."

Out of the large rock fragments, they created a picture-perfect stone path that wound from the garage through the trees and over to the court. They all had a job in completing the stonework, even Nate.

"This turned out great," Mitch said.

"Yup, right out of a storybook," Jen said, proud and content.

They took a weekend break to celebrate Nate's eighth birthday. Elbow deep in flour paste, Nate and Jen made his annual piñata.

"Look at that mess!" Mitch swiped wet flour from Nate's chin.

"Thanks for letting my friends come here this year. They are going to love this place!" Nate smiled at Mitch.

"You bet, buddy. I'm looking forward to it."

Nate and his friends had a fabulous time. Mitch and Ti took them on ATV rides, hiking, and fishing. Ti found an old piece of plywood and painted it black. He added white racing stripes. Jen made a spin wheel with different sayings about racing forward or back. Mitch bought each boy a different-colored ATV toy, which they used in the game and got to take home afterward.

"Whoo hoo! Go ahead two spaces!" Scott cried moving the copper one.

"Aw, man! Stuck in the pit." Nate frowned, then laughed as his dark red ATV was unable to move that round.

"I win!" Travis yelled.

"Great game, Mom and Ti. Thanks!"

Saturday night, Mitch grilled hot dogs while the boys gathered sticks. Ti whittled the tips. They roasted marshmallows over a campfire, under a star-filled sky. They pitched tents in the yard to camp for the night.

The next weekend, the Conners got back to their projects. They designated a site for horseshoes. Jen's father came to help them dig, rake, plant, and restack woodpiles.

"Mouse, I'm so proud to see you in the country, living your dreams."

"I'm at home in the woods, Dad. What can I say? I'm glad you could come and share this with me." Jen coughed to hide the squeak in her voice as she choked up with delight over her dad supporting her.

Ti and Mitch purchased seventy tons of stone and re-graded the driveway where tents would stand. Jen and Nate painted the garage floor with a light color and planted mums by the shed.

Through each effort, they attained the country feel they desired.

"Nate, grab that bucket. We're going to collect pinecones." Jen picked up a pail, and they walked through the woods. When they'd found enough, Jen made centerpieces using the pinecones, silk sunflowers and daisies.

"Mom, they look really good." Nate picked one up.

"Let's put some around the garage." Jen handed Nate a bunch.

"Okay!" Nate stuck flower stems in the wall beams, while Jen made eight large flower baskets to adorn the porch railing. She found silk garland that matched the blooms in her baskets. She tied it up the railing and across the front stoop where they would stand to say their vows.

Jen set each piece in place and stepped back for a good view. She studied the dark logs with white, yellow, and green accents. "Amazing!"

Ti reached from behind and hugged his soon-to-be wife. She smiled. Mitch and Nate came to check out the view too.

"Nice, Mom!" Nate ran from one side to the other to check both flanks.

"And I have just enough silks left for a matching bouquet," Jen said.

"Nonsense," Mitch said.

"Huh?" Jen asked.

"Dad, don't you like the flowers? They look awesome." Ti turned.

"Of course I do. But Jen will have real flowers, as is proper."

"But these match, and real ones can be expensive," Jen said.

"That is my contribution. No daughter of mine will carry a fake bouquet at her wedding. Her flowers will be alive, vibrant, and fragrant." He held firm to his opinion. Mitch wanted Jen to have real flowers, just like every corsage he had ever gotten for Mandy.

"What kind of flowers do you want, Jen?" Mitch asked.

"Well, how about yellow roses and white daisies?" Jen imagined small, budding roses among green leaves and soft petals.

Mitch worked with the florist. When the time came, he couldn't wait to show them to Jen. His eyes brimmed with tears.

"These are the most beautiful flowers I've ever seen," she gasped.

◆ ◆ ◆ ◆

At 6:00 the morning of their eagerly anticipated day, rain poured so hard that Jen wondered if the tents would collapse. "I know we took risks when we chose to be outdoors, but I really wanted to stand on the beautiful porch with those perfect decorations." She couldn't help but cry.

"The back-up plan means moving the ceremony and guests to the garage. The tables and chairs can stay under the tents." Mitch said.

"The caterers are prepared for shelter. They brought their own tent."

"I wanted our guest to enjoy the grounds, the volleyball, and horseshoes," Jen sighed.

"Well, either way, it's our special day. We have to make the most of it. There's plenty of room for visiting and dancing." Ti stroked her back.

"Good thing you guys built such a huge garage." Nate tried to help.

"Remember, you two have what it takes. Marriage isn't always easy. There can be disappointment, even hardships. You learn to make the most of what you're given," Mitch said.

"You're right, Dad; we are truly blessed. There's always a silver lining." Jen agreed and forced her chin up.

But the saints smiled on them. By 9:00 a.m., the rain had stopped and the clouds parted. Mitch looked up at the blue coming into the sky. *Thanks, Mandy. This means a lot to them. I know you're here with Ti today.*

A tear fell from his raised eyes before he returned to his tidying and preparing with gleeful anticipation for what was next. The weather was ideal long before prayer and promise time.

The wedding was the most incredible moment of their lives. With no overly fancy fuss, just everything that was truly them, they shared their joy with friends and family. Cassie's husband had volunteered to officiate the ceremony. He worked with them to make their declaration of love special and sentimental through each reading and prayer. He shared in their bliss as much as the rest of them. Cassie offered her musical talent. Her performances were incredibly beautiful, including an original song written just for them. Ti and Jen recited personalized vows, with Nate and Mitch standing by their sides.

Kay, Allie, and their kids sat in the front row grinning excitedly for their friend. Jen was pleased that her parents, sisters, and brothers-in-law had come around to support her new life. Mitch's sisters waved at father and son, beaming with happiness. Nate was glad to have his part, but even happier that his friends and cousins were included in the day's events.

During the ceremony, Ti and Jen looked into each other's eyes, held hands, promised, and declared their love freely.

Today I join my life to yours, to live together in holy marriage. Not merely as your spouse but as your friend, lover, and confidant. Let me be the shoulder you lean on, the rock on which you rest, the true companion of your life. With loving admiration, I cherish all that you are. I am devoted to you, and our future, forever and some. I will make my home in your heart from this day forward.

Jen and Ti glowed with such pride and happiness that they radiated beauty and joy from every angle.

All four had a role in the unity prayer. Instead of a candle, Ti had carved a wooden chime from four types of wood, each matched to represent one of their different yet beautiful personalities. One by one, they hung their slender piece of wood around the chime base. Ti's creation was as solid as any structure the Mitches had ever built. It reinforced the fact that the four of them were now a family.

So simple; so natural; so incredibly beautiful.

Their day's slogan was *Love-in the country*—meant both ways.

"Mitch, you look like the Monopoly man in your tux with tails." Betty hugged him as Mitch held back his tears of pride and joy. "And, Nate you look like a doll—so handsome and dapper. You must be five years older than the last time I saw you." Betty hugged him too. Nate blushed.

"Thank you all for participating in one of the most charming ceremonies I've ever had the pleasure to be a part of. Please join us for a fresh hot barbecue. The caterers are grilling a feast of steak, pork, and chicken filets, which are starting to smell divine." Mitch put his nose in the air and all their friends chuckled. "There are salads and fresh breads too!"

The kids ran around, the adults played horseshoes, and everyone joined in games of volleyball. Friends visited and danced.

"C'mon my old friend." Mitch grabbed Betty's arm to dance with her.

"Can I cut in?" Deirdre smirked.

"Sure, today is a celebration for all." Mitch indulged his admirer.

"I saved the best for last." Mitch held his hand out to Millie. They had fun gliding and twirling across the garage floor.

"Excuse me, excuse me!" Mitch called. "Time for the toast. As the closest thing Ti has to a best man..."

The guests smiled. Jen hugged Ti, who put his arm around her.

"I have a true story." Mitch cleared his throat. "I prayed to my favorite saint every night to find a special companion for Ti. St. Francis answered many times. As the patron saint of animals, he kept sending canines. Thus, the four Labs!" Mitch swung his arm around toward the dogs.

"After adding St. Anthony, per Betty's suggestion," he winked toward her, "...behold, an elevator door opened and Jennifer appeared in our lives." Hearts warmed as chuckles spread around the room.

"These two know what's important," Mitch added. "I pray they always remember what matters in life. It's not about wealth, or things, or what others think about you or your choices. It's about holding your head high, enjoying the life you've been given, and being true persons of integrity, despite the rest of the world."

He paused as he looked up before continuing. The entire grounds were silent as everyone waited for his next words.

Mitch's voice was strong. "Royal castles are built from bricks; majestic mansions are constructed with sticks. Everyday moments build a lifetime of love, friendship, and cherished memories."

He looked to his kids. "Find value in the little things. Don't forget what matters, what is real, and what is you."

Raising his plastic champagne glass, he finished, "May you enjoy deep love and a life filled with simple pleasures."

Before they knew it, they had cut the cake and the activities were winding down.

"Today went too fast!" Jen grabbed Ti's hand.

"I know. Every minute of it was great though." He smiled.

They spent the next tired day cleaning up the grounds and returning the rentals. The following day they flew to a little resort to share some time, just the two of them. Ti and Jen enjoyed their getaway. Then, ready to begin their life as husband and wife, they returned home.

The family started with a man, woman, child, father, four dogs, one cat, two houses, many friends, and a readiness for whatever others might be added to grace their lives.

CHAPTER 12

Mitch and Ti bragged about their team's record for weeks. According to the younger half of the duo, "You can't follow the season and not watch the playoffs, and ultimately, the football finale." They'd prepare for the men's pseudo-holiday occasion with cheese and crackers, chips and salsa, wings, and hoagies. Jen added one more item to their growing shopping list. "How are you guys going to eat all this?"

Mitch and Ti exchanged glances. Mitch said, "Special occasions and the food that goes with them are mandatory traditions. We Conners do it right, no matter how few."

"Even if one of us can't partake," Ti added.

"Huh?" Nate said.

Mitch cocked his head and frowned. "A few years ago on Thanksgiving I felt ill. I told Ti we'd better get the bird in the oven quick."

"I got the roaster. My father started the potatoes and stuffing."

"My head began to pound. I told Ti I needed aspirin and a good nap."

"Yeah, I had to go help."

"Ti was watching the game. But he got off the couch to peel apples and chop sweet potatoes. I felt worse and worse. The turkey baked. I slept."

"Yeah, Dad flopped on the couch next to Champ and Daisy and didn't move for three hours. Finally, when I told him it was suppertime, all he could say was, '*huh*,' and look around, disoriented."

"I couldn't eat a bite."

Ti grinned. "But of course, he told me to go ahead."

"Yup."

"I ate and ate, and even cleaned up while poor Dad cowered on the couch with his fever—too sad." Ti shook his head.

"So, you see, we are determined to have traditional celebrations no matter what. Our holidays may be simple, but we look forward to each minute and each bite."

Saturday morning they headed to the bakery and grocery store with a list Jen still thought was much too long. Ti drove with Jen in the front. The two playmates sat in the back seat, goofing around.

"*Found a peanut*," Mitch sang.

"Found a peanut." Nate joined in.

"Found a peeeanut!" they sang together. Ti beckoned over his shoulder, with a please-that's-enough look. The mischievous passengers played with the window controls. The couple looked at each other and sighed.

"*Found a peanut*," they chortled. After six long recitals, Ti proposed outlawing the peanut song for a week.

"I second the motion." Jen laughed, raising her hand.

As they passed the superstore's pharmacy, the impish pair found a vibrating chair on display. They both had to try the massage setting, first Nate and then the big kid, Mitch. After some goofing and giggling, they caught back up to Ti and Jen.

Sunday afternoon Mitch planted himself in his favorite couch recliner. He leaned forward, intent on hearing every word of the pregame show broadcast. Nate sat on the floor with Chip, asking questions.

"How come they're not playing at one of their home fields?"

"They pick the location long before they know who will be in it."

"Who's '*they*'?"

"The officials. There's a whole group that sets rules."

"Oh," Nate said. "But it's still weird."

"I must have a kidney stone," Mitch grumbled when Ti walked into the room. "I felt it last night, and it still hurts."

"You'll have to make a doctor's appointment," Ti said.

"Maybe it jarred loose from the vibrations in that massage chair yesterday," Jen said.

"I've felt a twinge now and then over the past few months, but it's always subsided." Mitch grunted. "I had a kidney stone before. It was no picnic, but I made it through."

◆ ◆ ◆ ◆

"Good day, Mr. Conner," the nurse greeted him.

"Hello." Mitch stepped through the doorway.

"Just step up here." She directed him to the scale. "One hundred ninety-one, same as last year."

They entered the examination room.

"So, Mr. Conner, what brings you in today?"

"My annual inspection and overhaul of rusty old parts," he said. "And, unfortunately, I think I have a kidney stone."

"Oh, that's unpleasant." The nurse with the polka-dot scrubs took his blood pressure and pulse. "The doctor will be in shortly, Mr. Conner." She closed the door. Mitch stared at a framed poster detailing a human heart. The one to his left showed a well-labeled skeleton.

Dr. Downey walked into the little room with his large smile, partially overshadowed by an even larger mustache. "How are you, Mitch?" He reached to shake Mitch's hand.

The doctor performed his examination and re-filled Mitch's cholesterol prescription. He tore off one more script. "Here's the order for an ultrasound to verify the stone's size and placement. I'll call once the results are in. Be sure to drink plenty of fluids."

Mitch scheduled the ultrasound for the following afternoon.

Later, at home, a couple of twinges made him wince. He'd brought the newspaper home, so he read his four companions his horoscope. "Brace yourself for the unseasonal storm ahead. Huh, that figures since the weather's been so nice the past two weeks." Then, he read each of theirs. He read aloud the highlights on the football finale, and showed the two in his lap the weather diagrams.

◆ ◆ ◆ ◆

Tuesday started as a typical day; Mitch thrived on typical. He anticipated his activity: dogs, repairs, small talk, and pot roast for dinner after his scan. He moseyed into the bathroom to shave. The electric razor hummed.

"Mandy, my love, I hope you are seeing Ti, Jen, and Nate with me." He gazed through the mirror into her pretty face. "It's so nice to feel like a whole family again." She came into focus, wearing an ivory blouse and a necklace with pale multicolored beads. He winked at the mirage in the upper-right corner of his mirror, and then set out for his day.

Later, Mitch chatted with the receptionist at the radiology center. "Hi." He took off his cap and approached her long mahogany desk.

"Good afternoon. You must be Mitch Conner; you're early." She smiled.

Mitch nodded once. "I like to be prompt."

"Oh, trust me, we appreciate a responsible patient."

"Have you been here long?"

"Over nine-and-a-half years. Fortunately I like it, since I had to work after my fourth started school."

"Four? Nice number. I always wanted a big family." He remembered the doctor informing Mandy that any more pregnancies could put her life at risk. They were lucky Ti survived. Considering the future, Mitch pictured more grandkids playing in the yard.

"Wasn't in my cards, I guess. But, I'm real proud of the one I have. So, you got a picture there behind the counter?"

"Of course." She gleamed, handing him the family photo from last Christmas. "The youngest is fourteen. The oldest will be graduating from college this spring."

Mitch handed the frame back to her. "Very nice."

◆ ◆ ◆ ◆

Ti worked a long day, constructing a wall of cabinets in the Publications office. He completed the woodwork and sanded the entire unit.

Jen also had a long, hectic day. Access to the Internet had failed that morning. She worked feverishly to check network components and get it back online. That afternoon, an administrative office computer dropped off for a second time. Jen and Sam spent hours tracking down the problem.

"Could it be a bad port in the switch?" After testing, and hashing out scenarios, they discovered the cause. A mouse had chewed a small hole in the cable. The remedy was hard to find but easy to fix. Her co-detective re-fit the line and all was well again.

Jen arrived at the cottage fifteen minutes later than usual. Mitch was just hanging up the phone, about to sit on the couch. As she dumped her bags in the kitchen, Jen barely noticed that he was quieter than usual. Nate was outside throwing the ball for Chip. She greeted everyone, kissed her handsome husband, and started to explain the mouse adventure as she unloaded the containers from her lunch bag.

"Yeah, after the first outage in the morning, everyone was eager to get caught up." Jen sighed. "The second problem was tough. Sam and I spent over two hours tracing parts of the network. Imagine—a mouse! Ha!"

"Go get your sneaks, my little mouse detective," Ti said.

Their evening walk was one of their most prized times together. Since Nate rode a few feet ahead on his bike, the two could speak openly, connecting with each other.

"Be right back." She changed her clothes and bounced down the stairs to join Ti at the back door.

"See ya' in a bit," she called to Mitch. He waved.

They began walking in the usual direction. Ti waited for Nate to ride ahead. He took Jen's hand. "I need to tell you something."

"What?" An uneasy prickle pranced over her skin—even with thick layers to protect her from the February chill.

"That phone call was from the doctor, calling about Dad's kidney stone. The test results came back, showing a mass in the kidney, not a stone."

"What?!" Her stomach plunged to the ground. "Oh my gosh. He was quiet this evening. No mention of his day. The dogs were outside." Jen babbled, suddenly realizing tiny, odd signs, which moments ago had gone unnoticed. "What does this mean? What's next? Does he need more tests?" A hundred thoughts ran through her mind.

"Okay, my little Miss Scatterbrain, take it down a notch." Ti teased, as a way to keep his emotions in check. "The doctor told him the first step is to see a urologist and bring the ultrasound." Tears welled up in his eyes.

She heard the strain in his speech as his voice grew softer. “Is this really bad?” She began to weep.

“There is no way to know. It sure sounds serious. But we shouldn’t worry till we know more.”

They continued to walk. Jen’s mind raced. She bent to pick up an acorn that had sprouted in a dip of swampy soil despite the cold. She touched the tiny leaves, pondering the life taking shape. *Dear God, please help him.*

Ti watched her gaze upward at the towering oak. He smiled, admiring her and her solace in God's creation. *Somehow, we’ll get through this.*

After a few minutes he said, “I worked on those cabinets today. I had to run out to the hardware store for stain, twice. The office people couldn’t decide. I made three test sections with different shades...”

When they got home, Jen gave Mitch a big hug, knowing he wasn’t ready for words. She set the table. Ti sat with Mitch while the newscast aired. Sitting together was his way of showing love and concern.

Jen observed her husband and father-in-law together—the connection between their spirits obvious even without words. *They make an amazing team. I almost envy how close they are. They have the same integrity, the same stubborn confidence. Ti is strong and trustworthy. Mitch is the mushy-man of the pair.* She giggled aloud. *‘Hey Jen, your hair looks great like that. Wear it that way more often,’ Mitch told me just yesterday. They really complement each other.*

After dinner, standing near the dishwasher, Ti said, “Hun, he won’t admit it, but he needs our support at that appointment. He’ll resist an offer from me. You should ask.”

Jen approached Mitch.

“Mitch, would you like me to go with you to the appointment? I mean, for note taking... and... moral support...” Jen stuttered. “But only... if you want... After the exam, you can call me in to review the information. It could be important to have a second pair of ears around.”

Mitch’s first instinct came out in a low grumble. “No, thanks anyway.”

But the more he pondered the idea, the more it made sense. *If it is bad news, I’ll need someone level-headed to comprehend all the details.*

For a long while, Ti lay in bed staring at the ceiling. His mind raced. *God, no. My father has to be well. We need information, details, and direction.* He broke the silence. "We shouldn't get worked up until we know more."

"Right." Jen twitched, full of worry for the man in the next room. She became lost in thoughts about how she'd just found Mitch and how he was like a father to her, as well as like another child, and how much an integral part of their family he was. *Nate is crazy about Mitch, who always includes him.* Mitch and Nate traveled out for Friday pizza, walked the dogs, solved riddles, and got into mischief together. Mitch had begun teaching Nate about oil changes and carburetors, building and construction. *So many good man-things a growing boy should learn.* Mitch had become a solid male role model, something the boy craved. *For years, I prayed for Nate to have such an honorable mentor. And gee, I appreciate the closeness between us too.*

All four felt lucky to have found one another. Each had experience, perspective, humor, and talents to contribute to the new family. The mutual respect that had developed as they adapted, either outright or through subtle adjustments, into their roles gave them a level of understanding that brought them closer. In the end, they were grateful for the sharing of household responsibilities—except for cleaning. Mitch was messy. Ti called Mitch "Piggy" often, making Nate giggle.

◆ ◆ ◆ ◆

Mitch scheduled a time with the urologist. Nate went to Scott's house after school, and the three adults met with the doctor. Jen brought a pad of lined paper and two pens. The discussion was intense. She listened to every word he spoke, scribbling all the while.

The gray-eyed man spoke candidly, expressing no major concern. "A CT scan will provide more details. I'll use a scope technique to investigate the bladder and tubes leading into the kidney. The ultrasound shows shadows that I need to confirm. The tests should be done immediately so we can assess the full extent of the problem. Then we can work to rectify it." He spoke without emotion.

"Shadows? In addition to the mass? What does this mean?" Despite his air of confidence, Ti sensed there was more to the story.

"Based on the size of the mass, I'm certain it is cancerous." The doctor didn't give them any reason not to worry. "We'll construct a plan to deal with the whole circumstance as we collect more data." He leaned back, relaxed in his chair, implying a positive outcome.

"Is he distant from the personal part," Jen whispered to Ti, "or really not concerned that Mitch's life is in jeopardy?" Ti gazed at her, tilting his head to one side.

Mitch and Ti headed to the car in silence. Jen stopped at the counter to schedule the tests. She booked the CT scan the following Tuesday, the scope procedure on Wednesday, and a kidney filter test on Friday.

Ti folded his arms and grumbled. "How come a week of Christmas vacation zooms past us like a racecar, and seven days awaiting something important crawls like a truck with four flat tires?"

That night as Mitch lay down and said his prayers, his thoughts lingered.

This is not right! Only two-and-a-half months ago, Ti and I were building a chimney for the basement wood stove. Deep in his distracting thoughts, Mitch imagined the warmth on his skin, caught a scent of burning wood, and envisioned the bright orange flames. He stood taller, remembering how all four of them had shared the work. Ti laid the brick; Jen and Mitch mixed the cement; Nate entertained the dogs and brought Ti drinks—just so he could scramble up and down the scaffold.

Mitch smiled. *That is how it should be... That's what I want. I'm looking forward to time with my new family, just plain-old-living time, and all the things we'll do together. Maybe we can start building again and be able to live in one state, one home. Please Lord...* He pleaded his case for good health and a happy outcome.

After a few minutes, he took a deep breath. "Mandy, I'm scared. This is a lot for our new family to deal with so soon. Ti, Jen, and little Nate... Oh, how you'd love having a grandson! And, God willing, there will be more of them to dote over soon." His mood swung from worry to hope. "My darling, your ring sparkles with new life and promise on Jen's finger. I'm so proud of her, of Ti, of your memory and our love living on through theirs..."

Mitch fell asleep, with his focus on family and what meant most to him.

◆ ◆ ◆ ◆

The Conners headed home Friday afternoon with a dreary sensation filling the atmosphere in the car. Partly cloudy, the air felt gray—not heavy, just gray. Conversation was intermittent. The radio played.

I'm glad we're traveling together. Jen glanced to the rear seat.

Once home, Ti and Jen attempted to lighten the mood without any obvious signs that they were doing so.

"Huh, another house fire. Looks like everyone got out." Ti said half to the television, half to Mitch.

"How about I make a homemade mac and cheese tomorrow?" Jen suggested with some pep in her voice.

"Yum," Nate said. Mitch nodded.

Keeping busy, Ti worked Saturday on a new storage closet in the basement. He hammered the nails forcefully.

Nate ran back and forth. "Ti, why does that piece have to connect this way, but the other one didn't? And how come those have to double up?"

Mitch snorted as Ti tried to answer the eager boy with short statements between swings. Mitch was the more patient, experienced mentor, even though he had forgone the role of foreman years ago.

Still somewhat numb from the news, working with tools and wood was good for them. The foursome ran errands and completed chores, while also thinking about the week ahead. A swarm of emotions swept over them. The lack of details, although leaving room for hope, only caused anxiety and confusion. At times, it felt like a tornado of turmoil.

"Ti, Jen..." Mitch called Saturday evening, while Nate was playing with a toy construction set in his room. He'd been sitting in the family room in his favorite blue-and-tan-checkered couch recliner, with his elbows in the air and his hands folded behind his head. He sat forward. His voice was firm. "I don't want to say anything to anyone about any of this."

"Dad, are you sure? Your sisters will want to know. Everyone at work will ask. You're never out of the office." He took a breath. "Some of them really care about you."

"No." Mitch's palm pounded the armrest. "I don't want to talk about it. They'll call or want to visit and make a fuss. That's no good."

Ti and Jen couldn't recall a time when they'd seen Mitch upset about anything for more than ten minutes. If Mitch didn't like something, he complained and it was done.

Over.

This was new territory for them all. They struggled as if with blindfolds in a dark, cluttered room for the right way to act, speak, and feel.

CHAPTER 13

Mitch shuffled into the bathroom, pressed the button on his razor and touched his left cheek. "Mandy." He stared into the mirror, moving the razor over his chin. She appeared with sympathetic eyes; her hands were by her sides, her palms facing upward. Noticing how she stood ready to join the saints in prayer, he said, "Darling, keep praying." Mitch absorbed the glow that surrounded her pretty face. Grateful for her tender smile and intercession, he finished shaving and got dressed.

He headed to the hospital for his CT scan, pleased to be taking steps toward restoring his health. He called Jen less than an hour later.

"I didn't expect to hear from you so soon," she said.

"That's because they rejected me." Mitch's voice faded.

"What do you mean?"

He inhaled. "Someone forgot to mention that I need a blood test before this kind of scan. They tested me and my levels are off, something about hydration. They can't scan me now. I'm scheduled again in two days."

"Oh... uh well, I guess we want accurate results. So, if it's not good to do now..." Jen sought encouraging words.

Only silence responded.

"More waiting isn't what you need right now. I know it's difficult. I'm sorry," she sighed.

"It's okay," he mumbled. "I'm just aggravated."

"I know. Can I do anything to help?"

"No thanks. Gotta go. Bye."

The Conner family was famous for ending conversations abruptly, and Mitch was no exception. They were well-spoken conversationalists, but when they were done, they were done. No winding down, unlike Jen's relatives who'd say goodbye and finish five or even twenty minutes later. When a Conner decided they'd had enough, it ended.

"Luv ya'," Jen whispered into the dead receiver.

She dialed Ti's number, not only to tell him, but also to hear his voice.

"Hello."

"Hi, hun."

"What's wrong?"

"Your dad couldn't have his test; they...," Jen explained and felt better sharing with her other, often stronger, half.

"Oh, man," Ti rubbed his forehead. "He's got to be so let down. He's desperate to make progress with all this."

Meanwhile, Mitch strode toward the parking lot, staring at the pavement. *Maybe tomorrow will be better.* Thoughts surged around his wilted spirit, like the lines in a rotating barber's pole. He thought about Mandy and the parallels to her ordeal that were already apparent: tests, doctors, postponements, and fears. Although none of his reports substantiated a similar problem, he couldn't help but think about the difficult time they'd struggled through before she was finally at peace. Once her illness had begun, she was never truly well.

And that was a scary prospect.

No, my path has to be different. This is one problem; Mandy had many. The worst is not for me... not now... perhaps ten or twenty years...

His mind wandered. He missed his wife. Although she had to leave earlier than expected, they'd had many wonderful years. Together since they were twelve, Mitch relished his memories, which kept her close. Maintaining a lifestyle that supported devotion to his one true love made him proud. He'd turned down women that pursued him, sternly, but gently. As they'd expressed interest, Ti teased his father about having an animal magnetism. Mitch replied, "Nah, it's just my eligibility, perhaps mixed with a bit of charm and politeness."

But it wasn't.

It was his personality: his carefree attitude, cheerful manner, desire to help others, and truthful existence. Mitch said what he thought—not what you wanted to hear, not what might be appropriate—what he thought.

Sometimes his candor bit him in the butt, but most of the time it was fine, and all of the time it was right.

Mitch clicked the button to unlock the car. His thoughts about life and Mandy's journey gelled into questions. *What will I be up against? Will it be hard on my family? Will I be able to work? How debilitating will this be?* He opened the weighty car door with a heavy sigh.

Mitch started the car and looked in the rear-view mirror before backing up. There she was—his angel. She looked back at him, her pretty blue eyes shining, her yellow blouse cheerful. Mitch nodded to her. Knowing Mandy was by his side, he muddled through a day that began with disappointment but became bearable through his memories and her love.

◆ ◆ ◆ ◆

Wednesday morning the urologist entered the room. An icy sensation ran down Mitch's spine. The doctor moved energetically. *Well, I suppose his liveliness is a good sign.*

"Alright, Mr. Conner," the doctor's voice boomed. "We're going to see what's going on in there and get you all fixed up."

Yeah, he's optimistic on the other end of that scope! Mitch exhaled. "You'd better fix me up!"

The procedure completed swiftly. "I took biopsies and tissue samples, after finding a few polyps," the doctor said. Mitch inspected the flecks in the doctor's suddenly eerie gray eyes. "I'll send them to the lab; I expect results next week. Once they're in, we'll make a plan for surgery. That kidney should be removed soon." His words burned through Mitch.

Mitch left quietly and drove away with mixed emotions. *I'm glad that's over and answers are coming. But, what if the news is bad? And, a plan for surgery, big surgery...*

The process seemed to plod along. Uncertainty consumed his mind as the possible scenarios took turns in his consciousness. Mitch considered all of the people with whom he'd grown close. With dread, he mulled over the idea of having to hash out his problem amid each of them.

I can't imagine talking about cancer at every turn. Then again, I hated that I couldn't help Uncle Billy when he was sick. I know some of my friends will want to know. Not telling them would probably be wrong. But

I just don't want life to change. I like everything just the way it is. He huffed and pounded his pillow.

Saturday, before the sun was over the horizon, Mitch stretched and patted Chase on the head. His eyes focused on his wedding picture, a gift from his brother-in-law after the fire. Placed prominently on his new dresser where he could view it best, it remained a beautiful reminder of his lost seraph. He stared. Her face changed, as if she looked toward him. Like a sunbeam, her smile radiated heat he felt on his face as he sat mesmerized. Her full lips parted as if she would speak. Mitch felt her encouraging him, sustaining him, and he felt more drawn to opening up about his situation.

Chip jumped onto the bed, breaking his trance. Mitch dressed. He entered the kitchen, one of his favorite rooms where he enjoyed cooking one of his famed dishes from an old stained recipe. A sunny morning glow cascaded through the windows. He could see the garage out back. Nate's new bike stood in front of it.

"You guys picked the best bike ever!" Nate had jumped up and down when he saw it last Christmas.

"Do you like the red with silvery metallic lettering?" Jen had asked.

"Goes great with the chrome." Mitch had said. He smiled at the memory. *A good gift; Nate needed a bike at his mountain house.*

Mitch lifted his head to inspect the room. The cabinets were made of well-stained oak wood that matched the log walls flawlessly. The counter was country blue. The kitchen was rustic, with a touch of lace over the windows and a manly blue tile on the floor. As the heart of the house, it was often part of anything going on.

He sat on a stool at the counter and glanced at his watch. Jen was sorting laundry at the large table in the dining area. Ti leaned on the opposite counter drinking coffee, flavored with hazelnut cream. Mitch breathed in the faint sweet scent.

"Well," he blurted out, "I suppose it's time to tell the family."

Ti and Jen stopped in their tracks and held their breath. After his initial declaration, this change of heart was unexpected.

"You can call them. I do not want to speak to anyone. I don't want a fuss made or any extra attention. I want life to be *normal*. Make sure they understand. I don't want to tell them now, or talk about it tomorrow. The only thing I want is for everything to go on as it always has. Explain that you guys will be my liaison to keep them informed about... this."

He waved his hand and left the room. Catching their breath, Ti and Jen looked at each other, looked to Mitch, then looked back at each other.

"Humm," Ti breathed, moving toward Jen, pulling her into his arms.

"I wonder what changed his mind." She hugged him back.

"Dunno. Can you call my aunts? I don't think I could keep it together. Besides, they like hearing from the girl in the family."

"I'm not sure that's so, but I'll do my best."

"Do you think you can manage it alright?"

She shrugged, "I'll do my best."

Jen spent the day on the phone. She called Mitch's three sisters, as well as their friends Lenny and Camille. She called her mother and Millie. Everyone expressed concern, but she encouraged them to stay optimistic. She thanked them for their prayers and promised to keep in touch.

Later that evening, Jen and Ti joined Mitch in the family room. Mitch was resting in his couch recliner. He sat up. "I've been trying to decide how and what to tell our friends at work." His tone was soft and pensive. He breathed and cleared his throat. "I think it might be easier if you send one of those building-wide email messages. It gets notice to everyone at once, it's not quite as awkward as in person, and details don't get distorted as they're repeated. It'll get the job done. What do you think?"

"I like it," Ti said.

It wasn't arrogance. Mitch understood that he'd become a building cornerstone of sorts. He was the one who everyone else, whether director or janitor, relied on to keep it all functioning. Almost everyone there was some level of friend.

"There might be a few people I'd like to talk to, but I'm just not up for all those faces and questions." Mitch stroked Champ's neck.

"Would you like me to draft something?" Jen volunteered.

"Absolutely," Mitch said. "You'll be able to say it well. Remember, no talk, no fuss, no sorrow, just business as usual. No visits, no calls, no generous offers. You know most of them now; you know they'll try to do something. Tell them to stay away, but tell them in a way that cares for their feelings too."

"I understand." Jen sat down to type.

Dear Coworkers, Pals, and Friends,

We see many of you every day, and you've become our extended family. Each relationship is genuinely important. We would like to share something so everyone can understand our situation and feelings simultaneously and similarly.

We discovered some unfortunate news about Mitch's health. After much testing, the doctors have determined that he has a large mass in one of his kidneys. This mass is certainly cancerous. While it requires removal as soon as possible, there are more tests to be performed in order to know if there's any spreading or other serious concerns.

We are writing to you, first to thank you for your friendship, each of which is special in its own way. Your smiles and chatter make every day one worth being a part of.

The second motive is to make a request. The situation has been difficult for Mitch, and it is painfully uncomfortable to discuss. We would be saddened to have this issue become the focus of our contact with you. Should he not be receptive to inquiries, please understand his awkwardness, and that we do indeed gratefully welcome your support and concern. Please direct most of your questions regarding this particular topic to young Mitchell and Jennifer.

We truly wish to continue celebrating life and all its aspects with normalcy. Experiencing every day as it has always been is the best medicine. Your well wishes are appreciated and your prayers are cherished. We hope to see each of you as always, with greetings of camaraderie, fun, and lightheartedness. Your smile will show what you are feeling, thinking, praying, and hoping for us.

Thank you so much for your support and understanding.

Sincerely,

The Mitches

Mitch approved the verbiage and, with that, stepped onto the first rung of the ladder he was about to climb.

CHAPTER 14

"Your test results show cancer in the kidney, bladder, and adrenal gland, at minimum. We must develop a plan for treatment right away, Mr. Conner." The doctor stood in his white coat and plaid tie, uttering the life-changing words as if reciting a poem to his audience of three.

Mitch's heart sank.

All their hearts sank.

Back at home, Mitch said to Chase, "He can't be right. I can't have cancer. The doctor made a mistake. I have a grandson to mentor, chimneys to construct, dogs to spoil, people who rely on me, and a family I deeply cherish." Champ licked his hand. "I know; we have a lot to look forward to—holidays to enjoy, turkeys to roast, Christmas trees to decorate." He rubbed Daisy's ears. "Remember our first Thanksgiving together, putting up the new Christmas tree?" He snorted, "Our Jennifer with all her decorations, so eager to share the story behind each and every one. Then she gave Ti and me our own special ornaments." Mitch mused about Ti's tiny red toolbox with the hammer on top, the baseball ornament with the Mustang team logo, the Lab almost smiling with his tongue hanging out, and the one displaying their family photo. As Mitch had opened each one, its sentiment touched his heart. *Yeah, we'll be unpacking her beloved trinkets and recalling their meaning every Christmas for years to come.*

"This is supposed to be a kidney stone for goodness sake!" Mitch hollered, startling Chip. "This is not supposed to be a tumor the size of a football, with malignancies in other places." Anger bubbled up inside. *Surgeries... treatments.* He kicked the bottom of the coffee table. Dejected, he almost didn't know how to behave, or what to feel.

Mitch sat on the couch and put his head down, covering his face with his large right hand. Despair permeated through him like a heavy, damp fog.

Jen entered the room. Seeing her father-in-law, she moved closer and struggled with what consolation she could or should offer.

It will be okay... but would it?

I'm sorry... that was lame.

You can beat this... that denied his feelings.

You have great chances of healing... that wasn't bad.

We're all here for you... maybe.

Instead, she pulled him close and provided a shoulder on which to sob for about twenty seconds before the tough guy in him reined back his emotions. He sat up straight. He smiled at her and motioned with his hand that she could leave him with his thoughts.

Later, Jen rested her head on Ti's chest. With tears swelling in his eyes, he listened as she described that moment, her concern for Mitch, her fears, and her desperation.

"How can I help him? I have to do something."

"You're our tender one. Your job might be to console him in those moments." Ti released a long slow breath. "You'll probably do the same for me." Neither man would allow any such outpourings in front of the other. Strength was to be portrayed by each.

Solid. Confident. Sturdy.

"Periods of confusion and doubt are normal." Ti moved a wayward curl from her temple. "We'll pull through this and it'll leave us stronger somehow. As Mitch says, '*Things don't always go your way, but if you have your family, you can manage*.'" Although secure on the outside, Ti's insides felt torn—shredded like a bag of confetti. He'd already seen the suffering that serious illness could bring. He prayed with all his might, with everything he had ever believed in, that his father could be spared that tragedy, especially now.

The next morning, Ti called his aunt and explained the new information. She offered to relay the news, insisting he shouldn't have to repeat everything to each of the Conner sisters.

Many people were eager to keep up with Mitch's progress. Ti and Jen tried to keep them all informed. After making calls every evening for over a week, they sought a better way. Writing Mitch's coworkers had laid the foundation, so they created an email group of family and friends.

Jen and Ti used the messages to explain, vent, and digest information as well as to encourage everyone, including themselves.

Greetings! We would like to keep all of you informed about Mitch's progress, so we're using email messages to share news as things move forward. Thank you for respecting Mitch's wishes to keep his encounters with you "normal." The scope test did not come back as well as we had hoped. There is a polyp in the bladder that tested positive. The urologist scheduled an outpatient procedure to remove the lump in a few days. We can't thank you enough for your love and concern. We know that your prayers are with us and believe every single one helps! Know that we are holding together, sometimes better than others, but we feel lucky to have each other and all of you. We do plan to have occasional... no, make that frequent... bright spots!

Jen sat next to Nate on the side of his bed. "Nate, honey, Mitch is sick. It's important for him to do everything the doctor says."

"Yeah, he has to get better." Nate nodded.

"Some days he might feel pretty bad. You should never think his being worn-out or sad means he's upset with you. He will be tired and his stomach could be queasy. You know how that feels, right?"

"Yes," the young boy replied, listening while unconsciously spinning the wheels on the small silver racecar in his hands.

"We're all going to take care of Mitch when he doesn't feel good, and help him get better." She reached for his hand, attempting to balance her emotions while explaining. "And we're not going to feel bad if he's sleepy or even a little grouchy. Can you help us do that?"

"Sure, Mommy." Nate stood up. "I can help take care of Mitch. I can't wait for him to feel better. He's such a good grandpa. God will help him." The boy responded with concern but took the news well. She wished for his youthful innocence, natural optimism, and unshaken faith.

"Mitch is my best buddy," he said, heading out to show Mitch his car. Nate was confident nothing could change that, sick or not.

Days passed.

Mitch tried to maintain his routine and ignore his situation. He did not deny it; he performed all medical tests and procedures like a champ. But he did attempt to push it from his primary focus.

Ti and Jen continued working, tending to the house, and maintaining life as usual. Still, there was a different flare to each day. No one saw it, spoke about it, or tried to identify it. Living meant more than the old routines, with added concerns, and extra things to value. Appointments and prescriptions blended into their rituals, as well as a perpetual desire for Mitch to be well.

But how, and when?

Mitch woke at 5:00 a.m. every day to eight paws tugging at his blanket. He selected his striped shirt, shaved, spoke to Mandy, fed the dogs, and watched the morning news. He went to work, attended the breakfast club, changed light bulbs, tightened shelves, hung pictures, set up meeting rooms, ordered supplies, tuned the boiler, and negotiated contracts for cleaners, electrical systems, and plumbing. The nuns in the convent called for his assistance. Mitch continued doing everything as he had always done.

He greeted everyone with the same cheerful demeanor. He welcomed chatter about weather, sports, and families. Extending pleasant wishes for a nice afternoon, he bowed, waved, or winked to his coworkers. He kept anything else to himself.

That was Mitch.

To his surprise, many respected his wishes. They greeted him with warm smiles and conversed about normal events.

"My daughter is engaged!" Claire said.

"That's great! You know, I have experience planning a wedding now."

"I sprained my ankle playing volleyball," Rick told him.

"Ouch!"

"I can't wait for baseball season," Rose said. "My nephew gave me opening-day tickets!"

"I bet our Mustangs win!" Mitch put two thumbs up.

The happenings went on—just like always—just as he requested.

Gradually, Mitch realized that his friends shared intimate parts of their lives with him. He wanted to lean on some in return. They might offer an ear, or discuss a similar experience. Knowing with whom and how much he could share, he opened up, but he did it on his terms and they let him. His friends offered support through their eyes and from their hearts. This place and these people were his far-reaching family, his home away from home, the reason he traveled back and forth every week.

Just like a family, there were all kinds of personalities: Rose listened and never pried; Cassie always had a lot to say, but spoke in a soft voice; Rick understood, comparing details to his brother's experience; his supervisor, Jackson, respected his privacy, but was charitable about Mitch being able to do what he needed to do to be well.

"The doctor said I need another test; it's frustrating, but I want to be well, so..." The majority of his companions responded with sensitivity and diplomacy. If a conversation got touchy, Mitch changed the subject.

Some annoyed him. For example, the guy on the fourth floor, who insisted with a glad insensitivity, "Ah, you'll be fine! My down-the-street neighbor had no problems."

Like he'd know the horror of a neighbor's intimate experience. I'm sure he only heard one-tenth of the story... fifth-hand.

Others wanted to dwell on the sorrow of the illness. "Ooooh, I knoooow," one woman said. "My sister suffered so much; chemo was horrrrible; the disease is soooo awful."

Yes, those people are irritating.

Mitch was honest as honest can be. He said it like it was. If he heard something that did not appeal to him, he said so, and moved on.

◆ ◆ ◆ ◆

The day of the first operation arrived. *This procedure has to go well. If this one is troublesome, what will the big surgery bring?* Mitch stretched and peered at his face in the mirror. Starting the razor, he thought about his past with his angel. When Mandy appeared in the top-right corner of his foggy mirror, Mitch's eyes twinkled. The razor vibrated.

"Good morning, my love. I hope seeing you is a good sign... I'm scared." Mandy lifted her right hand across her chest and placed it on her heart. There was a breeze in the meadow where she stood, her purple-and-yellow flowered sundress swayed. Her sandy hair flowed behind her face.

"You give me strength, Mandy." Mitch smiled at her. "I remember when your water broke the day Ti was born. You were the calm one. How did you know it would turn out alright?"

She lowered her head, blushing slightly.

"Oh, what a day that was, and what joy you gave me. I wish I was still able to give you all that you deserve," he said wistfully.

Her head lifted and she shimmered, glowing with contentment from their life together, directing her serenity through the mirage and into his soul. A shiver ran down his back. Mitch clicked the razor's button off and studied her until the vision faded.

Mid-morning they piled into the car and headed to the hospital. Mitch reported in, undressed, and took his place on the bed in the outpatient cubicle. The nurse inserted the IV and took his vitals. They waited; and waited some more. Mitch crossed, uncrossed, and crossed his arms again. "When are they going to get this started?"

The doctor visited and reviewed the procedure. The anesthesiologist explained his role. Mitch nodded nervously. After some whispering with the nurse, the anesthesiologist returned. "Mr. Conner, I'm sorry, but we have to postpone. The nurse recorded a fever. I can't risk putting you under."

The surgeon agreed. They prescribed an antibiotic for Mitch to take over the weekend. Although the raised temperature was most likely due to the growing tumor, they had to be sure he was free of infection.

Heavy disappointment weighed them down as the Conners returned home. Ti picked up Colossal burgers on the way. Fasting before surgery, Mitch should have been hungry for the treat.

"Thanks, Ti." Mitch smiled at his son. Still frustrated, he nibbled; his pups got about as much as he did.

Once Mitch insisted there was nothing they could do for him, Ti and Jen hustled back to work since they'd be repeating the process on Monday.

Mitch kicked the foot of his recliner before he sat down. Flipping through the TV channels, he shook his head and grunted. Getting out of routine was challenging enough without all this emotional stuff to muddy his feelings. He sat with Champ in his lap, anxious to begin healing. The tumor, which originally felt like a kidney stone, now caused a constant, dull pain. He felt sicker. Knowing a cancer was growing inside him was enough to make him sick. The grey-eyed doctor's words echoed in his ears.

"Mr. Conner, your disease is advanced. I estimate that it's been developing over two years, probably more."

"But how can it be so far along? I never had any symptoms."

"I can't say. But, at this stage you will experience noticeable pain, fatigue, and worry. It's not unusual."

I just don't get it. Mitch shook his head and stroked his pup's belly.

◆ ◆ ◆ ◆

Ti did some work, but his mind was elsewhere. *I doubt Dad's having a decent afternoon. I wonder how he was after we left. Did he sulk, cry, rant, or rage? Did he sleep or watch TV? Did he put the surgery out of his mind; was it the only thing on his mind? I feel so helpless.*

Later, as they ate dinner, Ti spoke about his day; it was his turn to tell his father about the afternoon's events.

"Jimmy came by. They're forecasting snow in the morning. Can you believe it? He brought salt and checked the spreader just in case." Ti shook some black pepper over his food.

Jen added to the light conversation. "Sam and I worked on a design for new wiring today. It's time we update and consolidate the mess. Maybe the new lines can be mouse proof!"

They all smiled.

"Mom, I got an eighty-seven on my science test." Nate grinned with a dab of red sauce on his cheek.

"Good job, Nate." The three adults asked for details. Nate answered their questions, proud to share what he was learning with his family.

As they were just about finished, Mitch looked at Jen. "Are you going to write the family tonight?"

"Yeah, they'll be wondering how you made out."

"Okay, mention that I will speak to my sisters. I'm sure they're worried. Tell them they need to understand that if I can't talk at the moment, I won't, and they should try again later, without my having to explain."

"Gotcha!" she said, happy for him to have more love and support from family she knew was eager to offer it.

As you know, Mitch was scheduled for a procedure to remove the tumor in his bladder today. Unfortunately, even though he was as prepared as possible (all pre-ops were accomplished, we delivered him on time, packed him a care pack, kissed and hugged him duly, etc.), Mitch's procedure was postponed. He's running a slight fever, which causes concern when dealing with anesthesia. They gave him antibiotics. At least after our dry run, we'll know the routine for Monday. Distraught and irritated, poor Mitch alternated between utter disappointment and wild aggravation. Not eating, drinking, or medicating all morning left him feeling hungry and deprived. Yet he was most distressed because he thought he would start on his journey to wellness today. Our hearts hurt as we saw his every fiber consumed with anguish. We want him well, smiling, playing, even complaining and being stubborn. Thank you for your love, support, and prayers. We remain optimistic and hope that this will be the bad portion, as there is always a little good and bad in every endeavor.

Then she added a final paragraph to the aunts' copy:

I am pleased to say your brother is more interested in talking, after digesting this whole situation...

Jen clicked SEND.

Later, in bed, they lay awake. Ti stared at the wall. Jen fidgeted. *What will Monday bring? How will we relax for the weekend? Why does this miserable ordeal include so much waiting?*

Mitch studied the ceiling. He thought about a time when Mandy's chemo treatment had to be postponed.

"Come, love. I'm taking you out to eat. Let's keep those spirits up."

"Mitch, you don't have to take me anywhere."

"I want to. It'll be nice." They'd walked in holding hands. The place was dim. A pianist played a melody on an old baby grand and the lilting sound filled the room.

"The candles on the tables are pretty." Mandy smiled as Mitch pulled the chair out for her.

After several minutes, Mitch checked his watch. "Where's our waiter?" When one finally arrived, he took their order and disappeared. After thirty minutes, Mitch took his wife by the hand and stomped out the door.

"That's it! From now on, we stay close to home when we want to get out. No fancy-shmancy restaurants near the hospital. Nope."

He smiled, remembering the steam coming from his ears and the tenderness in her eyes.

"Mitch, I don't care where we eat... being together is all that matters. If you want to go out, let's go to our favorite little place." They went to Clancy's Diner where they'd had many happy meals.

"Oh Mandy, you always did have more patience than me. I hope you'll help me now." Mitch turned over. Chase moaned.

Mitch still prayed, even though he didn't have to ask for his original request. Ti and Jen were wonderful together. He couldn't have loved her more. And Nate was a bonus for having waited so long.

Dear Lord,
Thank you for my family, and for this lousy day,
  surely glorious in your plan, so a valued gift anyway.
Watch over each member—two legged and four,
  be with me and guide me through this mess and more.
This is what I pray.

As always, he concluded, "I miss you, Mandy."

CHAPTER 15

Dawn arrived, and a heavy mist filled the air. The weatherman predicted a potent sun would burn off the haze.

"I'm looking forward to some sunshine. This dreary weather is bringing me down," Ti said, lacing his work boots. It was easier to confess his sullen feeling when he could blame it on the atmosphere.

Hoping to ignite sparks of optimism, Jen selected a cheerful pink sweater from her closet. "Yeah, well, if the weather can influence our mood, perhaps a bright top can even out the cosmic powers." She completed her outfit with gray slacks and dangling silver earrings, and then bounced down the stairs.

Ti brightened as he kissed his wife goodbye. He muddled through his day, setting up two conference rooms, meeting the elevator inspector, and working with the electrician to fix a breaker panel in the east wing. *God, You better take care of my father!* Ti worked with forceful movements, banging the bent table leg with fury and shoving chairs around, unknowingly releasing some anxiety.

Later, their ride to Walleycito was normal; normal felt good. The skies were clear and the roads were active. After settling into their spots in the large family room, Mitch sorted the mail.

"Nate, look at this." Ti pointed to a page in an auto magazine. "Oh, this yellow one catches your eye, huh? The new Chevy Corvette features..." Ti read aloud with obvious admiration in his voice.

"Oh, cool, Ti look at this metallic blue Mustang, with sparkling chrome wheels!" Nate's eyes lit up.

"Wow, check out the lightning streak effects on this white convertible captured in motion!" Ti practically drooled.

Mitch sat back. "Nate, you know, my family owned a car dealership, and I was a typical car fanatic. Had a couple of really cool ones. I was around twenty when I got a candy-apple-red Corvette."

Nate's focus lingered on the next picture—a black Trans Am—before he turned to face Mitch.

"Once, when I was near the farm on a long stretch of road, a guy in a Dodge muscle car with wide tires drove up alongside me." Mitch moved his hands apart to show the thickness of the oversized tires. "He wanted to race; gave me the I-bet-I-can-beat-you look." Mitch imitated his villainous challenger by glaring over the rim of his glasses.

"What'd you do?" Nate's eyes were big as headlights.

"I took off, peeled my tires, and smoked him." Mitch smiled, shooting his hand in the air.

Nate sucked in a breath. His jaw dropped.

"Yeah, I kept the pedal down on the floor for a quarter mile, smokin' past everything in sight. It was a weird, but incredible feeling. When I looked down, I was going one hundred thirty-four miles per hour. I literally scared myself!" Mitch chuckled.

"Wow!" Nate blinked.

Jen cringed.

After Nate and Ti had gone through every page, Nate showed Mitch a picture of a Cobra. "This is what I want when I grow up."

Mitch smiled at his good taste and patted his back. "Nice one, my boy! You go for your goals!"

His kindred-spirit timekeeper nudged his arm as the clock chimed.

"Right, Nate, time to order. Who's having what tonight? I think I'll be adventurous and have plain pizza." Mitch grinned. "But also some fried zucchini sticks. Jen, you'll have a few?"

"Sure," she said, noticing his recent willingness to share takeout. She recalled their first lunch together. *Funny how things change. Back then, he'd offer me anything I wanted, except from his own plate. Those two obeyed their man-rule to finish a helping, as if ordering it were a commitment. So cute...*

"Well, I need pepperoni and bacon tonight." Ti stood and stretched.

Nate turned up his nose. "I'm with Mitch, just cheese. Mmmm."

Mitch called the pizzeria. Ti let the dogs out. Jen emptied the dishwasher. The more routines they accomplished, the more Mitch felt comfortable and content.

"C'mon Nate, let's go." Mitch counted out the bills. "'Cause, once I hit that couch, I won't be getting off it."

"On my way." Nate ran after him.

Exiting the kitchen, Jen grabbed the deck of cards and sat next to Ti. "We've got time for me to whip your butt at least once," she said.

"In your dreams!" He divided the deck and shuffled.

◆ ◆ ◆ ◆

Saturday morning the foursome went out for breakfast and shopping. Ti ordered his favorite coffee and fresh-baked cinnamon bun, which filled his belly and gave him a psychological boost to know that all was well with the world. Mitch and Jen chose big, fluffy muffins. Nate pointed to a donut, happy for any sweet treat. The bakery, originally Mitch's idea, also pleased Nate, who was becoming more like his grandfather every day.

Mitch sat quietly during breakfast. He observed a few folks come and go. He commented once, nudging Nate and tossing his head in the proper direction. "Hey, check out that lady's hat." Nate giggled and poked Mitch, who didn't comment further.

"I'll wait in the car while you finish shopping. I just have no ambition today." Mitch turned as Ti and Jen nodded, confused as to how to respond. Mitch had always found everyday activities appealing. But not now. Now he seemed lethargic and almost lifeless.

◆ ◆ ◆ ◆

That afternoon, the sun shone on the back deck, inspiring Ti to fire up the grill. "There's no better medicine than a grilled hot dog in February."

"Yeah, nothing like a good hot dog. Better than steak." Mitch sounded excited by the idea. "Not sure I have much of an appetite though."

"I wish we had some corn on the cob. I wonder if he'd perk up for his buttery favorite," Jen said.

"Don't think so." Ti watched Mitch recline and close his eyes.

"Well, at least he could tease me for eating it '*all wrong*.'" She smiled.

"He still thinks you're bizarre—insists he has to teach you how to eat corn properly." Ti wagged a finger at her, pretending to scold.

"I remember." Jen relived the memory with Ti.

"What the heck are you doing?!" Mitch had bellowed, the first time they ate corn together.

Jen looked up from her thrice bitten cob, "Who, me?"

"Yeah, where'd you learn, or should I say, not learn, to eat corn?"

"Uh...," she hesitated.

"Everyone knows you eat corn left to right, like reading a book."

"So I can look like a typewriter?" she joked, unsure what else to say.

"What's a typewriter?" Nate asked.

"It's an old thing used for typing before we had computers. The paper rolled into the top and, when you hit the keys, tiny metal arms with letters on the tips smacked the paper real quick, one after the other." Jen moved her fingers as if typing.

"Whoa, weird!" Nate said.

"I think Nana has one..." Jen relaxed.

"Now, don't change the subject. How 'bout you eat that corn like you're supposed to?" Mitch pushed.

"But I like going round and round. It keeps the butter on better." Feeling justified, she took another bite.

"She's got a point, Dad."

Ti received a sideways glance.

"No way! Nibble left to right; it's the only way."

Jen completed a full round circle on the far left side and moved to the far right end and took a bite.

"Oh-my-gosh! Now you're just trying to upset me." He put his cob on his plate and glared at her.

"What? This side's getting cold already."

Ti and Nate snickered and looked down into their own plates.

Every time, old Mitch was sure to remind her, and every time, they enjoyed a good chuckle reminiscing about one of his inflexible theories.

The hot dogs were delicious, yet didn't quite impact their temperaments as Ti had hoped—not because there was no corn, but more because of the anxious cloud that hovered above them.

"Let's play a game," Nate suggested. When it came to their family games, they competed with zest. Playing even more often in winter when there was less to be done outside, they'd each in turn held the title of Champion. Mitch claimed most word game victories; no one could even come close. He was also lucky with the dice.

But now he had no interest.

"The doctor gave me a note... for restricted activity, which includes that crazy drawing game Jen likes. It's at the top of the list, among other...," he paused to consider the phrasing, "...senseless games." Mitch smirked sarcastically and threatened to produce said note "in a minute." He pretended to search each of his pockets.

"Really, I cannot," he declared with a raised hand and slight force. He went back to watching the home improvement channel. He was down and out—just pooped from it all.

◆ ◆ ◆ ◆

As Monday approached, Ti didn't know whether to be frightened or glad for the surgery to happen. *I just want my father well again.*

The morning came, the nurse prepped Mitch, the doctor visited, and the procedure began. The attendant wheeled Mitch out of sight.

"Be brave!" Ti patted the edge of the gurney.

"We love you!" Jen waved.

They strove to ground themselves as all the anxieties, concerns, relief, and questions twirled inside them.

"He'll be okay, right Ti?"

"Sure love, he's gonna be fine. He knows we need him."

"I think he needs a few prayers though." She shut her eyes.

Jen despised hospitals. Gazing around the room, she considered why: the white walls and overcoats, the smells, the wires and tubes, the frailty of the occupants, the workers who feared neither needles nor blood. *The idea of blood—eww and yuck!* She couldn't take... well... any of it. She called it "the scary H-place" as a child, avoiding even the word "hospital."

Going through something like this was frightening, but Ti needed her. Fear or not, she'd be by his side, and there for Mitch too.

Ti got up, went out to check his voicemail and retrieved some surprisingly decent coffee on his way back to the row of green padded chairs. Watching his wife read her novel, he noticed her brow tighten, release for a minute, and then tighten again. He knew that meant she had to re-read the page because her mind had wandered. He stood up, paced, and went back to the coffee counter, where he rifled through the packets of sugar and tea. He found one decaf pouch at the bottom. *Ah, this will help.* He opened the mint tea bag and placed it in a tall cup of hot water.

"Here, my little ball of nerves," he said. "This will calm your belly, and your thoughts."

"Thank goodness I have you." She squeezed his hand as she accepted the cup with a smile.

After a full day at the "scary H-place," they got Mitch home and settled in bed. Drowsily, Mitch completed the long day with his vital habit:

Dear Lord,
Thank you for seeing me through this day.
Watch over my whole family I pray.

Short and sweet.

"I miss you, Mandy. I made it. One step down; one to go." In seconds, the synchronized dog-snores mesmerized him into a deep sleep.

The next morning, Mitch appeared a little brighter and more like himself. Completing the first step gave him a sense of confidence.

Hooray! The patient is home! Let me rewind and tell you... Due at 8:00 a.m., Mitch grumbled something about it being too early. After they led him away, the doctor didn't come out till 1:00. He told us the bladder cyst was larger than expected. He admitted Mitch for observation. Ugh. We knew how thrilled he'd be with that. When we saw him in recovery, our groggy Mitch barely knew where he was. They found him a room and gave him "the good stuff" for pain. Toward evening, we watched him perk up and a rumor started about letting him go home. Mitch did everything they asked to meet the criteria for release. Paperwork and process ensued. We got home around 10:00 p.m. His pals greeted him with tail wagging, snorting, prancing and just about every other sign of sheer pleasure they could offer. Happy to be home, he spent a quiet night in his own bed—no roommate, no noise, no poking, just lots of panting and mounds of fur cuddled up beside him. It was all worth it for his first day of action, after all that pre-stuff. He's already talking about doing as well with the big surgery. We see a spark of renewed spirit. Thank you! What would we do without your support? Your love is keeping us well!

Life progressed. Although the family hadn't felt normal since this hardship began, things were settling and they were gaining some control over the emotional squalls.

Mitch, while worried and feeling weaker, tried to stay positive until he had a reason to feel otherwise. He endured his medical consults and appointments with bravery. *All this effort has to pay off.*

He conceded that he was sick—sick in a big way. The combination of the disease's physical progression and its emotional burden weighed him down. Knowing the path to recovery would be a hard haul and coveting a victory, he began to barter with the higher powers in the universe. He vowed to give up Chinese takeout for a year.

No, make that two... or ten.

Mitch spent a lot of time watching television and sitting with his pups. Friends gave him books and magazines, but reading didn't interest him. Jen created crossword puzzles and word searches themed around his favorite hobbies. Mitch had little attention for those either.

"But Jen, I can't concentrate, and I have no energy for such silly things," he said, waving his hand.

"They'll be fun when you're ready." Jen knew the old Mitch would get a kick out of his personalized puzzles.

At the Center, the breakfast club continued to meet. Ti welcomed the break, which occurred hours after his increasingly longer day began. Often, they spoke about a husband who bought a new car, or the crazy nephew whose antics provided comic relief. Ti enjoyed times when the conversation turned to a Mitch story. Since an unexpected dusting had graced the hills that weekend, the topic focused on snow.

"I love it. Even though it's a lot of work, I look forward to a good snow." Ti pictured the log home surrounded by trees with white flakes clinging to every branch, the fluffy blanket covering the ground, and the tiny animal prints in the yard, all of which brought him a sense of peace. Winter came with fond memories of tobogganing, snowmobiling, and other sports he and Mitch had enjoyed over the years.

"One day," Ti said, "I took the snowmobile on the lake. I got comfortable jumping over the drifts. After a bunch of rounds, I took my father for a ride. I revved up the snowmobile and rode around, jumped the dike as I had before, but..."

"I knew there was a '*but*' in there." Betty smirked.

"But," Ti continued, "the unexpected bounce from my extra passenger caused me to slam my face into the windshield... ouch!"

"Ouch." Cassie frowned. Betty covered her forehead.

"Blood was *everywhere*! The deep red on the white snow looked horrifying. Turned out, I'd cut the underside of my lip on the edge of the plexi-glass. My mouth bled and bled. Dad took me to the hospital, where I got thirteen stitches. Fortunately, all the damage was behind the lip, on the inside. Nothing scarred." Ti grinned.

He shared his father-son memory, one of many where those two had gotten themselves into a heady situation. Pain and all, both Mitch and Ti knew they would never have skipped a single one.

◆ ◆ ◆ ◆

"Dad," Ti said, approaching his father that evening. "What do you say about getting a second opinion on your kidney surgery? There's a reputable cancer center not too far from here. After the complications with the bladder surgery, I'd like to hear their take."

"Hmm," Mitch touched his chin, "I never thought about going anywhere else." Ti, Jen, and Mitch debated the pros and cons of another hospital or treatment. Surgery was certain.

"It would be nice to get confirmation that we're taking the right steps to get you well," Jen said.

"Or, find out what more we can do." Ti didn't want to overlook any possible course of treatment in their quest to make Mitch well.

After deliberating the idea, Mitch said, "Yeah, I would like to hear another perspective."

Jen contacted the city cancer institute. Their procedures and requirements were more complex, starting with a full report on his entire medical history. The staff assured Jen that a pre-evaluation was best. Patience was low, but spirits were up knowing there were options.

The next day, Jen stopped at the store on her way home. *What can I get Mitch to cheer him? Not books or puzzles, perhaps a new shirt.* She paced the aisles. *Ah, this is the one.* She held up one of the button-down shirts that made the man: white with a blue-green stripe.

Perfect. She went to the next aisle and picked out a solid chamois flannel for Ti, and a blue-checkered one for Nate. On the way out, she passed a bin of socks. She grabbed one of those too, knowing how much Mitch looked forward to his new socks on Christmas morning. His feet would wiggle as he opened the expected but pleasing package. "Bright and cushy," he'd mumble, tapping his toes.

After the clinic determined the specialist most appropriate for Mitch's case, they called with an appointment for Friday.

"Jen," Ti said. "You should probably take Dad to this appointment. You're the best one to ensure an actual conversation."

"You mean more than the typical Mitch: 'yeah,' 'okay,' 'uh-huh-s'?"

"Right. You can take notes." Ti said, glancing to Jen's binder on the table, filled with contact numbers, doctor notes, dates, and test data. The records helped them remember what the mind alone could distort when left to wander through a maze of emotion.

"You go to the appointments; I'll drive him to tests. This way everyone has a part and no one will miss too much work. I don't want us to run out of time off before this is over," Ti said.

Friday morning, Ti went into work. He prepared the building for its daily occupants, and then phoned Jen. "What time are you leaving? Don't go without me. I changed my mind. There's nowhere else I should be than with my family and if we run out of sick leave, we'll deal with it then. I spoke to Jackson, and he fully supports my going today."

They were feeling more secure as all three of them set out, early, the way Mitch liked it. When they arrived, the receptionist directed them to the registration desk, where Mitch was asked to fill out yet another mound of forms. He accepted the clipboard. "Jen..."

"Of course." Jen took the pile and sat down. If writing and rewriting all that information helped Mitch in any way, she was happy to volunteer. They sat in the waiting area that Mitch called the 'how-to-spend-a-long-boring-day room,' because they waited over an hour for the doctor. Mitch didn't know whether to cry or get mean. He stood up, stomped over to the window, sighed, paced, thought about pounding his fist on the counter, but decided to pace again instead. He wore a frown, staring at his sneakers moving slowly across the anodyne floor.

Well worth the wait, the doctor covered Mitch's case with the care and detail of a professional painter, watching his lines and filling in with precisely chosen shades. An experienced physician, he spoke with confidence and patience, addressing all of their concerns.

"Yes, I can work with your condition and give you hope for the future. This is not the largest tumor I've seen treated successfully."

On the seventy-five minute drive back, they discussed the visit.

"This guy knows his stuff," Jen said.

"Yeah, I like his views on the whole thing." Mitch nodded.

"I want you to have the best care possible." Ti glanced at his father through the rearview mirror.

Mitch's expression was pensive, his jaw set, his brows low, and his eyes lost in visions beyond the window. "Well, we'll be home for the weekend. I can think more about the whole mess there."

Mitch went to his second-opinion appointment with a surgeon at Bestford Cancer Center. We took a little pilgrimage out to the big city... yes, us country mice. What we'll do for love! We saw a doctor whom I feel is very good, and the Mitches both like. He was extremely thorough, even a little amusing, but straightforward and open. The kidney must be removed soon, via conventional surgery with at least a week's hospital stay. We discussed Mitch's pain, fatigue and fever, all of which seemed reasonable to the doctor. He suggested additional tests that could influence the plan, which we are scheduling right away. We didn't get news. We got confirmation and advice. There's a lot to comprehend and a lot necessary to make him well. Pleased we made the trip, Mitch plans to choose where he'll be treated after his follow-up with the urologist next week. Wherever he feels most comfortable, and whichever will give him the best care possible, are our only concerns. Please continue to pray for

Mitch. I realize we are repeating ourselves by expressing our gratitude for your love and support. We've faced several weeks of shock, concern, fear, chaos, sadness, and many other emotions. Your positive energy is truly helping us pull through. These country mice are eager to spend time in the countryside before another busy week...

"I'm glad we went and heard more about all this," Ti whispered to Jen later that evening. "My mother's illness started when I was a teenager. She fought it for almost fifteen years."

"You must be tormented by memories of your mom's long, hard journey." Jen touched his shoulder.

"I'm fine. I want Dad to be fine too." Ti closed his eyes. He did not want to see his father suffer, or endure any of that horrible sequence. He prayed for a different voyage for his father. And a different outcome.

Please God, I never ask for anything...

CHAPTER 16

"Oh, Mandy and I played on three leagues at once." Mitch stood tall. "She loved being at those lanes."

"My mom liked to socialize more than bowl." Ti chuckled.

"Mandy was a shining star, and proud of her husband." Mitch's eyes twinkled. "I'd gotten real good. I bowled a two-thirty-five average—give or take a few pins. Pretty awesome, don't you think?" He patted Nate's back.

"Yeah, Mitch. I want to be good as you." Nate grinned from ear to ear.

"Nate, as soon as I feel better, you and me are gonna practice at home. I trained Ti how to handle the heavy ball by throwing it into the couch cushions over and over. Lucky we had a big, fluffy couch."

"No way! That's how you taught Ti to bowl?" Jen's eyes widened.

"Ha, yeah, Mandy stayed in the kitchen, certain we'd break something!"

"Hmmm," Jen muttered.

"But it worked." Mitch grinned. "Ti got pretty comfortable and bowled better for it."

Jen shook her head, picturing the scene. She chuckled. "Yeah, my father was a huge bowler. I remember going to the lanes and his pointers on how to control a natural curve I hadn't asked for."

As they reminisced, they realized how much Mitch's stories meant to them, now more than ever. Whether they were real or had a touch of fantasy, they listened to every word, even those they'd heard before.

"Ah, good times," Mitch said. "You know, good times are gifts of joy, wrapped in colorful paper and bows."

"So, let's go bowling," Ti said.

"Mitch, you can use the new shoes you got for Christmas." Nate smiled.

"Yes, it's good to get out, don't you think?" Jen looked at Mitch.

"Ah, I don't know." Mitch glanced toward the ground.

"How about a movie?" Ti reached for the paper.

"No, I'm not up for a long sit at a crowded theater—not when I have my comfy recliner, dim lights and surround-sound right here." Thanks to Lenny, they'd mounted speakers all around the family room when they re-built the house. Mitch perked up with his cozy plan. "Let's stay home and make popcorn."

"Yeah, popcorn!" Nate agreed. "It's dark and loud enough in here. Ti, tell me again how you got all the wires up those huge log walls."

"We'd add a log, and drill holes all along for anything needing a line—outlets, speakers, lights, see?" he said, pointing to different spots while Mitch chose a movie. "Then we'd repeat that for each log layer... all the way to the top." His arm rose, guiding Nate's attention.

They settled in for a movie in their theater-like room. The opening credits boomed.

"Mom, remember when we watched that funny movie with the silly monsters? You laughed so much."

"You did too." Jen started to giggle.

"Yeah, but Mitch..." Laughter overtook Nate's words.

"Ha-ha, he didn't like it at all." Jen finished for him.

For some reason, animation irritated Mitch. Although a good sport for the annual Christmas shows, he preferred the rest of their family movies be "real." Chuckling, they recalled his grumbling and her hysterics from the one animated movie they'd all watched together.

Mitch pushed back his recliner and tapped his toes together to ensure Jen noticed his new socks. Then he welcomed Champ in his lap, nibbled on his popcorn and appeared quite content.

◆ ◆ ◆ ◆

The family made the trip south for another week of work and medical appointments. Mitch still had to decide what he wanted to do and where. "I just don't know." Mitch turned up his right palm. "I'm impressed with Bestford, but staying close is important too."

"It won't matter to us. We want you to have the best care," Ti said.

"That's easy to say, but treatments can involve a lot of travel."

"We'll figure it out." Jen's voice was firm.

"Think... you'd have to run back and forth; it could be far, and could be a lot, even just to let the dogs out. Listen you two, family and spending time together, whether on a big project or doing nothing special makes up our most precious moments." That opinion showed through all Mitch's behaviors, even this decision.

Ti turned to Jen and whispered. "If we're to listen to what he wants, we have to accept whatever justification he offers."

"I guess. Our heads are in a constant state of swim. Who knows if any of us can think lucidly anyway?" She pursed her lips.

After dinner, Jen deciphered her shorthand that summarized their day.

Today we saw the urologist. He addressed our inquiries, reviewed the first surgery, and discussed what lies ahead. Here is the report:

-The pathology on the bladder cyst shows he has T1 type cancer.
-The adrenal gland, a section of bladder, and possibly the spleen will come out.
-Lymph nodes will be tested during surgery and removed as necessary.
-There is invasion to the psoas muscle, which exist in the back but controls the thigh. A portion must be removed leaving him with weakness in his left leg. The deeper they have to go into the muscle, the more severe his disability will be.
-Per the filter test on the good kidney, Mitch won't need dialysis.
-Surgery will take several hours and require a week's hospital stay.
-After eight weeks, Mitch will see a medical oncologist for chemotherapy.
-Surgery is scheduled for Monday.

Both Mitches feel this doctor is young, energetic, and self-assured. Mitch is drawn to his confidence, which borders on arrogance. He likes that a doctor doing such serious work has a big-shot attitude. Although he liked the surgeon in the city, he decided to stay close and have the operation here. With so many people praying, this has to work out. We are hopeful his health will be restored soon.

The next morning, the breakfast club gathered in the cafeteria. Mitch sipped a cup of ginger tea in his yellow Lab mug. Ti regarded the large rugged hand covering half the design. "I just remembered something. When we were building the cabin, we'd start early. My father always brought his mug outside. The car bumper made an excellent shelf."

"Ha," Betty grunted, anticipating the next part.

"Eventually, we'd need a part," Mitch added. "I usually volunteered for gopher duty. So I'd run out to the corner hardware store."

"He'd drive away with his mug sitting on the back bumper." Ti put his hand on Mitch's shoulder.

"Yeah, it'd take a little trip... or part of one," Mitch said.

"All those mugs! One by one, they dove to the pavement at the bottom of the driveway." Ti teased, motioning a plummet with his right hand.

In a way, Mitch liked it. *Being the butt of a joke isn't so bad as long as you're helping make life fun and interesting.*

◆ ◆ ◆ ◆

Back home on Saturday, Jen doted on Mitch, bringing him tea and cooking a favorite supper—pepper steak over rice. Afterward, Mitch watched his son beat her in yet another game. Ti and Nate often won board games. Card games were more favorable to Jen. They played cards on Sunday. The challenge board grew: one more for Ti, one more for Jen, both inching toward Nate's record.

Outside, Ti ran the dogs in the snowy yard. Chip fetched his tennis ball, while Chase fetched snowballs. He ran, pounced, chewed and returned, with his tail wagging, ready for Ti to throw another.

"We need more snow," Nate said. "Our driveway is a perfect hill."

Last year, they'd enjoyed sledding. Ti had hugged Jen on the wood toboggan, while Mitch and Nate rode the foam sleds. The dogs chased the riders, pouncing as they slowed at the bottom of the long incline. They'd glided down and trudged back up that hill for hours. Even Champ frolicked for a few rides with Ti, who held a slow and steady course.

When not sledding, they would skate on the lake. Mitch walked in his boots, insisting, "It's slippery enough without adding a thin blade." Nate raced back and forth, grinning and shouting. However, he stayed near the shoreline, certain the middle area would crack and swallow him up.

But this winter was different. They were not up for much activity.

Walking with Nate along the driveway, Mitch pointed. "This is a chipmunk hole." He moved a few feet over. "And this is a snake hole." Looking down the hill, he stretched his arm out toward a natural chasm in the woods. "See there, that used to be a bear den."

"Really? How do you know they're not in there now?"

"We haven't seen a bear in years. Did Ti ever tell you about the time the bear ate a bowl of spaghetti on the back deck?"

"No, no way!" Nate jumped back.

"Really," Mitch insisted. "Just ask him; he'll tell you."

"Oh, I will!"

"See this flat spot? The deer slept here."

"Yeah, I see. And here's a pile of deer poop!" Nate pointed.

As Ti played with the dogs, Jen watched everyone with a lump in her throat. *Nate's growing up so fast. And they're the answer to my prayers. Ti is a wonderful role model, and Mitch is a bonus. Nate adores them. Thank you.* She put her hands together and bowed her head, absorbing the heartwarming moment.

Silently, they each prepared for Mitch's big surgery. They prayed, worried, wondered, and treasured time together. Mitch showed Jen how to open the safe and locate important documents, including cemetery plot paperwork. She and Ti tried to avoid it, but it made Mitch feel better that she watched, listened, and repeated back to him the what, the where, and the how for those small essentials.

"Write it down in that scribble of yours." Mitch shook a playful finger to lighten the mood.

Sunday night, Mitch lay awake for a long, long time thinking about the day he brought Mandy to her first surgery all those years ago.

Dear Lord,
Thank you for my wonderful family
  and the gift that was today.
Watch over all under this roof.
  And help me get through the challenges you've put before me.
This is what I pray.

He ended with "I miss you, Mandy. Ask God to help me; I'm scared."

CHAPTER 17

With anxiety as captain of his emotions, and hope as the first mate, Ti sailed through oceans of waiting and wanting, into the hospital parking lot. *God, I'm counting on a successful recovery—it's the only outcome that makes any sense.*

Terrified, Mitch moved gingerly as he prepared for his operation. His hands shook. With a blank expression on a pale face, he dressed in his tan-with-little-green-squares hospital gown.

This time, his bed was directly across from the nurse's station. The doctors visited and offered a recap of the events ahead. Between vital checks, Mitch watched life happen for the group of people going in and out of the station. They discussed kids, what they'd made for dinner, what was on sale at the local market, and the morning headlines. Mitch smirked, while picking at his cuticles. Neither Mitch nor Ti spoke much during stressful times, but they were always watchers.

Ti leaned over and tossed his head toward the busy area. "Well, at least you've got a distraction, good as a live TV show."

"All this waiting is tough on the nerves." Mitch fidgeted in his hospital bed. The old, secure, take-no-crap Mitch began to grumble about being hungry, chilled, and tired. Finally, he couldn't take it anymore. "How stupid to bring somebody in so early, only to sit and stew in his fears!"

Soon after, things started to happen. The nurse checked his multiple allergy and identification bracelets. Ti and Jen kissed and hugged a tearful Mitch before the attendant wheeled him away.

The two walked to the waiting room hand-in-hand. Jen hugged Ti before they sat down. With her head on his chest, she listened to his heartbeat, strong, like a tribal drum, pulsing a rhythm: "family, faith, family, faith, family, faith."

Ti wrapped his arms around her, sniffed the minty scent of her hair, and felt more secure in her embrace.

Several times, he got up to move around and wound up consuming three cups of bland waiting-room coffee. Each time he checked, but could not find any decaf tea for Jen. He decided to check on the dogs, so he wouldn't miss anything as the surgery completed. Jen stayed in the waiting room, praying, reading, and realizing she was praying for and re-reading the same things over and over. Ti returned, with a hot tea.

"Aw, thank you." Jen smiled.

They took turns getting a snack, and using the bathroom. Ti made a few calls. Talking to Lenny at home or Jimmy filling in at work provided a good distraction and vent for his nervous energy.

"The only thing I want is for your dad to complete his first step toward restored health by the time that sun sets." Jen touched his shoulder.

The doctor approached them at 3:30 p.m.

Finally!

They expected good news. Jen and her notebook were ready to record his words. The doctor spoke quickly. "The kidney was removed, along with the adrenal glands and most of the lymph nodes. The spleen and pancreas were left alone. The trouble was the psoas muscle where I took a lot of tissue and tested several layers. Mitch will spend time in the hospital and at home recovering. Then I'll turn him over to the oncology department. Overall, I did well." Jen flinched. *I, meaning himself?*

"...The end result is good." Exuding confidence, he walked away.

Good!?

It didn't sound so good. It sounded scary.

The doctor clearly focused on the positive aspects, yet an underlying negativity hid in his report. They were sure they'd heard it and could not shake the sour pit in their stomachs. Yet they also knew optimism was all they could believe or show; doubts wouldn't do any good. A little while later, they saw a groggy Mitch in recovery.

"You did great, Dad." Ti clung to his wife's hand. Relieved to see Mitch with color in his cheeks, they spent a long while by his side before returning to Mitch's pups and their beds.

◆ ◆ ◆ ◆

Hello! Ready for the report on Mitch's big day? The nurse prepped him as his doctor reiterated the list of affected areas, which grew to include the colon. We looked at one another, thinking, "Gee, any more spots and we're not sure how much of him we'll be getting back!" His blood counts were already low, so he got a transfusion. Mitch was uncomfortable and anxious, but glad to be on his way to getting better. This morning, he looks wonderful compared to what we expected. Heavily medicated, he sleeps a lot. He can't eat, drink, or move. When awake, he speaks slowly, but he's alert. He asked about the world outside. Hard to believe our Mitch is curious, right? He joked a little with his nurse. Of course, she likes him. (Even in this condition, he wins over the ladies.) The surgeon's report left us puzzled. He removed the tumor but cancer remains. That's the only fact we understand. Apparently, he stopped cutting bad tissue from the muscle when he reached the main nerve that would disable Mitch from walking. Explaining how he "took as much as he could," he said Mitch absolutely needs chemotherapy to destroy the rest. For now, Mitch will stay in ICU. It's a strange place: awkwardly quiet, too dark or too light, just uncomfortable. We want to take Mitch home. We want the whole thing to be over, with the happy ending we're counting on. Please keep the prayers coming! Every utterance makes a difference.

Seeing Mitch after surgery, and again the next morning, gave Ti and Jen a spiritual boost. After work, they were back in his hospital room, getting the scoop on how he was faring.

"Mitch is doing pretty well. He told me about you two and your amazing wedding." The nurse grinned, hungry for more details.

"We'll bring Mitch's favorite album tomorrow."

Mitch loved to show off the scrapbook Jen's sister had made. It included their readings and vows, along with clever captions to highlight their favorite wedding pictures.

"Mitch is proud of you guys. He even confessed, due to his medicated state of course, that he is looking forward to more grandkids. I learned about Nate, the dogs, and your mountain cabin," she said.

Pleased to know that Mitch had been able to say so much, they enjoyed their evening visit. Once home, the two tired caretakers treated themselves to a bowl of ice cream with peanuts and bananas, adding a bit of nutrition since they'd skipped dinner.

"This ice cream is refreshing. What a good idea!" Jen giggled.

The next day they visited again. Mitch was a good sport about his situation. They were proud of him. He was not used to being stuck.

Sitting next to his father, Ti started to tell a story with his elbows on his knees and his hands holding up his face. "One Sunday, when I was about five, we were on our way back from visiting my grandmother. The old blue Ford broke down about ten miles from home. Dad walked to the nearest phone, while mom and I waited in the car. It only took the tow truck twenty minutes to arrive. Not too bad, huh?"

Mitch winked at Jen.

Ti continued. "Dad was eager to get home. You know, without the proper Sunday routine, his whole week would be off."

"Sounds okay so far." Jen shrugged. Mitch grunted.

"The man stepped out of the truck. I can still picture him—overweight, with messy hair and oil-stained hands. He sat the three of us in our car and then connected it to the tow truck." Ti cleared his throat and sat up.

"Letting us ride in our old clunker while it dragged behind the big truck seemed awesome to a five-year-old. We drove for a few minutes..." Ti paused with a contemplating look on his face. He shook his head. "...Covering n-i-n-e-t-y percent of the distance to the station."

"Ah, here it comes." Jen shifted her feet.

"To our surprise, the driver pulled into a fast-food parking lot. Yes, with us in tow. Dad watched as the man walked in, ordered at the counter, and sat at a booth to eat what must have been his dinner."

"No way!" She sat forward.

Mitch grumbled.

"Oh yes, Dad could almost see the station ahead. I thought the whole thing was great, until I saw him so upset."

Ti continued to describe the scene. Mitch lay in his hospital bed smirking, adding a few "ah-s," "humph-s," and moans when appropriate, feeling annoyed all over again.

"He steamed more and more each second; for exactly nine-and-a-half minutes as the man ordered, ate, and used the restroom!"

"Ha!" Jen laughed, knowing Mitch timed just about everything: driving, sermons at Mass, cooking, and waiting.

"Boy was he stewed! As the man approached the truck, Dad rolled down the window and yelled at him." After demonstrating Mitch's rage with clenched fists, Ti relaxed to imitate the driver's unemotional response. "'*Don't worry, you get charged by the mile, not the minute—it's all good.*'" Ti raised his arms, and his voice. "This guy had no clue! You were really out of sorts for a few days, huh Dad?" Ti touched his father's leg, understanding him well.

"Even though deep down I believe upsets like that are supposed to build character, I couldn't help letting it get to me." *That was tough. Funny now though. Definitely a brick among the many events that built my life.*

"Well, Dad, you survived that mini nightmare, out of your hands and stuck. You'll get through this one too. This one's bigger, but this time you have both of us to help till you're un-stuck."

"Now, that's what counts." Mitch smiled.

◆ ◆ ◆ ◆

The two maintained a steady visit schedule that seemed to work for their spirits as well as the patient's: early morning stop-ins, then after-work stays until all three were sleepy. Mitch was not faring as well later in the week. The recovery process was slow and patience was not a Conner forte. According to Mitch, waiting was a waste of time.

On the way home, Ti told Jen, "One time the snow plow left a huge pile at the end of our driveway. I was in the Jeep. I couldn't wait to get home after a long week. Jeeps are four-wheel-drive after all."

Jen smiled. "I can guess where this is going."

"C'mon. Jeeps are made for any terrain. I figured I'd skip parking, trekking up the hill for a shovel, clearing the pile, and wasting all that time. I just wanted to get in and settled for dinner."

"Yeah, your tummy usually rules." Jen patted his middle.

Ti flinched from an unexpected tickle. "Ah, funny. So, I drove up the snow pile. But I didn't exactly get over it; the mound was high and wide, but not long. So, the front half of the jeep went over, while the back half hung over the other side." Ti motioned like a teeter-totter with his hands.

"Oh my gosh!"

"Yup, the middle of the Jeep sat perched atop the snow pile. No wheels touching meant no traction, no driving, no anything."

Jen shook her head.

"So, instead of wasting an hour clearing snow before getting inside, it took me and Dad two hours to dig the mound out from under the Jeep."

Patience didn't come easily to either of them, and they knew it; they also knew they occasionally paid for that trait. Eager to see Mitch well, they didn't see any downside to their impatience this time.

On one hand, the Conners did well, supporting each other, making time to visit, work, and accomplish a minimum of household chores. On the other hand, it was tough. They needed Mitch, and missed Nate, who had been staying with family members all week.

It's been a long week. Wednesday, Mitch appeared worse. The nurse explained that patients are initially eager to wake up, see family members, and feel that all their parts are still attached, so they're more awake their first day. Mitch also had trouble moving his right arm. The doctors feared a stroke but decided the cause was his position during the long surgery. Still, being stubborn, he worked to lift that arm over his head—that's our Mitch. Considering the "Mitch scale," he doesn't talk much, imagine that! But, when he's awake he asks about... well... you know... everything... to keep up on the mundane to the important. Yesterday, he was convinced it was Friday and that he'd lost a day. After some debate, Ti persuaded him it was only Thursday, and that he'd actually gained one in that case. He's on a lot of medication. Once, Mitch claimed to have seen little men climbing over the curtains... no aliens... just brightly clothed little men... He met his physical therapist this morning. All he had to say was 'ouch!' And the doctor upped his diet. He's had some ginger ale, gelatin, and lemon ice. Wow, is he a happy guy! We enjoy seeing even a sparkle of the real him. It's been tough on Little m... seeing his father so weak weighs heavily, not to mention the long days of opening the building early and visiting late. But it's worth it. Mitch brightens with our visits. Thanks to all of you helping in countless ways. Your kindness means more than we can say!

Friday, Jen asked, "Nate would you like to see Mitch tonight?"

"Oh, yes!" Nate's smile lit the room.

"I don't want you to worry. There's a lot of sick patients and machines in ICU. But it's to help them get well. Mitch will look weak, but he'll be real happy to see us."

"Okay mom, I can't wait to see him."

Mitch's eyes widened and gleamed at the sight of his grandson. "Hey, Nate, buddy!" Mitch spoke in the most stable voice possible. "How are you? How's school? What have I missed?"

Thrilled, Nate talked about math class, his last science test, and a scuffle during recess. Mitch beamed as Nate spoke. However, he wasn't himself. Perplexed, he had trouble speaking. "That's great, Nate. Did you... pretend... your project?"

Jen leaned to Ti and whispered. "He seems drug-dazed."

"But they cut back on the heavier medication."

Aware that he was not making sense, Mitch tried harder. "Pre...stint, pre...stent... uh!" he huffed. The more he tried, the more the phenomenon frustrated him. Nate was somewhat amused as he watched him search for the correct language. After Mitch's attempt to speak regular sentences didn't work, he started to recite favorite rhymes and poems.

"*Found a peanut, found a peanut!*" Nate sang the peanut song with him. Mitch fared well with a partner, but other rhymes they did not know were much tougher.

"You got it that time," Jen encouraged.

"Good job, Dad," Ti said, hoping Mitch was satisfied.

"Hey, that's right," Nate added.

Sadness engulfed them as they observed him attempt to articulate words, while fully comprehending that most were off. Ti, Jen, and Nate kissed him good night with a promise to return early Saturday, bartered for his promise to stop rhyming and go to sleep.

"Tomorrow we'll try again, okay?"

"Yeah, you've pushed your tired brain too much for now."

Mitch snuggled down, and they left the room with the lights turned out. On the way past the nurses' station, they explained Mitch's condition. A doctor overheard their concerns. “Mitch needs to progress through more daily stimulation,” he said. “I want him moved out of ICU.”

Ti called Aunt Colleen on the way home. After filling her in on their evening, he got an earful of the poem that had given her brother so much trouble. Ti hadn’t heard his dad’s favorite Irish chant in years. During the third recitation, now on speakerphone, Ti rolled his eyes. “Got it.”

“Maybe tomorrow we can fill-in-the-blanks,” Nate said.

The poem brought back memories, and Colleen reminisced about her childhood with Mitch. “The four of us had so much fun as youngsters! We played baseball and tag. On the tar roof over our parent’s auto place, we built a fort out of cardboard boxes.”

“I remember,” Ti interjected.

“We’d swim in Cook’s Creek,” she continued, “even when it filled with suds after Bobby’s Laundromat released their water.” To this day, when driving by, they always pointed to that stream—a family landmark.

“We rode our horses in the countryside.” She reminded Ti for the umpteenth time that the horses’ names were Candy, Pretzels, and Coconut. Ti’d heard much about the famed chestnut Pretzels. Riding was their favorite childhood activity. “Your father loved to ride. I’m not sure which of us was the better rider. We galloped all over the farm meadows. We rode, brushed, and fed the horses. We cleaned their stalls constantly.”

Ti remembered his father saying he had a ninety-two acre backyard. *No wonder he’s so comfortable around nature.*

“Yeah, thank goodness we had cousins. Your poor father had to grow up with three girls!” Aunt Colleen chuckled. “We would pretend he was a horse and make him pull us in the wagon down the dirt path. We called him Lollipop because he was such a scrawny kid—skinny as a lollipop stick.”

Ti felt sad they’d lost the farm after his grandparents passed away. He thought about how wonderful it would be to take his father there now, and imagined what fun all four of them might have.

CHAPTER 18

"C'mon, Mitch!" Mandy tugged his arm. "C'mon. Look!" She led him through the tall entrance, pulling open the thick, glass doors by their long, silver handles. "Look at all the toys!"

Mitch smiled, focused on her enthusiastic bounce. "Christmas time is the best season to be here, isn't it?"

"A dream come true! I always wanted to visit the big city toy store!" She skipped ahead in her little white sneakers.

"This is a sight to behold, alright." Mitch arched his neck, circling his head around the enormous room.

Mandy's eyes sparkled and widened as they explored the shelves of dolls, trains, games, and puzzles. She looked and pointed; her voice squeaked. "Oh, we have to see the stuffed ones!" She hastened down the aisle, then stopped and stared at a wall filled with stuffed animals of all shapes and sizes. Her eyes swept across the long, tall rows of fur, and settled on a white polar bear wearing a blue sweatshirt. She picked up the velvety-soft toy and hugged it.

"We'll take it," Mitch said, handing the clerk two crinkled bills. Turning to Mandy, he locked her arm in his. They strolled through the travertine aisles, surrounded by copious displays of toys and filled with the wonder of the season. After enjoying their time, she leaned her head on his shoulder, and they walked out. Mandy's fingers interlaced with her sweetheart's, while her other hand snuggled her new best friend to her chest.

Mitch dreamed peacefully, feeling the happiness of that afternoon as he pictured them together on one of his favorite dates.

◆ ◆ ◆ ◆

Saturday morning, Jen and Ti woke early. Jen breathed deeply, standing at the open cottage window. Spring air wafted in, carrying the scent of hyacinths mixed with fresh rain. The birds had returned from their southern pilgrimage, singing garrulously in the tall pine tree.

"Beautiful day," she said.

"Listen to that racket." Ti rolled over with a soft moan.

"Oh, stop your teasing; their song is so sweet. You know Mitch's old adage: appreciate the small things."

"Yeah, you're right. I guess if we can't be home, we should at least enjoy the nature here." He stood and stretched.

Ti, Jen, and Nate dressed in comfy clothes and set off to visit Mitch with a knapsack full of books, cars, games, and a bunch of Nate-approved snacks. Scary H-place or not, they would spend the day together.

They found Mitch in his new room sipping his breakfast of broth and tea. "Ugh, who can live on this?" he grumbled.

Ti winked at Jen, telepathically sharing his thoughts. *Ah, hunger. A good sign the old Mitch is coming back to us.*

Ti said hello as he passed Mitch's roommate and sat down. Not being home on a weekend, Ti felt out of sorts. He rose and paced by the window. After hearing about Mitch's night, Ti stepped out to call his friend in Walleycito. Knowing he could count on Lenny for anything, Ti dialed the number. He caught Lenny in the garage, tinkering with his car.

"Hey, how's Mitch?"

"Much better."

Lenny sensed Ti's uneasiness. "You should see if you can watch some of the game this afternoon."

"Yeah, we will. Would you mind gathering the mail and checking the thermostats? You know, just look around at home."

"Of course," Lenny replied. "I'd planned to stop over this afternoon."

When Ti returned to the small white room, nodding past the roommate, he heard Mitch reading a riddle from the book Nate had given him before surgery. Mitch used a few to taunt his nurses. It was the only book he'd opened, other than the photo album.

"Riddles are like brain exercise," Mitch told his protégé. The boy put his hand on his hip and pursed his lips as he considered the answer.

Looking at Ti, Mitch said, "Hey, how about helping me? I need a shave!"

"I don't know. Those white whiskers are attractive." Ti whistled.

While they were busy, Jen opened her laptop.

Friday afternoon was quite eventful. After scolding and threats that I'd cover his hands with mittens, Mitch finally stopped itching at his gauze and scabs. We've also threatened to staple his socks to the sheets, to prevent him from crossing his feet, which they keep reminding him is bad for clots. (And he says I'm a nudge, can you believe that?) The Bishop, Vicar General, and Chancellor all visited, making him feel both privileged and utterly exhausted. When we arrived, Mitch was delighted to see Nate, but was drowsy, disoriented and had trouble speaking. The doctor told us Mitch had ICU psychosis, which comes from staying in ICU too long. He upgraded Mitch's diet and ordered a bath and a transfer. He instructed Mitch to walk more. Turns out, he wasn't worse, just ready for bigger challenges and a change in venue. Today, Mitch is bright as a summer's morning. He knows his name, the day of the week, the current president of the United States, and can once again recite "Colin McCarthy" from start to finish. The poem that distressed him last night is once again his own. We heard about his voyage to his new room at 4:00 a.m. Ti just gave him a shave. Boy, does he look handsome! He has not ventured beyond the doorway. Our hardheaded patriarch feels a walk down the hall would be like climbing Mt. Everest. Mitch sends a big thank you for the prayers, flowers, and cards, many of which have inspired our conversation today. As you know, we are grateful for your love and support. We'd be lost without you!

"Hello?" Ti answered the room phone. "Hi, Rose. Yup, he's better."

"Brock and I want to visit. We're planning to come around 6:30. You and Jen deserve an evening to sit and do nothing."

Ti did not entrust his father's visit time to just anyone. But he knew he could count on Rose. "That works. Nate's going to his father's later."

Hospital visits left no time for winding down. They laundered and cleaned the essentials and ate quick meals. Last week, Rose had dropped off a pasta casserole. Calling themselves "the pray-and-feed club," she and three friends took turns sending a meal, which was a blessing since Jen and Ti did not want to give up time away from Mitch—even to cook. The amount of kindness that came to them throughout this ordeal astounded them—and it wasn't nearly over.

After Rose and Brock arrived, Ti and Jen went home and enjoyed lounging on a full couch rather than the hard, narrow hospital chairs they knew so well. They watched a fun movie they'd seen before.

"Wow, what a difference a day can make, huh? Mitch was awesome today." Chase leaned on Jen. Champ sprawled on the floor, snoring, pleased to have evening company.

"Yeah, and his shave really cheered him up." Ti rubbed his throat, noticing the stubble that had accumulated over the past two days.

"Dad was talkative, showing interest in his cards, who was up to what, and the riddles." She looked up at Ti.

"He has been asking about more. Last week, he asked about Jackson's sister and whether Betty had baked recently."

"And he really enjoyed his meal. Solid food today. Whoo-hoo!"

"He told me twice to bring a toothbrush and comb when we go back tomorrow." Ti felt relief with Mitch's desire to clean up.

A gust of wind blew their wooden chimes, as if an angel had whispered. Jen heard the message in its song. The wind chime Ti had made for their wedding represented their becoming a family. Four personalized limbs had come together, each to play an important role. *That sound is a good sign.*

"This must be so hard for my father. He's always been healthy, aside from bumps and scrapes, the occasional flu, and a nasty kidney stone." Ti glanced out the window. The yo-yo of up-and-down emotions had exhausted him. "I don't know how he managed during Mom's illness. He was always with her; he never tired. Even I got bored and frustrated with the life of a sick person being our only focal point. But, my father made me go out with friends. He knew better than I, what I needed to feel normal." He closed his eyes. Jen touched his shoulder. "I was... no, I am... astonished by his devotion: reading to her, doing crosswords with her, playing cards, and when she couldn't see her hand, describing it to her. He'd let her win. It was... adorable." Ti paused. "She was his queen."

Ti decided his father deserved at least this much care and attention. He pulled Jen closer and she rested on his shoulder. They fell fast asleep before the end of the show.

◆ ◆ ◆ ◆

Back in his hospital room, Mitch visited with Rose and Brock. "Thanks for coming. My kids are here all the time. They won't let me be alone. They really are special."

"We know, Mitch. You are blessed." Rose patted his arm.

"I am at that." Mitch smiled. "I'm gonna beat this, for them. You'll see. We have a lot more living to do as a family. I feel much better today."

"That's the spirit, Mitch." Brock leaned in. "God is listening to your deepest desires. He knows what's right, and He'll follow through."

"So how are our Mustangs? And what's going on at work?"

◆ ◆ ◆ ◆

The next morning, Ti and Jen picked up Nate and returned to visit Mitch. Jen dealt with her hospital-phobia, coaxing her stomach away from brutal nausea through her resolve to be by Mitch's side. Ti was more familiar and comfortable with the hospital scene. However, if there had been no TV, then that would have been a different story.

Jen would never forget the day she discovered that the Conner television turned on early in the morning and didn't lose power until bedtime. While the men worked, the television kept the pooches company.

"What?" Jen and Nate had asked in stereo. "Keep them company?"

Jen looked at Nate. "There are four of them, how much more company do they need?" Nate lifted his shoulders.

"It's vital. Labradors need audio and visual stimulation. I read about it before our first puppy. It was all over the research. You know us, gotta do everything big... and right," Mitch had explained.

In the white room, Ti watched television between telling his curious father about the happenings in the outside world. He simply raised or lowered the volume depending on the discussion.

Nurse Vic walked in. "Hey, you guys are glued to that program. Anything good happening?"

"Not really," Jen said, looking up from her magazine. "They tired of chatting. They're having what Ti calls '*a man visit*' at the moment."

"Good thing they have something to watch," Vic replied.

"You're not kidding," Jen said. "I never want to see either of these two without a television again."

“Uh oh. I sense another Mitch story.” Smiling, Vic checked Mitch’s blood pressure. “How about a walk down the hall, Mitch?”

Mitch sat up. “I don’t have any idea how I’ll make it, but I’ll try right after you hear this.”

“Ah, the weekend we lost TV.” Jen grinned.

Nate giggled and drove his red Ferrari along the windowsill.

Ti held his stomach. “I was physically ill when I realized we had no television during football playoffs. I contacted tech support. They told me we were stuck till the part shipped.”

“Boy, did he whine.” Jen closed her magazine.

“You can’t watch an entire season of football and miss the playoffs. You just don’t understand.” Ti scowled at her.

“Yeah. So?” Vic, a die-hard football fan, needed to know.

“After listening to us groan for an hour, Jen called customer service again, while her men remained skeptical.” Ti smirked.

“That’s us.” Mitch circled his hand around the room, “Her men, who insisted they’d reported all the facts and asked all the right questions.”

“The agent came up with an idea, involving a certain electronics store, an hour car ride, and seventy-nine bucks! We missed a day of TV, but only fifteen minutes of that playoff game.” Ti’s stance relaxed.

“Whew!” Vic said.

“You’re not kidding.” Mitch snickered.

Looking back, they laughed about that event—much less traumatic than what they were presently going through. Ti looked at his father. *Huh. Funny how life reminds us of proper priorities.* Mitch’s wedding toast resonated in his ears, although he didn’t admit it aloud. *Bricks and sticks… everyday moments… don’t forget what matters…*

Vic and Ti walked Mitch out of the room, past two doors and back again. Nurse, family, and patient were pleased.

Later, Vic returned. “Have you run your marathon down the hall again?” Mitch cooperated with all the poking, prodding, rules, and protocols imposed upon him. But he seemed to have a psychological block about walking. Headstrong, Mitch always found a way, given a will. Yet for some reason, he didn’t believe he could walk.

Then, Vic mentioned a scary word: discharge.

"Discharge?" Mitch mumbled in a shaky voice.

Jen eyebrows rose as she whispered, "No way, he likes it here?"

"Maybe he feels a little safe?" Ti breathed.

"Seems like you could be ready sometime Monday." Vic clipped the chart back to Mitch's bed and exited.

The hospital was a tough routine. Then again, it meant constant care. Mitch tolerated it, which was about as odd for him as it would be for Champ to skip a meal. *Discharge, so soon? I just got on solid food. I can barely get to the bathroom. I don't know about this.*

Sunday afternoon, Millie visited. She brought balloons, smiles, and almost flirty teasing. Happy to see Millie with Mitch, Ti and Jen took the opportunity to run an errand. Nate dropped the comic book he'd been reading, and the threesome headed toward the mall.

The morning after leaving ICU, Mitch had commented about hospital conveniences, implying concern for the furniture back home. So Ti and Jen had started searching for a comfortable recliner that would let him sit up and lay back with ease once he returned to the cottage sunroom.

They passed a going-out-of-business sign in front of a furniture shop.

"Why not check it out?" Ti pulled into the lot.

Initially, all the chairs looked the same, and none were right.

"Mom!" Nate called, "Over this way. There's some over here."

In a spacious rear room, they found a suitable chair: large, plush, and comfortable, with pockets, a nice color, and a good price. They took turns testing it out, and all three agreed.

Perfect.

With a quick favor from Jimmy and his pickup truck, they were able to get the chair in place and return before supper. Glad for their company, Mitch felt half-content. His other half remained nervous as a baby chick about to break out of its safe, comfortable eggshell.

CHAPTER 19

"Okay Nate, let's get you off to school." Jen handed him his lunchbox.

"Is Mitch coming home today?" he asked.

"We think so. The nurse will call when he's ready. I'll pick you up right after school."

"I'm so happy he's coming home!" Nate leapt to his feet.

"I know, sweetheart, me too. Remember, Mitch will be weak after his operation and probably a little scared. He'll need our help."

"I'm nervous, but I'll help him."

"I know you will," Jen said. "Remember, hardships can help us learn and become stronger."

"You know what Mitch told me after I lost the big race at school?"

"What did he tell you?"

"He wrote it inside my blue notebook, see?" Nate held out his notebook.

Everything in life is a gift
All of it —
good, bad,
happy, sad,
you just have to unwrap it and look inside

"That's a pretty great saying. Even hard things can be an invitation to something unexpected. That's where faith comes in."

"Mommy, do you think Mitch has faith he'll be even better after he's not sick anymore?"

"Yup. Faith can help us when things are tough."

"I know, mom."

"Good. Now have a good day." She hugged him.

◆ ◆ ◆ ◆

The nurse called about 3:30 p.m. Millie accompanied them to offer moral support during the tedious discharge process. With her notebook and no less than a dozen questions, Jen gathered information about his care, restrictions, and medications.

I guess this is it. Well, I made it this far. Mitch swallowed. Vic helped him into the wheelchair.

Ti drove around the hospital circle to see his family waiting, wearing big grins. A wave of pride flooded his body. His nerves revitalized; they soaked in joy as he parked the truck and helped his father into the seat.

They pulled up to the cottage. Barking ensued. Ti exited first, and led the flurry of tails to the yard. Then, he opened the door for Mitch, who swiveled his quivering legs toward the opening. As soon as Mitch was stable, he bellowed his old familiar tune, "Heeeeeey, dooog-gies!"

The barks grew louder and more excited. One under each arm, Ti and Jen steered Mitch into the house. Nate carried Mitch's travel case. Millie followed behind with the walker she was loaning him. Leading Mitch to the familiar sunroom, they watched his expression. *Something's different.*

Jen and Nate beamed while Ti feigned normalcy. Mitch looked from side to side. "Oh, a new recliner where the loveseat was!" he realized.

They lowered Mitch into his chair, where he raised his legs and reclined into the soft cushion—perfect for his tender body. Touched, Mitch's eyes brimmed with tears, elated to be home and grateful for his kids, who were proof of God's grace in his life.

Jen and Millie stuffed pillows on either side of the chair and folded blankets over Mitch. Fully padded, he prepared for his canine welcome. Millie said her goodbyes and dashed out. She loved Mitch dearly, but the exuberant Labs, not so much.

As the dogs raced in, Ti prevented them from jumping into Mitch's lap. In turn, he allowed each to put two paws on the recliner's armrest where they licked up and down Mitch's arm, delighted at the return of their best friend. Ti reached over and opened a window, knowing his father would appreciate a fresh breeze after so many days of stale hospital air.

Mitch sucked in a deep breath. "Ah!"

To celebrate, Ti went out for Colossal burgers. Jen filled a pillbox to organize Mitch's many medications and labeled each compartment. She made a list of things she had to do to get him settled in his new routine. At the bottom, she wrote *walk* with a smiley face.

"The nice weather should help entice him into a few trips down the driveway," she whispered to Nate. He nodded.

Nate joined Mitch in the sunroom and paced. "Mitch, I really wanted to buy you a coming home present. But, well, I don't have enough money for what you deserve. I want to buy you a Corvette."

"The best present I can get is being home with you, buddy. I want you to remember something, okay? Life isn't about what you have. It's about what you do. How about we do something together this weekend?"

"That sounds great." Nate smiled, rising up on his tiptoes.

Mitch ate slowly. Jen washed dishes, and Ti swept the kitchen. Then, tired from rushes of adrenaline, they all slept soundly—Mitch fully reclined in his new chair with his pups scattered on the floor.

Good Morning, we have news! Our Mitch is home! Yup! Really! A scary rumor started Sunday that they might discharge him. Monday, they said, "Come n' get him!" We arrived home about dinnertime. He overcame the hurdles to get up and through the side door, and settled into his new recliner. Gleeful pups drenched their long-lost master in loving licks. This morning, Mitch confessed that now that he's here, he's happy to be home. His fears are subsiding. He has my full attention and will be spoiled rotten by the day's end. Mitch has no restrictions. He can try anything that feels comfortable and should continue walking daily. We are trying to organize his medication to manage the plentitude of pills with varying schedules. Short-term we'll establish a plan with the visiting nurses. Next week, we will meet with the surgeon to discuss pathology and future treatments. We can't tell you how wonderful it is to have our patient home and how incredible it's been to have you pulling for him. Your love, kindness, and prayers give us strength. Thank you with utmost sincerity!

Jen spent the day doting on Mitch, catching up on chores, and establishing a routine for his 3Ms: meals, meds, and movements.

"Jen, how about a clean shirt? Maybe that new one you got me." Mitch recalled the day she brought it home, just to cheer him up. He placed each arm into its sleeve, pleased to sit in one of his favored garments again.

Jen brought him a snack around noon.

"Mmmm, this is very good," Mitch said. "What's in this tuna salad?"

"You know I can't share the secrets of my recipes," she teased with a slight grimace on her face, knowing she didn't remember every ingredient.

"Humph," he grunted, annoyed but not surprised. "I don't get the way you cook with dashes and pinches here and there, never measuring anything, always experimenting, throwing this or that into the mix."

As he nibbled, Mitch patted the wide armrest of his recliner so she would sit next to him. "I love good recipes, and pepper stuffing is a good one." He swallowed. "One time, I mixed the meat, rice, tomatoes, and garlic. I stuffed the goop into ten large peppers. I was checking the recipe for time and temperature when I realized I'd missed the basil. I was so mad! I couldn't leave it out."

"Seriously?" Her brows rose.

"I had to tear them apart and remix it. It took sixteen minutes to do them a second time, and you know I don't like to be late for anything, especially supper." They both giggled.

Mitch relaxed. While he was home healing, he spent a lot of time pondering his relationships. He felt strong, determined, and grateful to have so many good things in his life.

◆ ◆ ◆ ◆

The family settled into new routines. After school, Nate came home to a door full of snorting and prancing, dumped his knapsack, and helped Mitch herd the dogs out to the yard. They both waited all day for that moment. Proud to help his hero, Nate got him up to walk the sneaky way, even if only from one chair inside to another outside on the patio.

Nate adored Mitch's sense of humor. He fed on his wisdom and experience. This man had cool stories. Mitch claimed to have had "snowball fights" in the summer using balls made of dried up horse poop.

"Yeah, like all kids who grew up on farms," Mitch said with a shrug.

"Yuck," said Jen.

"Wow," said Nate.

Mitch told Nate all about his cars, building homes, and many of his construction mishaps. They sang silly songs, explored how things worked, and exchanged corny jokes and mind-bending riddles. They laughed about the time Mitch pulled Nate on the old lawn tractor with a chain tied to the other tractor after the first ran out of gas. One of Jen's favorite photos, it portrayed two guys, two tractors, two waving arms, and two big grins, all heading across the long driveway.

Nate learned a lot from Mitch without even knowing it. Mitch taught the boy more in the last year than anyone, save his mother, had in all eight thus far. He'd become a respected confidant, supporter, and mentor.

Nate was not the only one who benefited from knowing and loving Mitch. Jen adored her second father who awarded her attention, encouragement, challenges, and led her to discover her own courage. She too was better from his influence.

Others had been blessed through Mitch's effect on their lives. His friends yearned for his return to the office. Mitch was Claire's right arm, fastening her bracelet every morning. He empathized with Cassie over thousands of animal stories. He laughed with Millie, deliberated with Rose, visited with Betty, and was a valued buddy to Rick, who knew he could ask Mitch anything. Mitch was best friend to Lenny, who considered Mitch his little brother.

Mitch was eager to share his knowledge—about cars, people, traditions, nature, and whatever else touched his simple life's journey. If it met his existence, he learned about it. Mitch could not fathom hording any possession, feeling, thought, or idea. He was an average guy characterized by his striped shirts, his dogs, his son, his faith, doing his best, and caring for those around him. He spoke honestly and from his gut. Just as bricks and sticks built grand structures, segments of Mitch's life affected others, shaping their dwellings in a profound way.

Most of all, Mitch Senior was Tiger's guiding force, best friend, role model, fan, and rock. Ti had become the man he was thanks to his father.

Now, they all needed to know what was in store for their beloved Mitch.

CHAPTER 20

With the patient home and thriving, Jen and Nate rejoiced. Ti acted calm and cool, but euphoria surged through his veins as he witnessed his father's increasing strength. The more Mitch had something to contribute—big or small, important or unimportant—the more it meant his old dad was returning.

Mitch's doctor gave him clearance to travel. Delighted, Mitch and Ti looked forward to their mountain haven more than ever.

"Look at you guys," Jen said to Ti on Friday morning. "I see five wagging tails today." She giggled, nodding toward Mitch.

And so they went.

Thrilled to be back to normal and off to his favorite place, Ti drove them home. Jen and Nate sang along to the radio.

Mitch chatted for a short time and then napped. He awoke in plenty of time to enjoy his homecoming. Experiencing his mountain routine again was as exciting as getting a new power tool. He savored each sensation. His eyes glowed like fluorescent lights; his ears buzzed as if hearing a whirling saw blade or his favorite drill; he could smell fresh sawdust and taste the energy. He sat forward, holding the back of the driver's seat, looking through the windshield as the car climbed up the long driveway to view the log cabin ahead. He beamed as they disembarked.

Inside, he skimmed through the envelopes, needing to touch the larger-than-usual mail-mound as part of his regular activity. When the grandfather clocked chimed, he called for pizza.

"Friday night pizza on the couch with a movie... Ah, what could be better?" He pushed his recliner back.

Ti grabbed his keys. "Hey Dad, you need to be up for making the pizza run again. After all, you should continue serving your son as is proper." Nate giggled as he followed Ti out the door.

That pizza was the best-tasting pizzas the Conners had ever eaten. Missing the end of the movie, Mitch fell asleep in his familiar chair with Champ in his lap, Chase on his hip, and Daisy and Chip lying at his feet.

He woke long enough to stroke Champ's neck while he prayed.

Dear Lord,
Thank you for my wonderful family
  and the gift that was today.
Watch over all under this roof.
  Help me continue to get better.
This is what I pray

He finished by telling his special angel, "I miss you, Mandy; I know you're here with me. Today was awesome."

Saturday, Ti, Jen, and Nate cleared the winter debris from the yard. The weather was pleasant—an unusual mix of flurries and rays of sunshine glistened on the tree limbs. The clean scent of a not-too-distant spring hung in the air. Although it was cool, thoughts of campfires and days on the lake spawned feelings of warmth and an uplifting sense of anticipation.

"Hey, look!" Nate pointed at a sprout uncovered by his rake.

Mitch enjoyed the all-encompassing weather pattern, which reminded him of good times and gave him hope for a future filled with many more seasons. By Sunday, the hidden wear from the car ride began to emerge inside his fragile body, as if thousands of tiny inner bruises filled his weak middle section. The fact that the trip back to reality was never quite as nice as the trip up to paradise magnified his aches and pains. Still, he wouldn't have traded the time away for any comfort in the world.

◆ ◆ ◆ ◆

Ti began the new week with his breakfast companions after organizing the contractors outside. Alongside two large trucks, the crew prepared to mend curbs and realign parking delineators. Amidst the breakfast chatter, Ti reminisced. "When my friends and I worked for my father at St. John's, we filled potholes and repainted the parking lot lines every March. We looked forward to that first warm-weather job. Whenever I smell fresh asphalt, it reminds me of spring and new beginnings."

"It smells stale and burnt to me," Cassie said.

"I guess it's like gasoline. Some people like it." Rick shrugged.

"Anyway," Ti continued. "I'll never forget one year, on a Friday night. After painting lines all day in the sun, I drove home, walked through the front door, and got a call from the rectory. I had forgotten to unlock the kitchen for bingo and had to race back. I apologized to the people waiting, unlocked the door, and ran out—only to wonder, *what happened to my truck?* It took a minute to register the yelling, far across the parking lot."

"Uh oh," Betty said, both desiring and fearing his next words.

"Ha." Ti sensed her apprehension. "A man was screaming and waving his arms. His fence was down, and my truck was up against his swing set, which was now half in his pool."

"Yikes!" Cassie gasped. Rick stopped chewing.

"In my hurry, I left the truck running, but I guess in gear too. The parking brake must have come loose. I posed as much charm as I could to convince the homeowner that I worked maintenance at the parish and would repair all the damage."

Ti exhaled.

"The next day, the man spoke with the Maintenance Supervisor, who, after hearing a description of the culprit, figured out what had happened."

"Well, what did you expect?" Betty rubbed her nose.

"I wanted to handle it on my own, but... well..." Ti sighed. "Although Mitch oversaw the repair, took the expense from my pay, and disciplined his favorite employee, he still totally supported me. I can't tell you the number of jams that guy helped me squeak my way out of."

Amused, Rick sat back chuckling. Cassie and Betty shook their heads.

◆ ◆ ◆ ◆

Mitch strolled into the bathroom and turned on his razor. He inhaled as it buzzed. He rolled it back and forth on his left cheek. "Mandy, I know you're with me. I need to see you, to feel your love, to have your faith." He waited, knowing she would come. Her image emerged. She wore a blue blouse and her matching eyes gleamed with love. Her affection penetrated his soul as a warmth flowed over his cheeks, ears, and down across his shoulders. Studying her in the mirror, he guided the razor under his chin, not wanting the chore to end. He felt her daily, and knew she was present as he lay down at night, but in the mirror he could picture her—foggy, but there. "I love you." He shut the razor and picked up his toothbrush.

◆ ◆ ◆ ◆

Attempting to mask his anxiety, Mitch sauntered into the surgeon's office, eager for results and clarity. Ti and Jen followed. The visit was short, but informative. Before having time to absorb all the details, and still somewhat numb, the two dropped Mitch at the house, planted him in his recliner, repeated the repertoire of where all needed items could be found, and headed back to their jobs.

Mitch flopped in his chair. The phone rang. "Hello."

"Hey old man, how's my favorite maintenance duo?"

"Oh, it's just you," Mitch said with a chuckle. "What do you want?"

Millie laughed. "The usual, just to pester you. My daughter was by last night. The baby's getting bigger by the minute. Nice visit..." Their light conversation distracted him. *I've got so many people in my corner. I'm going to pull through for them all.* Relaxed, Mitch drifted off to sleep.

Mitch had a follow-up with his surgeon to review pathology and look toward the next phase of recovery. The doctor reviewed everything. He removed the kidney and surrounding tissue. The psoas muscle is the area most afflicted and will be the most challenging to treat. In five weeks, Mitch will begin chemo to destroy the remaining cancer. We feel cloudy about his report. So if you're wondering, "Hmm, is it good news or bad? How long will chemo take? How will he feel?" you're pretty much up to speed. We've decided the bottom line is: the news is neither very bad, nor very good, and it is optimistic overall but without assurance. How's that for a conclusion? Mitch is frustrated by his continued fatigue. Yesterday, he insisted on climbing three stairs, which he did oh-so-slowly yet miraculously well. But he needed a good nap afterward. The doctor confirmed what we've been telling him: his body's healing on the inside, so his energy's temporarily diverted. The doctor said it is time to walk, but not time to do more than that. Although moving around might wear him out, it will give him more strength in the end. When feeling well, Mitch speaks of driving to the burger place—a scary idea. I might have to hide his keys! We look forward to his wellness, grouching and grumping included, if that's what it takes (he's an adorable little grouch). Thank you for your greetings. Mitch gets more mail than Santa Claus these days. We are grateful for your kindness and support.

Jen and Ti went to work; Nate went to school. Jen urged Mitch to walk. He moseyed out, giving into two of her five pleadings. His willingness to walk swung from fear and refusal to confidence and success, and then back again, like a slow moving pendulum.

After dinner, Ti attempted a bribe. "Hey Dad, after we walk, I'll get us all some ice cream. Remember The Old Cream Shoppe?"

"Yeah, the owner knew our order by heart: triple-scoop banana split, brownie sundae, and two small vanilla cups to go."

"Why extra vanilla?" Nate asked.

"For the dogs, of course." Mitch laughed.

"Sounds good, doesn't it?" Ti hoped an old favorite pastime would motivate him. Alas, his valiant efforts were lost.

"Not tonight, Ti." Mitch leaned back. "I'm okay. But I feel like there's lead in my veins weighing me down."

Standing in the sunroom, Jen hugged her husband. Ti kissed the top of her head. "I remember when my parents took me for ice cream. Not only for celebrating a baseball victory, we'd go on Sunday afternoons just because. My dad will want it as soon as he's in a better place."

"I hope so," Jen said, looking at Mitch in his recliner. He was wearing his maroon striped shirt and gray sweatpants. Not pale, not thin, just tired. *I guess that's okay for now.*

◆ ◆ ◆ ◆

As time passed, Ti felt greater relief. His father grounded him and gave him a sense of security. Sitting on the couch one evening, Ti recalled a memory. His younger self had a knack for finding mischief, a streak he knew he'd inherited. But the man who gave him the inclination also rescued his butt repeatedly.

"So, this one time," Ti began.

"Oh goodie, an M-&-m story." Nate scooched next to Ti.

"I was playing in the woods across the street from my house with a bunch of other boys. We had many adventures in those woods."

"But sometimes their craving for mischief overtook them," Mitch added.

Ti was thrilled with his father's interest in the story. "One time we hid behind trees and threw snowballs at passing cars. We rarely hit anything; it was too far. This went on for a while. Then we hit one."

Mitch grunted a half-laugh.

"The car pulled over," Ti said. "We scattered. But the man ran into the woods after us. He yelled, '*Stop!*'"

"Two of them, Ti and Luke, stopped," Mitch said in a low voice, eyes dazed, as if he was watching the scene.

"The man asked my name. I told him. He asked where I lived, and I recited my address as a proud youngster would do." Ti began to snicker. "Then the guy held us both by the collars and walked us home. Luke first. He banged on the front door, feeling empowered to deliver a delinquent to his parents." Ti puffed out his chest and shoulders. "Then, he did the same for me. My father was calm yet protective, pushing me inside with both arms as the man complained. After the old man was done, Dad said, '*Apologize.*' I looked around from behind him. '*I'm sorry, Sir.*'" Ti chuckled. "Dad closed the door, looked at me and..."

Mitch cut in. "I said, '*How on earth did he know your name and where you lived?*' And Ti told me, '*Well, Dad, the man asked me.*'"

"To which my father's forehead wrinkled and he muttered, '*And you told him? Huh. Okay son...*'" Ti laughed. "I knew he had mixed emotions. Dad banned me from TV that night and had me paint old man Miller's shed the next weekend, hoping to teach me respect for the older generation. It worked. But from that point on, I thought about how my dad would handle something before doing or saying anything again. Even before we built homes, my father gave me a concrete foundation."

"WWMD," Nate said with a giggle. "What would Mitch do?"

Ti turned to his father and looked at his hero—the source of all he had become. He appreciated how his father had let him find his own way, yet had always been there to back him up when needed. The man was the best father anyone could ask for. "Thanks, Dad."

Mitch grinned.

Ti started the next day with the breakfast club. Rick entered and pulled out a chair. “My wife bought two fresh-baked pies and a slew of plants at the flea market yesterday.”

“My mother loved flea markets,” Ti said. “We’d go every weekend in the spring. I remember watching the man make those soft, hot pretzels. He’d roll the dough into a strip like a long cigar. Then, with a flick of his wrist, he’d twist it on the tray, adding a squirt of water and a dusting of salt. After a trip on a conveyor belt through the oven, they’d come out bronze and steamy. I’d wait like an excited puppy.” He licked his lips.

Betty giggled. “I’ll ask Ernesto if he can make some hot pretzels.”

“Yum. So, my parents found a Ruby Rag clown dealer there, which is where we got most of my mother’s collectibles.” Ti’s expression sagged as he recalled her treasures consumed in flames. It seemed like only yesterday, when he and his father survived those back-to-back tragedies: his mother’s death and then the fire. He prayed they could weather this storm too. Starting over wasn’t easy. There were times they’d been downright depressed about where circumstances had forced them. Yet the clouds had parted and sunny skies returned. They were not building houses, but they were building family, and memories, and love. Ti’s mood shifted from distress to hope.

◆ ◆ ◆ ◆

At the cabin the following weekend, the temperatures taunted with more previews of spring, inspiring Jen to visit the lawn and garden store. Boasting their colorful petals, the flowers lifted her spirits.

“Ti, how about I plant some flowers near the shed?” With a finger to her chin, she surveyed the plants, selecting carefully. They had to be hardy to survive the hot, dry summer, as well as deter the agile four-legged bandits who liked to nibble off all their blooms.

She’s got such a hopeful spirit… a black thumb, but a vibrant, hopeful spirit. Ti snickered as he carried them to the car.

Standing on the back deck, overlooking the yard, Ti and Jen inhaled and welcomed the warm air just as they had the first snowflake back when the earth was turning cold. Jen leaned into him. *Ah, spring!*

They walked to the yard. She removed the rocks from the area. Organizing the gray slates, she outlined her new garden wall.

Mitch watched from his lawn chair. *Nice, just as it should be—the family enjoying fresh air and making the grounds even homier...* He breathed deeply and looked around.

Before Jen knew it, Ti approached. "Time to go in for supper."

"It'll take time, but it's going to be worth it." She stepped back, brushing a curl from her face. A dirty brown smudge followed the glove across her forehead.

Ti licked his thumb and rubbed her face. "Look at this mess, and for what? Not like any flowers you touch live very long." Ti nudged her shoulder with a devilish grin.

"Hey, that's not nice." She stuck out her bottom lip and turned back to stare at her rocks once more before following him inside. "Hey, wait up."

◆ ◆ ◆ ◆

We had a nice weekend. The extra pillows and time healing made a big difference with the car ride. Ti, Nate, and I worked outside. Don't tell my husband how handsome he is in his lost-for-winter tanks and tan arms! Mitch made it out twice each day. He walked around enthralled by the scenery, which was great for his body and soul. Sunday he was more tired and grumped about everything from Ti's driving to the temperature to the radio volume. We saw right through his motives. He's trying to gear us up for the [foolish] idea that he can drive himself soon. Once we got home, he became super tired, beyond tired. On Monday, he was so sleepy we called the doctor, who wanted to run tests. Ti thought he'd have to carry poor Mitch into the place. Mitch fell asleep while the nurse was drawing his blood. The results came back with low counts, but no clear need to intervene. Our dejected Mitch declined a Colossal burger on the way home. We see the medical oncologist tomorrow for the first time to review his case and discuss a plan for recovery. Please pray that the news and suggested course of action are both positive and manageable for him. We are ready to have our old, healthy, lively Mitch back!

With a different daily tone, they settled into a survival reality. The Conners were willing to do whatever it took to get back to where they belonged. Ti, Jen, and Nate cared for their patriarch. When he was limited in his ability, they lingered nearby, ensuring he felt included. They cooked meals rich in protein, juggled schedules so someone was always around, delivered him to tests and appointments no matter what the hour, offered game play without pushing, asked questions about classwork to remind him how much knowledge he had to share, and updated his curiosity with the latest office happenings. Not one of them complained; not one of them would have been anywhere but by his side.

During his busy Tuesday morning, Ti visited several offices. He passed Youth Ministry on his way to move some furniture.

"Hey, handsome Junior." Deirdre swooned past him with a half swirl, as her long skirt swelled. "How's your father?"

"He's doing okay."

"Of course he is. He's got to get well so I can finally win over his affections. He's going to go out with me, you know."

Ti smiled but imagined rolling his eyes.

"Not that dying is a bad thing. Passing on is the way to our next life, our better life. So, either way, he wins," she said in an effervescent tone.

"Well, I'm set on the getting well option."

"Yes, you would be." She looked over her shoulder. "Ta-ta."

As Ti finished moving a credenza, he received a call from Sister Judy. He sauntered into to her cubicle. "Hello, Sister. How can I help you today?"

"Thanks for coming so quickly. This drawer is sticking, see?" She tugged; it moved jerkily. "How's your father?"

"He's okay. Well, I hope he's okay. Some days, I just don't know. He felt pretty lousy yesterday. He's got to catch a break. We meet the oncologist later today."

"I'm praying for you both." Sister Judy put her palms together.

"I just ran into Deirdre, who talks about looking forward to death, to get to the next place. Sometimes I don't get her. I know you believe in heaven, Sister, but who wants to die?"

"Existence is a natural instinct. God made us that way. Of course, I believe in heaven, and when I see Him, it will be wonderful. But He also gives us a marvelous gift: life. We must respect life as God gives it. So, you see, there is merit in both, but one follows the other in His time."

"Thanks, Sister. That makes a lot of sense." Ti realigned the drawer rails and head off to his next task.

CHAPTER 21

He made it! "Your recovery time is complete and you're ready to begin chemotherapy, Mr. Conner." The grey-eyed man shut the thick folder and met Mitch's gaze. Mitch swallowed, feeling fear and joy in the span of two breaths. *Guess this is a good thing.*

Ti and Jen looked at one another. Although not a pleasant experience to consider, they believed that chemo was the obvious next step to recovery. Accepting the need for treatment, they all prayed for a silver lining.

They drove four blocks to the oncology center. Mitch watched the landscape go by his window. *Yeah, I want this. It might be hard, but it will make me well. Let's get started... and get done.*

Tuesday, after the surgeon released Mitch, we went to his first oncology appointment. Dr. Leslie spent a good deal of time with us, reiterating the need for chemo to cure the remaining cancer. She described a regimen of six three-week cycles: an infusion during weeks one and two, followed by a third week off to check health levels. After more tests, she'll solidify her plan and meet with us again. Therefore, we don't know much more than we knew before, which is becoming an uncomfortable pattern. Wednesday Mitch felt exhausted. Each time we called to check in, he complained of feeling "terrible." When we arrived home, he was flushed with a one-hundred-two-degree fever. We called Dr. Leslie's office. The on-call doc sent us to the ER, where they juiced him up with IV fluids and antibiotics. They say he has pneumonia. What? Sigh... We have no idea how long they'll keep him. We're not sure about our much-needed holiday, but we'll have a good Easter one way or another. Any sacrifice is worth his restored health. He needs your prayers turned up a notch. With your strength and support, he is plodding along.

Another setback... geez. How am I supposed to get well, when each step forward is outdone by one backward? Mitch stared at the wall, reading and rereading the date on the whiteboard across the room.

"Hey you." Ti entered, dragging the chair closer. Jen smiled.

"Hey guys." Mitch pushed himself up on his elbows. The sadness in his voice was clear as crystal.

"I'm sorry you're stuck in this yucky place again." Jen reached for his hand and held it for a moment.

"Yeah, me too," Mitch sighed. "When am I going to get back on track?" He straightened his shoulders and cleared his throat. "Hey, you have to be grateful for the gifts you have, like you two. What's up at home?"

"That's the spirit." Jen sat down.

Ti looked at her. *Mitch is hiding his disappointment for our sake. Hopefully, we can help him focus on better things. Not sure how, but...*

They visited for an hour and went home praying that the special blessings of Easter would grace their family in a big way.

Jen sent Nate to celebrate with his cousins. She and Ti spent Sunday with Mitch. On the way back from an afternoon doggie run, Ti insisted they stop at the trail that ran along the creek. After all that hospital sitting, he needed to stretch his legs. Walking with Jen's hand in his, he paused and pointed to a hawk soaring over their heads.

He looked down at his wife. "Have I told you how grateful I am that you are with me... now... and every day? I couldn't do any of this without you. You are my beautiful salvation."

Jen's eyes filled with tears. "And, you are mine!" She exhaled. "I'm grateful for the knight who rescued me... and Nate too. I was extra lucky, because I got two knights. I wouldn't be anywhere else. You—all three of my men—mean the world to me. Ti, I admire you every day."

Ti's heart swelled. They watched the hawk for another minute, got back in the car, and drove back to Mitch with serene spirits.

◆ ◆ ◆ ◆

When work resumed after Easter, the breakfast club met at 8:00 a.m.

"My sister-in-law cooked a ham, and I made a turkey. We had twenty-eight for dinner," Rick said.

"Holy cow," Ti said.

"We had about seventeen," Betty added.

"My wife sliced the ham and put it on a platter," Rick continued. "The kitchen bustled: dishes clanking, people talking, gravy simmering. So, then, the cat jumped up on the counter and stole two slices of ham right off the plate and ran under the bed!"

"No way!" Cassie said. Betty raised her eyebrows.

"Yup, I crouched down in time to see him licking his paws."

Ti snickered. "Ha. That happened to us once. We were at my cousin's for Thanksgiving. My uncle carved half the turkey. The counter was full, so the other half went back in the oven with the door open."

"Hmm," Betty said. "I know where this is going."

"They had a dog named Frog, half beagle, half spaniel. Frog found the turkey and snagged the leg."

Ti's friends giggled.

"My father found Frog in the kitchen holding the drumstick with the turkey hanging from his mouth. He broke the leg off and put the rest back on the pan as if nothing had happened. Both of us turned down seconds."

"Not like you to decline food," Cassie laughed.

"He actually got it back from the dog? Hard to believe," Betty said.

"Didn't anyone notice a whole turkey leg missing?" Rick asked.

"My father said he'd taken it for soup or something. I just remember him saying, '*Hey, what they don't know won't hurt them.*'"

The breakfast table continued to hum with memories of Easter Sunday.

"My son got a ticket for not completely stopping at a corner stop sign," Betty said with a huff.

"Bummer," Ti said.

"That stinks," Cassie agreed.

Eager for distracting conversation, Ti chimed in again. "When I was about twelve, my father took me and three friends snowmobiling. We went to our favorite spot near his old farm. Since he had no idea if there was enough snow, he called a neighbor pretending to be a radio DJ from California. Excited they might be on the radio, they answered all his questions. My friends admired what they called his '*Mitch-manner.*'" Ti shook his head, still in awe of his father. "He has guts."

“That he has.” Betty nodded.

“My buddies thought he wasn’t afraid to try anything.”

“Okay.” Rick waved his hand. “On with the story.”

“Since there was plenty of snow, our full van headed out. Behind a big rig, we crawled like a convoy of turtles. My father found an opening and took advantage. He passed the truck and two cars.”

“Humph.” Betty snorted, curving one side of her mouth.

“Trying to make up time, he drove a smidgeon over the limit.” Ti showed a smidgeon with his fingertips and grinned. “But the police caught him. The officer pulled us over and asked for his paperwork. He left to record the offence. One of us noticed a duck-crossing sign and started to quack. Everyone joined in. There was a virtual van full of ducks!”

Ti couldn’t keep a straight face. He could hear the quacking now—silly, perhaps, but still funny. “Heh... it was contagious, even to Mitch. Heh, heh. The officer returned, upset my father wasn’t taking the issue seriously. He lectured Mitch on driving responsibly. But all we could think about were ducks!” Ti chuckled and made a mental note to share the story with Nate later, knowing they’d all benefit from a good belly laugh.

His day began on a happy note. Jimmy was due in to help with some of the growing maintenance tasks. A trusted contractor who cared about his father, Jimmy wanted to lend a hand for more than just the job.

“Hey,” Jimmy said when he arrived. “How’s our ol’ Pops today?” He’d always wished he were related to the Conners. Yet Mitch told him many times, “You don’t have to be blood to be family, Jimmy.”

Ti filled him in as they walked out of the office and down the hall.

◆ ◆ ◆ ◆

Days passed as their routine continued: rise early, hospital visit, work, another visit, quick dinner, crash on the couch, repeat... repeat... There was no telling how Mitch might be on any given day.

Thank God my kids want to spend so much time with me, else I’d go crazy here. Mitch gazed around what he now called his ‘*cell block*.’ He and his IV pole cellmate took a daily walk up the hallway. He chatted with the patients. “Well, the menu’s decent. So, where you from? You like dogs? What are you in for?” Three roommates came and went.

Great news! The eagle has landed! The patient is home! Boy, is he happy! The doggies are happy! Everyone is feeling good. Finally, the abscess in his surgical site cleared. We got Mitch home to his chair and best friends, who greeted him with abundant adoration. The sunroom is nice this time of year, overlooking colored blossoms that saturate tree limbs throughout the yard. Although still weaker than he'd prefer, Mitch is more like his old self. He is pleased to be home with his normal roommates (both fur-covered and skinned). Even better, we are eager to go home to the mountains for our belated Conner Easter. Thanks for your prayers, love, and friendship!

Their cabin in the woods beckoned as they rode up to their long-awaited paradise together. The mood was upbeat, despite a heavy rain. At times, raindrops the size of quarters poured from the sky. The wipers slapped the bottom of the windshield with perfect timing.

"I wonder what this will be like at home—a chilly rain or lingering snow showers." Ti leaned forward and looked to the clouds through the top of the windshield. Mountain weather averaged fifteen degrees cooler than the suburbs where they worked and stayed all week.

For the first time in a while, Mitch wasn't sleepy. He was excited to be with his family, heading to the spot that gave him the most joy.

He rambled. "This is a pretty good storm. Ti, do you remember the year it snowed for, like, two weeks? You were about Nate's age. We had this snowstorm." He turned to Nate. "It left twenty-some inches. Everyone shoveled three and four times as the snow kept coming. Ti and his pals had a blast. Remember?" He took a breath. "It lasted two days, off and on."

"Oh boy!" Nate said.

"There was no mail, no deliveries, no traveling, no shopping. If you didn't have it, you did without. The town shut down. After a day of sun, two passes with the plow, and a day of clouds, things started to move. Then the sky dumped another fourteen inches on us."

"Oh brother," Jen moaned.

"It was even too much for us snow lovers," Mitch said. "They couldn't deliver mail or pizza to our street for a week and a half—like we were quarantined. Our road barely got any attention, being the last one in the neighborhood before the woods."

Ti smiled, knowing where this was heading.

“On day nine there was an article about the town pulling together and the dependability of each business.” Mitch sighed. “Heck, those storms consumed the front page for two entire weeks. The writers praised the mail carriers and plow guys. I wasn’t happy.”

“Yeah, ha,” Ti laughed. “Was mom mad at you.”

“Why?” Jen asked.

“Yeah, how come?” Nate added.

“Because my father called the paper. You know how he enjoys his routines, including his mail and his pizza. And he wasn’t getting either. The blabbermouth got us in trouble. The next article included his name along with a ‘complaint’ as interpreted by the reporter, with a much worse spin. The postman and the garbage guys were annoyed. It stuck with us for a while, which is weird because my father makes friends with everyone.”

Mitch snickered. “Believe it or not, they were both new to our street—the mailman had retired and the guys got promoted to a better route.”

“He just couldn’t keep his mouth shut.” Ti chuckled.

Nate snickered.

“I can see that.” Jen giggled.

“That’s our busybody… always needing to be in-the-know and always having something to say about it.” Ti’s mouth arched upward.

Mitch sighed. “Whew, I can’t wait. I’m glad we are almost there.”

As they pulled up to the house, Mitch felt as giddy as a child on a merry-go-round. *Whoo-hoo.* He smiled, squirming in his seat.

CHAPTER 22

As she loved to do, Jen filled three dozen plastic eggs with treats for the Easter egg hunt. With a pink egg to place behind the mantel clock, she stretched on her tiptoes and reached out with her right arm. Suddenly, her feet were no longer under her. She was almost flying, dipping and rising as Ti scooped her up in his arms.

Realizing what was happening, she laughed and smacked at his chest, "You startled me!"

"Hey, I caught you." He grinned. "I had to give you a hug and tell you how adorable you are. You sure do love bunny duty." He looked around the room. Putting her down, he chuckled, "That Easter bunny pooped all over the place."

"They are not rabbit droppings; they are chicken eggs!" Jen giggled.

Mitch watched; he heard his son's chuckle. A wave of joy flooded his chest and bubbled up to the top of his head. *I'm so happy for those two.*

The Conners' mood remained cheerful as they appreciated their home even more than usual. They colored eggs with creativity and camaraderie. "Nate, let's work on one together." Mitch grabbled a wax crayon and drew the first of four stick dogs. Nate drew the second. When they'd drawn two each, Nate dipped it into the blue dye.

"This is the best egg." Nate held it up, admiring their workmanship.

Jen and Nate baked lemon cookies, cut out as ducks and bunnies and covered in powdered sugar.

"Jen, these are amazing. They melt in your mouth." Mitch sighed, with white powder on his chin. Since they were one of her father's favorites, she hid a few to bring back to the suburbs. She hoped to see her family the following week, even for a short while.

"How long does the ham need to heat? Shouldn't we start it?" Mitch asked Ti for the third time. "Jen, don't forget to make your green bean mush. I'm hungry for it."

At dinner, Mitch bowed his head. "God, thank you for our many Easter blessings. And all these goodies. Today was worth waiting for."

"Amen."

Mitch barely thought about being sick. He may not have eaten a quantity fit for the old Mitch, but he gobbled up his ham and green beans with great delight. He devoured two helpings of scalloped potatoes. Even Nate ate well, balancing dinner's nutrition with desert and candy.

Mitch is super! We had a great weekend and finally ate that ham. I'm happy to say, he's back to the old Mitch—a little skinnier, but back. He's lost eighteen pounds since last year. He's stubborn and ornery and picking on me as if it were back before January. He wants to drive all over and eat everything, determined that he's 'had enough of this patient crap.' Perhaps it was all a big act so I'd have to file his taxes for him this year. The nurse found it amusing when he signed them in the hospital last week. He has much to say, offering his two cents (which was more like fifty cents) about our big dinner. There is no satisfying him. Seven weeks after surgery, he's moving around the house, discussing classes with Nate, helping with dinner, doggie-duties, and other things which bring him back to regular life. Yesterday, he took a ride to the office where he saw how Little m was handling things and was impressed! His son has done a great job managing everything at work on his own. Mitch greeted a few of the early birds, all of whom were delighted to see him. After the morning excitement, he rested, of course. We're expecting more days of healing for his body and spirit as he gears up for chemotherapy. Having him feel positive is important, especially after the initial delay. Keep your prayers coming because they are working! Mitch is a little brighter with each new day and gaining strength for what lies ahead.

As long as Mitch was in reasonable health, the chemo would begin on schedule. Jen was anxious. She'd never been this close to someone receiving chemotherapy. Yet she knew that whatever it entailed, she would pour her heart and soul into Mitch's comfort and care. The way he and Ti spoke about work and dog walks, she got the impression it would be okay. Her gang seemed confident, but rumors on the subject sounded sickly and discouraging. She didn't know what to think.

Ti, on the other hand, was optimistic on the outside. He kept fears of anything but a full recovery to himself. It did not matter if Mitch lost weight or strength, as long as he kept everything precious: his wisdom, his character, his spirit. Ti transferred all his efforts into giving back to the man who'd built him. He knew that if it didn't go well, it could get ugly. He had seen the horror of fierce illness. But his father seemed strong and, more important, happy to be on his feet and getting well. Ti focused on Mitch's progress, and that's all he let anyone see.

Nate had no clue. The word sick had many meanings. Mostly, he didn't understand long stretches of Mitch feeling yucky and not wanting to play or talk. But it seemed to be better, so he went about his eight-year-old business of school, riddles, and bike rides. He could share just about anything with his smart and caring grandfather. Nate interacted effortlessly with the man whom he hoped to grow up to be just like.

Mitch had all of these feelings: Jen's uncertainty, Ti's previous experience, and Nate's confusion, along with everyone's joy in things going back to the way they were. The ability to perform normal activity was all he desired—to go to work, come home, dine with his family, visit the mountains, ride in the jeep and the boat, and walk the dogs. Even homemaking appealed to him. That was all he needed and all he'd ever want again. Ordinary, perhaps, but being a part of it meant the world.

Mitch was worried but hopeful; he was scared but strong.

Dear Lord,
Thank you for my wonderful family
  and the gift that was today.
Watch over all under this roof.
  Help me get through this next step.
This is what I pray.

He ended with "I miss you, Mandy. Ask God to help me; I think I can do this with the Holy Spirit to lead the way."

Stars shone against a dark night sky. The warm night was not hot or muggy. Mitch's window was wide open and the humming fans lulled him.

◆ ◆ ◆ ◆

We saw Dr. Leslie, who reviewed the chemotherapy process with us. Mitch's treatment will start in mid-May. After three full sets of weekly cycles, he'll have a CT scan. The hope is that all tumor tissue will be gone and after six cycles, he will be well! The nurses are nice, and Mitch thinks Dr. Leslie is both smart and cute. Handing Mitch a wad of prescriptions, she asked if we had any questions. Mitch asked whether he'd be losing his hair. She admitted that it would get thinner. Ti and I wanted to laugh; that's the least of his worries. But dignity exists in being as much of one's normal self as possible. As caretakers, we say, "take the hair, keep the man!" Mitch will still be Mitch to us. However, we also respect his desire to remain himself throughout this process. We'll be helping him to look his best, first with a new hairstyle. So don't be alarmed the next time you see him. Thanks for your prayers, love, and support.

Mitch loved life. Standing in his blue jeans and navy-blue pinstriped shirt, he gazed into the mirror feeling stronger and more optimistic. "Mandy, I'm so pleased. I feel better—almost well. I know you are walking this journey with me. So, my love, what do you think about my going back to work?" He waited. Her image, surrounded in pale pink, came to him like a gorgeous sunrise. She smiled and blinked twice. Mitch felt her love. *I am ready for whatever lies ahead.*

Later that day, Mitch approached Ti in family room. "I'm considering coming into work, between treatments, as much as I am able."

Ti expected Mitch to feel this way. He knew his father loved to be a part of things, to do, to learn, and to help others. "That's great Dad. Everyone hopes to have you back, even part-time."

Until now, Ti had been running their two-man show on his own. No one said anything about Mitch's share of the work. Ti had always gone in early, now he just stayed past closing so he could keep his father's place covered and available for his return. Although swamped all day, and worn out most evenings, Ti stood tall. Visits with Mitch often included dozing off, but it was what they both wanted—to be together as much as they could during the process, and to return to the way it had been as soon as possible. Ti welcomed the idea of having his father by his side. *It should be good for us... for all of us.*

During his time as maintenance supervisor at St. John's Church, Mitch led his crew of upper-grade kids. For many years that had included Ti and five of his buddies. Mitch taught them handyman lessons like how to paint, how to mix oil in gasoline to fuel a chain saw, how to measure with accuracy, how to know when to use a nail or a screw, and many other soon-to-be-men skills. Ti's dad was just cool—not easy, not a pushover, just a good guy. Mitch worked with kids from sixth through twelfth grade, which for most of them meant six years of Mitch-mentoring.

Ti thought a lot about those years. That evening, he hugged his pretty, curly-haired, bebopping wife. "C'mon we need to go for a walk. I've missed doing that with you."

Awesome! Sneakers on and ready, she went to the recliner and kissed Mitch on the head. "Be back in an hour."

Happy to see them share quality time together, Mitch saluted as Ti nodded in his direction and pulled the door closed.

"I'm so glad my dad wants to work. He loves work, and people," Ti said. "In fact, he made work fun for us growing up. My friends and I started every Saturday at 6:00 a.m." Ti's memories were vivid.

"I wish I'd known you guys back then. You have amazing stories."

"Yeah." He nodded. "By 9:00, we'd meet for a break. We'd walk two blocks to the convenience store. Summers were hot, so we'd each get a big bottle of soda and some snacks."

Jen smiled at her handsome companion.

"This one afternoon, we bought soda and a bunch of our favorite munchies: cookies, donuts, and licorice. Oh, and I'd always bring back a king-size chocolate bar for Mitch."

"Very nutritious," she said.

"Sound staples for young teenagers." Ti flexed his bicep. "We walked back to the church parking lot, gulping, chewing, skipping, and goofing with smacks upside the head." Ti demonstrated blithely.

"Ha, ha!" Jen laughed.

"We put our soda bottles in the commercial ice machine and headed back to various jobs. We'd meet up again at noon, but anyone could go for a drink anytime," Ti said.

Jen listened to his husky voice and walked in the fresh air, feeling content as if they were strolling along a beautiful Caribbean beach.

"One day, Tony had the bright idea to super-glue the cap on Frankie's soda bottle. He snuck back to the ice machine, pulled out the green bottle, and dabbed a bit of glue in the threads of the cap. We all had a bit of prankster in us."

"So I've heard." She nodded with a smirk.

He ignored her teasing. "He thought it'd be funny. Frankie wouldn't know how the cap got so tight. After Frankie gave up, and Tony had a good laugh, Tony planned to fess up and cut the top off."

"Oh brother."

Ti took a deep breath. "Well, the lack of air must have preserved the glue... wet. Frankie opened the bottle. The poor kid took a gulp, placed the cap back and twisted... He closed his lips."

"Oh, no..." Jen covered her face with her hands.

"Yup." Ti winced. "His lips stuck together."

"Oh my gosh!"

"Once Frankie realized his lips were stuck he panicked and mumbled like crazy. He found me outside and we went to my father. Again, Dad had to rescue us from our own shenanigans. He was so great. He reined us in if he had to, but he allowed our pranking. It was a group effort, and our intentions were playful." Ti felt guilty defending their mischief even now.

"Yeah, yeah, you were so sweet and innocent. C'mon, what happened?"

"Dad took Frankie to the emergency room. Something he experienced quite a lot between himself, his adorable, amazing son, eh-hem... and the teenagers he supervised." Ti grinned and walked tall. At least ten memories of the ER ran through his brain.

"Sooooo?" Jen prodded, tugging his sleeve.

"After applying an ointment, of course the staff wanted to know what happened. Frankie said, '*Well, I was fixing an old chair in the cafeteria, and it was hard to hold, and I didn't call for help, so it got on my hands and then I touched my lips, and...'* And that's what Frankie told them. It was awesome."

"I'm not sure lying is so awesome."

"Yeah, but that's not how us boys saw it. My father asked him after we got back, *'Frankie, why'd you make up the chair story?'* Frankie looked him in the eye. *'Because you're always there for us. You've shown us a million times how to be a loyal friend and look out for each other. I'd never want anyone, especially you, to get in trouble for a stupid mistake.'*"

"Hmmm. Well, your pranks are the strangest methods of learning or growing up I've ever heard, but I kinda see your point."

"That was one we all remember well. My father too. It wasn't the first or the last, but we appreciated every one of our adventures. The way I see it, they were lessons for becoming well-rounded people. And as we grew, my dad became more proud of us. We may have done dumb things, but when it came down to it, we learned about being trustworthy, dedicated, and responsible. Actually, I had the best adolescence possible."

For a few minutes, Jen talked about Nate's classes and his art project. Then, Ti and Jen headed up the driveway after a great walk.

◆ ◆ ◆ ◆

Mitch was ready to see all those friends on the other end of Jen's emails. Longing to have a purpose, he went back to work for several hours each day, managing small, yet necessary jobs. The first morning, Jackson stopped in to say hello and they talked about his car problem. Mitch spoke little of himself. He debated sports, bragged about his pups, and supported his friends' accomplishments. He even enjoyed Deirdre's flirting. *It's nice to be out... to feel important and like I belong to a community again.* Being there was good and normal, just as he had hoped.

Mitch glided like a paper airplane as an entire week passed without turbulence and a weekend destination approached. Being in the mountains would refuel his soul.

The Conners spent Saturday in the yard. They'd not seen such a perfect day in a long time. Ti fertilized the lawn. His bronze shoulders glistened in the sun as he paced with the spreader.

Wearing a red bandana to hold back his wavy hair, Nate helped Jen till the soil and plant her flowers. Then, they hunted for large flat slates to finish off the new stone wall.

Mitch sat in his lawn chair noticing the new buds, petting his pals, and offering advice. "I think that dark triangular one should go in the middle."

He got up and shuffled toward them in his worn sneakers. He kicked a few stones at the driveway edge as he paced near the two rock seekers.

"Nate, over here," Mitch called pointing. "There's a beauty." Jen and Nate found several large stones behind the garage.

Soaking in the country atmosphere, their spirits were energized with spring hope. Mitch felt good, which meant the other three did as well.

As evening approached, they spent time on the front porch drinking cold root beers. Nate ran up and down the stairs singing a silly song about nothing. Mitch sat with half-closed eyes, taking it all in: the pine-scented air, the chipmunks' chatter, the deep blue sky, the serenity. Even the dogs lounged contentedly, sprawled across the wooden floorboards. Jen looked over the yard. She imagined her bushes loaded with tiny indigo beads. "Our blueberry pies will taste better than ever this year, I can feel it."

Mitch opened one eye and twisted to glance at her over the rim of his glasses. "I expect big, fluffy, blueberry pancakes with extra syrup." Then he turned back to his relaxed position and pulled his cap down.

As a gorgeous sunset filled with promise shone out in the distance, they went inside to prepare supper. Mitch chose their Saturday movie, pleased to sit in his reclining chair with clear lungs, a satisfied belly, and a smile.

Nate heard him groan and laughed. "Mom, Mitch only made it through twenty-three minutes of the movie this time."

As many of you had seen, Mitch was looking, feeling and acting better every day. Never liking to keep still, he strolled around the yard, folded laundry and chose our menus. He was in what we call happy time. Back at work, he established new routines—all while preparing to start chemo next week. But... I don't know how to say this... Sunday after Mass, he developed pain similar to the last infection. We contacted his oncologist. Her staff responded. She waited for test results. By Tuesday, the pain had worsened, enough to admit him to the hospital... again... His morale is low after yet another setback. He said it was like giving a kid an ice cream cone, but only letting him have a few licks before taking it away. We're trying to stay optimistic. We loved seeing him back at work and play. It's hard to believe he's laid up again. Mitch holds your prayers in his heart.

A streaming ticker tape of questions ran through Ti's mind. *What is going on? Dad was doing great. Geez. How much more messed-up is this going to get? Hasn't he been through enough?*

Jen prayed. *God, Mitch deserves to heal and live out his wise philosophies. I've never seen a more generous, faithful, caring person. He's already been through a lot in his life. Please make him well.*

Mitch sulked. *God, are You still here? Are You on my side? This just stinks. So far, I can't find anything good in this one, Lord.*

Thursday evening, Jen was preparing a quick supper before heading out to visit Mitch. "What time is it?" She glanced up.

"Mom, you keep looking at the empty spot where the clock goes."

"I know, we gotta put that back up," Ti said.

"I'll go get the hammer," Nate said.

Ti got a long nail with a large head and tapped the soffit. "Here we go, better than ever." He continued to talk as they scurried around the kitchen. "One time, we were framing a wall and my father just about knocked himself out. He had to align a two-by-four by tapping the top of the board an inch to the left. He hit the wood hard because it was wedged in. But on the second swing, the board shoved over too far. My father reached his hammer around and hit the board toward himself... and... he missed." Ti snorted. "The handle hit the side of the wood just right, I mean wrong, and broke. The hammerhead flew back and whacked my father."

Jen and Nate shook their heads.

"It flew off the handle and landed square in the middle of his forehead, leaving a perfectly round, quarter-sized bruise."

"I love hearing about your old times, even the crazy ones," Jen said.

"I can't wait to build with you and Mitch. But I hope I don't get smacked with a hammer or stabbed with a screwdriver like you guys!" Nate rolled his eyes and pretended to fall backward as if fainting.

Ti patted Nate on the back and then pivoted to reach for a glass in the cupboard. *It makes no sense. My father's body has endured so much abuse over the years. It can't be sickness from inside that breaks it. This chemo stuff is going to work. We have more stories to build as a foursome.* He blinked his watery eyes before turning back around.

Ti gathered the dogs. Jen packed Nate's things and grabbed a jacket. The phone rang. "Hel—" Jen started.

Mitch bellowed, "Where the heck are you guys? If you're still home, you're two minutes off schedule." She opened her mouth to answer, but before she could, Mitch added, "Guess what? I'm outta here!"

They hurried to the hospital. Nate ran ahead. "Mitch, I'm so excited that you'll be home for my birthday! I'll be nine, you know."

"Yes, of course. I couldn't forget such a special date, even like this." Mitch spread his arms over his white blanket.

"Well, don't worry. Your being home is the best present. I'm not going to have a party this year. It'd be too noisy for you. I'm going to have Scott and Travis over for a ravioli dinner." He smiled at his big buddy and turned around. "Would that be okay, Mom?"

Tears welled up in Jen's eyes. "Yes, Nate, that would be great. I'll call Kay and Allie and see if we can celebrate with a special dinner and some games. What kind of cake would you like?" She held back a sniffle.

Nate thought for a moment. "I think it should be something Mitch likes, what do you think, Mitch? A Corvette cake, maybe?"

"I think a round cake with a huge happy face would be fine," Mitch said, winking toward Jen. *We've got a great kid here.*

"Well, we have time to decide. I'm just glad we'll all be home to enjoy it," she said with a grateful smile.

We have news. We got a surprise call last evening as we were leaving to visit Mitch. He said, "Come and get me!" They're not sure what caused the second infection, but we're sticking to the schedule and chemo will begin Monday. He's looking forward to starting (and finishing) treatments, which he truly believes will put him on the road to full recovery. He's a bit anxious, but his upbeat mood has returned after a two day hiatus. Even Nate knows when the air in the house is happy or sad. Happy is making a bigger comeback every day! Please continue to keep Mitch in your prayers!

CHAPTER 23

Mitch stood at the threshold of the next phase of his cure. *Ah, Mandy, I am ready. Let's do this!* He'd waited long enough to begin this medicine. Any more waiting would have driven him over the edge.

Jen looked into Ti's eyes without saying anything. Of course she was nervous, and he could tell.

"Dad will be okay." Ti sat on a chair and put his thumb under Jen's chin. "My father is a mule. He will outlast anything if his mind is set on it." He spoke softly. "I'll give you an example. One winter morning, Dad brushed the snow from his windshield and drove to work. It was early. He went about his business." Jen leaned into Ti, picturing Mitch's distinctive gait shuffling through the hallways.

"He opened the building, figuring they might call a snow delay. He'd say, '*This area is so wimpy, not like in the mountains*.' Back in his office over coffee, he listened to the radio host complain about '*all those people who were too lazy to clear the snow off their cars*.' Callers complained about snow spraying from the car ahead. '*It's as bad as driving in another snow squall*,' they exaggerated, calling the lazy drivers '*morons*.'"

"Oh, dear." She knew where this was heading.

"You know my father. '*What babies*.' Fed up, he called and argued on air with the host. '*So what if there was snow on my roof? It wasn't heavy or icy*.' After some debate, the guy told my dad, '*Get your head out of the sand*,' and hung up on him."

"Yeah, that sounds like Mitch." Jen gave Ti a hug. Reminded of Mitch's doggedness, she felt better.

Monday arrived—the big day—the day he'd start a new direction on his road to recovery. The nurse directed him to a wide-armed chair. Emotions of relief, fear, concern, and wonder, each like a different color stirred together inside him. He closed his eyes and saw only brown.

Jen waited while the nurse inserted his port, then dropped him off at the treatment room. Mitch phoned Ti a few hours later wearing a big smile. "I'm all set." The process and the week went smoothly.

Last week, I was ill, which left the men in charge. Actually, they did great. Ti stepped up and Mitch felt good helping take care of someone else for a change. Nate caught a bad cold. Keeping germs away from Mitch proves challenging. I spray disinfectant every time anyone touches a doorknob, light switch, or refrigerator handle. The house smells very clean! Mitch started treatments, receiving the first last Monday. He was fatigued by Thursday and worse on Saturday. Yesterday, he started the second treatment and felt great. In fact, I may like steroid days if this pattern holds. He feels well enough to cook and vacuum. His appetite is steady, and he's reading nutritional pamphlets. Funny, when I talk about a proper diet, he calls it nagging. Hey, whatever works! Thanks for your support. It's comforting to know that when things are tough, we have your love to hold us up. And when things are good, we have you to share them with too!

Jen clicked SEND.

Ti tapped her shoulder, swung the desk chair around and pulled her up into his embrace. After a deep hug, he grabbed her wrist, led her outside, and gave her a boost onto the truck seat.

"Uh, Ti, what are you doing?"

"I wanted to give you this and I wanted to do it alone. We get such little time to ourselves." He held out a small thin square.

"What is it?"

"Open it and you'll see."

Jen tore the paper off a new CD. "Oh, Texas Star!"

"Yup, and it's got their new song you love so much."

Jen had fallen in love with their song "Family Ties," about the pride, courage, and strength of families pulling together. It brought her to tears every time she heard it. "Oh Ti," she whispered. "This is so sweet."

"I knew you'd like it, you mushball. It reminds me of our non-date, the night we saw them at the fair... the night that changed my life."

"Mine too," she told her hero.

They popped the CD into the truck's player and listened to the first three songs. Then they returned indoors with a special little bubble of joy in their hearts.

Ti's amazing. No doubt he's strong, but I also know he's soft and caring to the core. He's been hurting too. Jen knew it, but didn't say so since she also knew it was important for him to appear tough. He spoke mostly of cars, tools, and workouts.

Holding a tissue smeared with dark red, Ti dabbed his thumb. Jen's mind returned from her thoughts. She looked from his hand to his eyes.

"Guys have rough hands—calluses, cuts, and dry finger splits." With each new scrape, he reminded Jen that bumps and scars were appropriate.

"You should use lotion."

"Man hands don't take lotions."

She rolled her eyes.

Mitch laughed, seeing himself in his son. "One time, back when we built homes, we were working on a garage for Mr. Leonard."

"Yeah, Leonard always watched us work," Ti said.

"He was retired, with time on his hands and curiosity on his mind."

"Yeah, a bit nuts, but cool too," Ti said. "One day, we went to his house. He was on the front porch, all bundled up in a blanket. A big thermometer rested on the concrete. When Dad asked him what he was doing, he said, '*I'm testing these boots. They're advertised to keep feet warm down to ten degrees.*'"

"Anyway," Mitch butted back in to tell his story. "Leonard hired us again to build a garage. From a window across the yard, he watched us frame it. We started nailing the header for the opening. The wood was slightly warped, twisted." Mitch wrung his hands.

Ti nodded. "Often long sections of wood are bent. The high side goes up. Carpenters call it the crown."

"We mounted the first end, crown up. Ti pulled the other end. I was ready with the nail-gun. You know, we demanded that our wood cooperate." Mitch winked at Nate, reveling in the memory.

Ti explained, “Most of the time, carpenters will hold a finger on the trigger and just tap the wood to make the nail fire.”

“So, what happened?” Nate asked.

“Mitch tapped twice. He shot two nails!” Ti blurted out.

Nate stared.

Jen sucked in a short breath. “So...?”

“In that case, when a nail gun fires twice, the second nail hits the first, which fish-hooks back out the side of the wood. The hook-nail caught my finger, pinning me to the board. Dad knew Leonard was watching and insisted I stay calm. He made me pretend like I was still holding the wood.”

Nate’s jaw hit the floor.

Mitch grinned. “It was important. Our reputation was crucial to our business. We were quality builders. Not everyone needed to know about our little mishaps.”

“Yeah right. No one, mishap or not, wouldn’t hire you guys. Your work is too good,” Jen said.

“Dad insisted we keep up the charade. He had me wait, stuck to the board with a little stream of red running down my arm.”

“Ti stayed put, cursing under his breath for almost five minutes till Leonard turned away.” A few grunts of laughter escaped Mitch’s lips.

◆ ◆ ◆ ◆

“Hey Mitch,” Nate called, “look at my new bathing suit. I picked it out myself.” Nate romped across the room, sporting a navy-blue suit with a colorful patch on his left thigh. It showed a fire-orange horizon, blue-green water, and a diving Orca.

“Very nice,” Mitch said. *Gosh, he’s getting bigger every day. Lord, I’m so happy to be a part of these things. Please let it stay that way.* “You all ready for swim class?”

Nate nodded.

Jen checked supplies—towel, goggles, change of clothes—and they were off. Inside the recreation center, Jen could smell the chlorine. The air was weighty and humid, the odor strong but still pleasing. Nate dove into the water. She looked at her son and felt a swelling in her throat. *I’m lucky. He’s a great kid. And Mitch and Ti adore him. He’s good for them too.*

She smiled as Nate took his turn swimming across the short end. The hour flew by, and he came out bouncing with energy.

Mitch has officially survived his first full treatment cycle. He's been tired and has trouble sleeping. But he's pleased it's moving along. When they checked his levels week three, his platelets were so low he required an emergency transfusion. They ordered the blood and sent us home to wait. Nate headed off to Nana's. At 9:45 p.m., they called us back. The ER staff completed the first half of the transfusion, and then sent us home at 12:45 a.m. If that wasn't enough, at 2:06 a.m., the mountain house alarm triggered, causing a crazy run back and forth by my poor, exhausted husband in the middle of the night. Mitch had to go back in the morning for the second half. He insisted he was well enough to drive but became frighteningly weak and had to pull over. He's decided that driving himself is no longer sensible, at least during chemo. It's a huge blow to his independence. Of course, we don't mind driving him anywhere... but he does. His emotions are strained; his anxiety is up. We hope the second cycle will go a little more smoothly. Nate's good, playing cards with Mitch whenever he'll put up with it. Little m appears strong, but I know he could use some prayers too. I don't know how he's managing the worry and pressure, but I admire him every day. We both appreciate your friendship and love. Thank you from the bottom of our hearts.

◆ ◆ ◆ ◆

Looking forward to getting cycle two under his belt, Mitch prepared for a day of drugs and cure. "I'm ready for round two, Mandy." He stared into the mirror. In a moment, she was there. His beautiful wife always made him feel like a sunflower facing a warm, blue sky.

Meanwhile, Ti opened the building, unlocking the doors on the first floor. His mind flashed back to his old school, where he and his buddies had made up "Mitch's crew." *It's ironic, how I've taken on so many of my father's daily routines.* Back then, Mitch would be in before most people were awake, opening classrooms, placing bus lane cones, and prepping the building for activity. Ti continued his morning tasks.

"Hello," he said, entering the cafeteria for breakfast. "Hey, I remembered one of my father's stories this morning. Wanna hear?"

"Always. Mitch stories are fun." Betty spread out her napkin.

Ti cut his bagel in half. "One day, Dad went to work in a great mood. He skipped down the hall."

Rick raised an eyebrow.

"Yes, I said skipped. Hey, this is how my father tells it." Ti met three scrutinizing expressions. "As he skipped, he hummed, '*la-de-da-de-da...*' He turned the corner to the next hallway, singing louder. '*If only I were rich, la-de-da-de-da...*' He went into the boy's bathroom and came back out, singing as he moved to the next few doors. '*If I were rich, la-de-da, I'd never fix poopy toilets again, la-de-da-de-da...*'"

"Oh!" Betty almost spat out a mouthful of muffin crumbs.

"Then he saw something out of the corner of his eye. Sister Jean Louise had appeared, obviously seeing and hearing his whole act."

"Ha, he must have blushed!" Cassie laughed.

"Well, he stood there in his jeans and striped shirt, in front of the straight-faced school principal, mortified on the inside but calm on the outside. He cleared his throat and said, '*Good morning, Sister.*'"

"That sounds so Mitch-ish," Betty said, picturing the scene. She was sure he'd bowed politely to the nun.

"He must have been mortified," Cassie said.

"That reminds me of another Sister Jean Louise story. One time, his assistant hung a swimsuit calendar page in the school boiler room. He added a speech bubble that read, '*Hiya Mitch.*' Later, Sister and the vice principal came to see Dad about a building expansion plan. You know my father, eager to talk and show off his stuff. He brought them into the boiler room to explain the heat pipes and pumps needed for the construction. He saw the picture and his jaw dropped. He tells me that he casually ripped it down, put it behind his back, and kept speaking. I can just imagine." Ti finished with a chuckle.

Meanwhile, Jen dropped Mitch off for his treatment and went to work. Mitch was to call Ti if he was ready before noon and Jen if he was ready after that. They had it all figured out.

"Hi Ti," Mitch grumbled. "I need a ride."

"No problem, Dad, on my way."

"I couldn't have my treatment. Levels are too low. I can't believe another darned delay... now my whole schedule will be off."

"I'm sorry, Dad." He paused. "Hang in. I'll be right there." *Things never coast for him without a bunch of bumps and potholes in the road.*

Mitch put the phone down. *I like Monday cycles. I don't feel lousy till the weekend. And I want this to finish. I can't wait to be well.* Sulking, he sunk into a waiting-room chair.

Later, when they got home, Ti took Mitch, Jen, Nate, and the dogs for a walk in the fresh air. All twenty-four feet made it up the street and back. The slow-setting sun shone between the houses on the block, and the air was tepid. They looked at colorful rosebushes and evergreen landscapes outlined in decorative brick, commenting on how the shrubs had grown. Nate balanced on the white curb, and Chip yanked his leash, hoping to go further and faster than they'd planned. The walking was good for them, each in different ways, and it was good together too.

◆ ◆ ◆ ◆

By Thursday, Mitch's spirits rose. He received his drugs with steroids and was happy to be back on the track to wellness.

When Ti and Jen got home, Mitch said, "You two need a break. Why not head to the nature trail? The weather's perfect. I promised Nate I'd watch him shoot some hoops. I tossed the chicken in the oven already." Mitch sounded resolute.

"Thanks, that sounds great. I'll whip up some potatoes when we get back." Jen bopped up the stairs for her sneakers. She came down holding a blue bottle with turquoise letters reading *Have a Sip* and handed it to Ti.

"What's this for?"

"I thought you'd like to have an easy way to carry your water. Look, it has a clip." She held it up with a grin. "Plus," she said, reaching for the door, "I adore you, and you should be shown." She turned the knob, and glanced over her shoulder, "often."

Mitch winked at Ti, who followed her outside. As they reached the street, she hugged his thick right bicep. Her adoration warmed him.

Their hands met and laced together.

"It's gorgeous out here." Jen sighed.

Ti and Jen had a nice walk, talking and connecting over nothing special, but it brought them closer anyway.

◆ ◆ ◆ ◆

Jen sat cross-legged on the linoleum floor holding Toby and daydreaming about what they'd renovate after Mitch got well. She looked around. *Probably start here in the kitchen.*

Mitch shuffled in to peek at the roasting chicken. "Hey, Jen. Did I ever tell you about Ti's first cat?"

"Nope." She stroked Toby's sleek fur.

Nate saw them chatting. "Hey, is it time for another M-&-m?"

"When Ti was about four, a coworker told us he had kittens that needed a home. You know us animal lovers—just couldn't help myself."

"I bet this'll be funny." Nate swiped his car across the counter.

Mitch touched Nate's shoulder. "Growing up, Ti had bunnies, gerbils, birds, you name it. But the cat..."

"Here it comes," Nate said with another swipe up the refrigerator.

"We went to bed that night and the little fur-ball stayed with Ti. Apparently, the kitten's kneading on the blanket annoyed him. When he heard us awake, he came down the stairs and dropped the kitten off the final step. He declared at five years old with one hand on his hip and a bottom lip out, '*I do not like kittens!*'" Mitch gestured to imitate young Ti.

"Did the poor thing get hurt?" Jen asked, while Nate giggled.

"Oh, no, he was fine. My neighbor took him. They were happy for years," Mitch said, concerned they didn't miss the point. Although Ti adored Toby now, he'd stayed away from felines ever since.

Days passed, while they made the best of every minute. Jen put silly notes with hearts and smiley faces in lunches, under place settings, or in a clean pants pocket. Although her men made a macho comment about them being 'girly,' the appearance of a random Jen-drawing melted their hearts.

Mitch opened the medicine cabinet. Out fell a white square piece of paper with a crooked heart surrounding '*Thinking of You*' in red marker. *Ah, it's good to feel loved.*

Chapter 24

"C'mon, Jen," Mitch said. "You know you can't alter supper plans. It'd throw me off for the rest of the week."

"I just thought you might like the fresh meat. I couldn't put it in the plan. Who knew Allie was going to have extra steaks from her family cookout? She thought they'd be good for you."

"That's nice of her, but I'm prepared for the plan." He paused. Mitch was never a picky eater, just a picky planner. "Do we have corn?"

Before she could answer, he said, "Hey, are these regular steaks? You know, Lenny and Camille invited us over for supper one time, for Italian pasta and meat sauce."

"I know. When you saw the strange chunks floating in the red gravy on the stove, you got concerned." She'd heard this story twice.

"Who'd have thought she'd add pig's feet?" A sour wince covered his face. "We were not about to eat that!"

"But Camille swore it was normal."

"Yeah, I never let either of them live it down."

"Okay, I'll make the ziti as planned and put the steaks away. How about tomorrow? Can you mentally prepare for a change tomorrow? I'll pick up some corn." She shook her head, though a thrill rushed over her skin seeing Mitch care enough to debate the issue.

"I suppose that would be okay." He tilted his head.

Mitch is doing well on his adjusted regimen. He's confident in his doctor. He even likes steroid days and I agree, since that's when he wants to help with chores. We try to tease about it because we see how disheartening it is for him to feel uninvolved in things he used to do. His recovery is all that matters. We remind him of that often. He continues to work, eager to be productive. Work helps him physically and mentally. He gets a little exercise, some socializing, and affirmation that he's helping others. He's nervous about tiring, but he's giving it his all. Little m has done an amazing job holding the fort down. Thanks to Mitch's own insistence, Jackson named Little m the Maintenance Supervisor. Big M is officially the assistant. Congratulations! The role reversal makes sense and should be good for them both moving forward. I'm proud of my guys. We'll keep in touch as we gear up for Fourth of July, which is great at the lake. We're happy to be experiencing it together. Thanks for your love and prayers. We keep every good wish close to our hearts.

◆ ◆ ◆ ◆

When the weekend of the Fourth rolled around, life had resumed a reasonable pace. Long weekends were anticipated as they'd been before so much medical stuff had blended into their existence.

They looked forward to the exploding bursts of color that reflected so splendidly on the lake. The best seats were along the shore at Lenny and Camille's or on the water. Since Mitch wasn't up for company, they decided to watch via boat. Their friends understood.

Knowing the docks would be crowded, they prepared to set sail before dinner. Jen packed the camping stove, hot dogs, chips, pickles, chocolate chip cookies, and red licorice.

At the last minute, Mitch changed his mind. "I'd rather stay home, but you guys get out there and enjoy."

"But Mitch, you'll miss the fireworks," Nate said.

"Are you sure?" Jen asked.

"Yes. There's nothing wrong. Really. I'm just not in the mood for an adventure. I feel like relaxing, that's all."

After significant cajoling, they gave in. Jen left his hot dogs ready to warm in the microwave. Smothered in mustard, relish, and onions, they were just as he liked, although he liked all hot dogs. Mitch savored every bite, shared a cookie with his pups, and napped until they returned.

His family returned with bright eyes. "Those were the best fireworks I've ever seen!" Nate said. "You have to come on the boat next year!"

"I had a nice quiet evening." Mitch sat in his chair, quite content.

Both Mitch and Ti had been hanging around blue spots on the map most of their lives. They enjoyed outdoor activities on the lake in all seasons.

"You know, when he was twenty-one, Ti got a new eighteen-foot sport boat. It was a fantastic midnight-blue metallic color with white accents."

"It had a good motor—a large six-cylinder inboard/outboard," Ti cut in.

"Learning to handle the boat took time. We practiced, feeling the way she turned as the wheel curved." Mitch motioned as if he was at the helm. "Our dock was on the windy side of the lake, and the wind coerced her to the right the minute she faced the slip."

"So we tried different things to find the right combination of timing and turning," Ti said.

"We did best when we came in quick. So our strategy was to get as close as possible while still ninety degrees off the slip," Mitch said.

"Huh?" Nate asked.

Mitch motioned with his hands to make a T.

"Oh. Hey, we learned that in math—perpendicular, right Mom?"

"Right, Nate."

Mitch continued, "So we stayed *perpendicular* until the last minute, but once we turned toward the slip, we had to gun it to get the nose in straight. Once the nose was in, we'd have to hit reverse so we didn't hit the dock with the front of the boat. Tricky, huh?"

"This was your parking solution?" Jen raised her brow.

"One morning, when the boat was still new, we took Lenny and Camille out for a ride. The sun was shining, and many families were out on the lake. After an hour or so, we were due back for lunch."

"Mitch drove," Ti said. "An elderly lady sat on a milk crate on the far end of the boat dock, crocheting and watching her family water ski."

Jen put her palm to her forehead. *Oh, this is about to get messy.*

"Mitch followed our new process. He approached the dock, gave it gas with a quick jerk, but forgot to switch into reverse. Nervous, he hit more gas and put the nose of the boat—"

"—And then some," Mitch interjected.

Ti corrected, "Put the entire front end of the boat up on the dock, shook the whole pier, and knocked the old woman, knitting needles and all, into the water!"

"Oh my gosh!" Jen gasped, despite her foresight.

"Boy, did we get an earful that day!" Mitch said. "I'm not sure if her son was more upset she went for an unexpected swim, or that he had to stop water skiing in order to help her out."

Nate giggled so hard, he held his middle. "You should've got a video!"

"Nate, my boy, our stories are funny, but there's almost always a lesson." Mitch sat forward.

"Don't crochet on a pier?" Jen chuckled.

"Mistakes are gifts of humility, wrapped in black-and-white newspapers. They're not-so-fancy ways of building character and reminding us that we're all flawed." Mitch pat Nate's back and headed down the hall.

They went to bed smiling, happy to be home, happy to be sharing fun memories, and counting on making many more together.

Mitch laid his head on the pillow. The dogs jumped up.

Dear Lord,
Thank you for my wonderful family, and for this glorious day.
Watch over my family, and let me see those fireworks next year.
This is what I pray.

"I miss you, Mandy." As he drifted into a tranquil slumber, Mitch remembered the fireworks they saw together in the park when Ti was three. Then he dreamed about the explosions Mandy's spirit ignited in his soul every day of their lives.

◆ ◆ ◆ ◆

Mitch had a knack for portraying an appealing attitude and getting through life's trials with determination. He carried on, dealing with the difficulties and discomforts as they came along. He'd seen wonderful times in his life, but he had also seen pain and heartache. Although he missed Mandy, he learned to appreciate each day as presented to him.

One afternoon, Nate came home flustered. "Danny was yelling stupid, mean things to the kids on my team. Everyone got mad."

"Nate, bullying is a sign of cowardice. It's wrong. But the best way to deal with it is to let it go."

"But it's not fair."

"Sometimes things aren't fair, and you're not able to understand why, or change it when it happens. You do your best to deal with it, and if you can't fix it, you try to let it go." Mitch stretched. "Want to hear a story?"

"Yeah!"

"One day, Ti and I were splitting firewood. We rented a heavy-duty log splitter from the shop... you know, the one we pass near the bank."

"Oh, yeah." Nate's eyes widened. "Where all those big diggers are. And the tall gray shed."

"Yup, that's the place," Mitch said. "We'd cut a huge pile of wood that we needed to split and stack."

Nate nodded.

"No matter what I did, I was doomed." Mitch raised his shoulders and turned up his palms. "I kept standing in the wrong place. Everywhere I moved around that machine, I got hit."

"Oh, man." Nate scowled with a tight jaw.

"The wood was dry and hard, probably maple. Anyway, the splitter popped the wood after each slice. It sort of flew off and wedges kept hitting me in the shins. I got whacked at least every other log. My shins were polka-dotted with little bruises."

"Like the machine was spitting it at you." Nate thought the tale was funny, especially the way Mitch told it. "I would have called you Spot." Regardless of how the metaphor related to the playground bullying, Nate relaxed. He perceived Mitch's stories as often amusing, sometimes astonishing, and always awesome.

◆ ◆ ◆ ◆

Mitch dealt with his metaphorical whacks as he continued treatments, accepting all the demands of his illness. The week for his midway checkup arrived. Counting on good news, he carried his emotions like a cast-iron backpack. Imagining every possible outcome, the hoping, wishing, and worrying weighed him down. Yet he dug deeper every day, and every hour, for more. He believed in the depths of his soul that this test would tell him everything—about where he was now, and what would happen at the end of the run, no matter how long or rough.

"Mandy," he said turning on the razor. "This is it. We've hoped and prayed for weeks. I know you are pulling for me." He paused. "You know how much being with you meant to me." He pictured the day he proposed. He had stood in front of her, lost in eyes that shone with the prettiest color blue he'd ever seen. They'd planned to walk along the rippling creek. He almost couldn't wait as he helped her out of the car. Bursting with excitement, he grabbed her and turned her toward him, pulling her into an intense hug. Mandy smiled, a bit confused by his sudden embrace. He mustered up an ounce of willpower to wait and time it just right.

Now he felt that same rush of adrenalin. Staring at her reflection, he saw her as she looked that day, her lips plump and red as her mouth dropped open. She smiled the biggest, brightest smile as only she could, vibrant and beautiful. Mesmerized, he almost dropped his razor.

"Mandy, my love, send me strength and hope. You know how happy I am with my family. I know you will help me through all this."

She blew a kiss to her number one man. Mitch felt a whisper on his cleanly shaven cheek. He was in wonderful spirits for his scan. He greeted the radiology staff with his usual charm. "Nice day, huh?"

Later that afternoon, Nate entered the side door with a skip in his step. "Hey Mitch, guess what? Mean old Danny tried to mess up our game again."

"Oh?" Mitch waited.

"Yeah, they are so lame. Me, Scott, and Travis just moved, but we kept on playing and ignored what they said. We just kept playing our game. Danny stopped yelling at us and went somewhere else."

"I'm glad you didn't let them intimidate you," Mitch said. "Seems their messing around was only fun when it bothered you guys. Good for you!"

Nate grinned from ear to ear. "The wood didn't spit on me today." His grandfather's talk had lessened the impact of the playground monkey business, and Nate's attitude had helped his friends.

Nate's story made Mitch feel important, and replaced his dense, anxious mind with lighter thoughts before the news he awaited.

That evening, Jen carried a load of laundry into the room.

Staring ahead and wringing his hands as if in a trance, Mitch stood up to reach for the basket. "Here, let me fold that."

Jen handed off the basket. *I don't blame him, looking for a distraction. We're all on pins and needles waiting for Dr. Leslie's call.*

Ti and Nate were in the yard. Wiping his brow, Nate followed Ti into the kitchen for a drink. Ti poured two cups of cool, sweet tea. They sipped while they spoke about trimming the big tree in the back. Jen stretched for a casserole dish. With his hands on her hips, Ti lifted her aside, grabbed the dish, and set it down on the counter. He gave her a hug.

"What was that for?" she asked.

"Oh, nothing." He grinned and walked toward the door.

Nate put his cup in the sink. He went over to his mother and squeezed her around the middle as hard as he could.

"What was that for?" she asked.

"Oh, nothing." Nate giggled and ran after Ti.

They're so good for him. Jen smiled as she turned toward the sink. *That's funny—only one cup.* Her eyes scanned the room twice before finding it. "Hey, my tall hunk of a man, can you reach up and get this cup off the refrigerator?"

Ti and Nate were just stepping onto the porch.

"Oh, sorry Shortie."

Nate giggled and repeated, "Shortie."

"It's a good thing short is so cute." He handed her his empty cup.

"Ti, tell her about the time you left that hat somewhere high," Mitch said, failing to contain a snort.

Ti burst out into laughter.

"Aw, c'mon," Nate said. "Tell us the M-&-m story!"

"Nope," Mitch said. "Just m. This one is all Ti's."

"Okay." Ti exhaled as he sat on the couch.

Nate took a seat with Chip on the floor near Ti's feet.

"The old church at St. John's had a big, rounded area at the front—up by the altar." Ti gestured with his hands. "Along both sides was a lowered ceiling with classy light fixtures. The high center and front section had recessed lights. The front lights pointed to the new statue of the Risen Christ, which had replaced the old crucifix."

"Our chapel at school has a Risen Jesus. I like it," Jen said.

"We always waited for a few bulbs to burn out before replacing any because it was a big deal to set up the scaffold."

"C'mon, Ti, get to the good part." Mitch fidgeted. "Just before Thanksgiving, as the flowers arrived, the pastor asked us to replace five or six lights behind the altar."

"Hey, who's telling this?" Ti glanced at Mitch. "So Tony, Luke and me assembled the scaffold. Tony brought the long-handled broom to dust the wall and ceiling. Luke was wearing a baseball cap, and it gets hot up under the lights. From the ground, the rounded ceiling seems spacious. But on the scaffold, it's a bit closed in." Ti ducked for effect, and Nate squirmed.

"Luke took his cap off and put it on the scaffold landing. I moved it to one side as I replaced the first bulb. Then, I moved it again as I did the second. I got tired of moving it around, so I put it on the statue."

"No way. On the statue? Of Jesus? Isn't that irreverent?" Jen grimaced, exposing clenched teeth.

"No... well," Ti said.

"Did Jesus look cool?" Nate giggled.

"Yes... We finished replacing the lights, dusted for cobwebs, disassembled the scaffolding, put it in storage, and went home."

"Oh no." Nate leaned back.

"Yup, guess what the pastor saw Thursday morning as he came in for the Thanksgiving Mass?" Mitch laughed.

"Along with splendid floral arrangements around the altar, he saw a baseball cap resting on Jesus. He was not amused. He called us right away. Without time for scaffolding, we used a ladder and a long pole to relieve Jesus of his excess wardrobe," Ti said.

Jen stood to go back into the kitchen, giggling and shaking her head.

"Hey, you never know. Didn't Luke's team win the championship that year?" Mitch said.

The ringing of the phone brought them back to the present moment. Their laughter subsided and silence cloaked the room. Jen and Ti stopped and held their breath. Nate swallowed.

Mitch picked it up with a shaky hand. "Hello?"

CHAPTER 25

We have wonderful news! Mitch went for his mid-treatment CT scan to verify that the chemo is working. He spent the day on the edge of his chair. Finally, around 7:00 p.m., the doctor called to say the scan was very good! There's no new growth, and less fluid buildup. Even the uncertain area she's been watching is smaller. God is hearing our prayers, and we are ecstatic he's getting well! We dream about life getting back to the way it should be. Therefore, Mitch is doing great. He likes to be at work in his comfortable routine. He has some issues with clear vision and remembering details, even though he will tell you he is absolutely right on everything. (In case you were wondering, chemo does not diminish stubborn streaks.) But seriously, this news confirms it's all been worth the struggle. We might just get our old Mitch back very soon, as this one grows stronger and healthier. What perfect birthday wishes come true for Ti and me! Thanks for your love and support, and all you do for us. You are an important part of his journey, and his recovery.

The report renewed their faith that Mitch would overcome his illness and assured them that all four would get back to doing the things they loved to do, starting with a construction project. They'd play more too: fishing, boating, riding in the jeep, and maybe fixing the old ATV. They'd hike near the lake shore, where they'd find old sections of broken dock. The two child-like family members pinned notes to the foam chunks and sailed them out on the lake.

"Who needs a bottle?" Mitch would say. Of course, with Mitch's input, the clever notes often rhymed. For Nate, hikes focused on searching for dock foam just to see what Mitch would write on the paper.

They planned to install another chimney and wood-burning stove at the mountain house. The bathroom could use updating, along with the cottage kitchen, and they'd finally finish the basement. The projects would require two skilled builders and two apprentices. Yes, they had plans for all four to work and play hard again.

As if Mitch and Ti shared the same essence, their thoughts, behaviors, and tastes intertwined. Ti didn't admit it aloud, but wore it like a medal of honor. Working with his father gave him security, contentment, and pride. The things they had done and the creations they would leave behind were impressive. The happenings—every bump and bruise—led to teasing, and more important, close bonds and unique memories.

As they spoke about the renovations, Ti laughed. "Mitch is famous for doing electric repairs with the breakers on."

"Hey, that's intentional... to test my skill." Mitch flicked the nearest light switch off and on, with a little spark in his eyes too.

"He's gotten zapped so much, it's a wonder he doesn't light up." Ti chuckled, ignoring Mitch's excuses. "Every time he does circuit work for Lenny and Camille, she leaves the house. Her nerves can't handle it."

Over the years, Mitch had achieved many things, but completing an electrical project without a shock still eluded him. *Soon... we'll do more work... and soon I'll remember to turn the darn breaker off... and soon I'll get through a wire job start to finish without a single spark.*

He chuckled aloud. "It'll be done; I can feel it."

◆ ◆ ◆ ◆

Away for the weekend, they celebrated Mitch's improving health and held a combined tribute for the two humans and two canines who all had summer birthdays. Jen made a cake at Ti's request—chocolate with chocolate chips. They gobbled up the whole thing before the day was done.

Mitch relaxed as they took the boat out. Jen read. Ti tried to fish. Nate splashed around on the raft, still not certain he wanted to swim in a lake where he couldn't see his feet. The water disturbance gave Ti a good excuse to find few bites on the end of his line.

After a few hours, Mitch's usual post-treatment fatigue kicked in. They headed back home where he rested on the couch. Nate played with his camo-colored truck set, using a sleepy Chase as his mountain range: two trucks on one side, two on the other, and a low-flying helicopter over the patient dog's head.

That afternoon, Ti and Jen hiked their favorite trail. "Jen, do you remember the day we hiked in the rain?"

"Yeah. It's one of my favorites. We saw the bald eagle. Oh, and the mommy and baby raccoon!" she squealed.

"Yup, don't forget the bear prints near the lake edge."

"And tons of salamanders. There's so much to see on these trails."

"And it's better exercise than the gym!" Ti raised his arms as if pushing up a heavy dumbbell.

"Who wouldn't love it, even in a misty rain?" Jen concluded with a grin.

To his left, Ti noticed branches swaying. Moving judiciously, he tapped her arm. They froze... watching, listening. After a moment, they both pointed, each to ensure the other didn't miss the white tails bouncing through the trees—two full-grown deer, and one spotted baby.

"You don't have to travel far to see beautiful sights," Jen said.

They walked, laughing about that crazy hike where they sopped along like two soaked sponges. That day, they'd had the whole forest to themselves. But this time the trail was busy. They met a lone man and two families, one with two kids, one with three kids and a dog.

Ti diverted away from the path and led her to the lakeshore. He lunged, stepping onto a big rock. Jen climbed up after him. She turned her face up toward the deep blue sky, and reached for his hand.

Ti held it for a few moments. "I'm glad we found this ring. I'm glad we didn't sell it to pay for my mom's funeral. And I'm glad I see it on your finger every day."

She heard his voice strain.

"I finally understand just how my father felt about my mother. Do you have any idea how you've affected my life?" He corrected, "Our lives?"

"I'm pretty sure I do," she said in a soft voice. "You and Mitch have done the same for me and Nate. We are blessed, and it's good to take a few moments to soak that in now and then." She arched her head back.

"Yup, it's been a bit chaotic lately." He sighed. They sat on the rock for about ten minutes with the sun shining on their faces.

Still savoring our good news, Big M enjoyed a short outing on the boat. Spending time with his family where nothing but the sun can touch him boosted his morale even more. We also did some used-car shopping. Mitch's old faithful has had enough after a hundred ninety-two thousand miles. Problems arose one after the other, and the final straw hit. What do you think of the criteria for his replacement?

-needs to travel in snow

-needs to carry dogs

-must have four wheels, an air conditioner, and a radio

-does not need cup holders, since he's used to throwing everything (and we mean everything) on the floor

-does not need doors that lock—he hasn't locked his car in years

-needs to be reliable and last him more than five years because he's confident its services will be required at least that long

Good to see a positive attitude for his future, no? You would think our task would be easy. We're looking for an affordable and appropriate vehicle. So far, those two adjectives are mutually exclusive. It's one more thing to manage, but someone said that's supposed to make life interesting. I'm rooting for boring next month!

"I can't wait to find a car for my father," Ti said. "He needs it. That, and neither of us was ever good at waiting."

"Yeah, patience is not a virtue either of you possess," Jen said.

Mitch taught Ti about instant gratification his entire life. You wanted something done, you did it; you needed something, you got it. They may have had slanted views, but they owned them. Sometimes they were right to be annoyed by a delay, sometimes not, and sometimes that was unclear.

"Hey, did my father tell you about the time he got in trouble at Mass?"

"What? Mitch, in trouble? At Mass?"

"Yup," Ti said. "Dad would go to Mass every Sunday in tan slacks and his dress sneakers—just like now. He's such a creature of habit."

"Lucky it's so adorable on him." Jen grinned, picturing Mitch.

"He liked the early Mass with most of the older parishioners. He'd get done and have the rest of the day to himself. Most of the priests understood these folks had places to go and things to do. He'd say, '*They abide by an unspoken pact to move things along.*' But sometimes the sermon still got a bit long-winded."

"And he did not appreciate that." She understood Mitch's attitude.

"You got it. He preferred speakers who got down to business and made their point. He timed every sermon, adding a dollar to his donation any time they preached well and for less than five or six minutes. Pastor Paul was not a concise homilist, and his favorite topic was the Holy Trinity. Dad had heard that homily dozens of times and could recite it himself."

"Really?"

"Once he started to prove it, and after two minutes, I gave in to his spot-on impersonation of the pastor."

"Ha, ha, okay." Jen rotated her hand for him to continue.

"So, on Trinity Sunday, Pastor made a mistake. He began by saying he didn't want to talk long, telling the congregation that if he spoke over ten minutes, someone should let him know. Mitch took him at his word."

"Oh no!" She covered her open mouth with her right hand.

Ti nodded. "Pastor Paul brought out his red, white, and blue two-foot-wide wooden triangle, like he did every year. He explained yet again how one or two pieces of wood did not a triangle make. The triangle needed all three, no matter how you held them. Not sure he'd gotten his point across, the pastor began the analogy again using different words that meant the same thing. Mitch's watch beeped. He stood up and announced that eleven minutes had passed—he'd added one for wiggle room."

Jen let out a puff of air.

"The old folks turned to stare at the obviously disrespectful fellow. But Dad didn't see any problem; after all, Pastor Paul did make the request."

"That's him. A clock watcher and a literal person."

Mitch was not a patient fellow, not then, not most of the time, and certainly not now. He appreciated speedy resolutions. '*Do it*' was the best slogan he'd ever heard. However, his cure process dragged on like filling a five-gallon jug off a maple tree tap.

"Yeah, so we really need to figure out this car thing. He's upset he drives such an old, run-down car."

"Do you think he's afraid it's a reflection on himself? On his health?"

"Maybe."

"A car will help him get around, but I think it could also help his mental edge. So what if it adds to the rising expenses? It might make a difference. And we need all the help we can get to guarantee he beats this."

Thursday afternoon, Nate and Mitch toyed with a riddle. Jen listened as she sewed a button on Mitch's shirt. She could see half of her husband's red T-shirt and one denim leg stepping forward and back in the yard as he threw the ball. Even with his busy schedule, Ti was sure to make dog time.

◆ ◆ ◆ ◆

Summertime was calm and cozy. The air was warm. The bright yellow sun permeated their worries. Jen and Nate walked Mitch up and down the block often, sometimes a house's distance, sometimes all the way to the end. They felt good about sticking to it either way. Jen would yield to a candy-bar reward, as long as it was not too close to dinnertime.

One evening after a walk, Mitch sat in the sunroom watching two brown bunnies in the yard. He knew that as soon as Daisy saw them, there would be much commotion, so he turned his attention to his son and grandson at the gate. Ti, wanting to teach Nate the way his father had taught him, was explaining parts of the lawn mower and passing on his tricks-of-the-trade.

Nate paid attention, excited to do a good job on the section of grass Ti was entrusting to him. "This'll be cool!"

Keeping one eye on Nate, Ti began fixing the storm door. The abused door stood up well to the eight pushy front paws. But the latch finally gave after one too many pounces during a competition for the highest, most forward spot at the door.

Looks like we'll need a new screen soon. The top portion was screen or storm window, depending on the season. While they used the screen in the summer, the storm glass recessed down into the bottom half. Ti took note of the door innards. He'd seen fiascos with glass, and every time he or his father worked with it, one memory in particular surfaced. He couldn't wait to go in and relive the tale with his dad, wife, and stepson.

Jen and Mitch watched their boys outside. The windows were open and the air smelled fresh and clean.

When Nate completed his grass cutting, everyone gathered inside.

Ti sat on the end of the couch, popping the top of a soda. "Dad, do you remember the time we ordered replacement windows for the west wing of St. John's Grammar School? Remember Luke's loud moped?"

"Uh oh," Nate said. "Sounds like another M-&-m disaster."

"Yeah," replied Mitch. "Your stepfather and his buddies were always causing some kind of mischief."

"Something tells me we should not be telling Nate all these things." Jen put a hand on her hip.

Disregarding Nate's impressionability, Ti continued. "We were seniors—about seventeen or eighteen. Some of the guys who went to the local college still worked for my father, so I'm not sure. Luke was old enough to be driving his moped. Anyway, Dad got a shipment of replacement windows. The windows came in shrink-wrap, outlined in cardboard. The delivery guys put them by the rear wall of our workshop. Oh, wait, I forgot to mention. The parish had built a barn-like garage behind the school. My dad made the front into a maintenance workshop. We had a table and chairs, a microwave and a refrigerator—no more throwing our soda bottles in the icemaker. Tractors, plows, and machinery filled the middle section. There was a long workbench with all kinds of nails and supplies running the length of the left wall. We'd start about 6:00 a.m. on Saturday with coffee and a bagel." Ti took a gulp of soda.

He swallowed. "Ahh. We all left our bikes outside—motorized or pedaled—except Luke. He always pulled his moped into the building. One day, Frankie sprayed oil on the cement at the entrance, figuring Luke would slip, and we'd all get a good laugh at his expense."

"Oh no," Jen said.

"He didn't spray much. The oil was thin, but slick. Luke steered into the shop. The moped went out from under him. Sideways. The bike left its rider behind and somehow kept sliding all the way to the back wall. It slid thirty feet and, of course, right where the new windows were. It was like an alien bowling game."

Nate's eyes widened. Jen's shoulders went up as she cringed. Mitch winced, as he did every time he heard the tale.

"Strike! Not one window survived. The sound of breaking glass echoed through the whole garage." Ti recalled the noise of shattering glass.

"Yeah." Mitch shook his head. "The pastor was not pleased to have the window replacement delayed."

"Dad, I'm not sure how you managed to console the school officials. I only remember giving up a month's pay and spending two hours sweeping up every crumb of glass. I can still see that darned bike sliding across the silver-painted floor." Ti put his hand to his brow. "Oh, it just kept going... like it was pulled by a magnetic force into those windows."

"Maybe aliens," Nate said.

"Maybe!" Mitch chuckled in agreement.

Ti and Nate had a good laugh, recalling yet another M-&-m escapade.

Jen too let out a giggly chirp. "Oh. You guys were such delinquents."

"Don't forget, there are hidden gifts in everything we experience," Mitch said.

"Another secret meaning, like what?" Nate asked.

"Excessive pride. I think this one shows what can happen when we dare to judge someone. Attempting to teach Luke a lesson backfired."

Chapter 26

Whew! I don't get the expression "lazy days of summer." We seem to be in a state of weird flux. Ti had some kind of stomach bug. Nate's recovering from a nasty fall. He skinned his knee skidding out of a wild squirrel's path. Mitch saw the doctor. Once again, his levels were low, and poor Mitch needed blood and platelets. Even though he expected it, he was disappointed. At least it gave him a little more spunk. Gee, he gets chemo to kill cells so the cancer can't thrive, then he gets a transfusion of healthy cells because he loses too many good ones. What a strange and murky method. But as long as it's working, we are pleased... no... we are relieved, joyous, and ecstatic! This time, even though he got the new blood, his levels remained borderline. They had to reschedule his treatment twice. That really bothered him. We're proud of his being such a good sport about everything. You forget when you have it, yet it's soooo true: good health is one of the most precious gifts you can receive. As Ti and I approach our first anniversary, we know how fortunate we are. We're getting away for a few extra days to enjoy a dreamy vacation at our cabin in the woods, where we can keep a close eye on Mitch. We feel joy in having each other to share both the good and the not-so-good times.

Ti, Jen, and Mitch geared up for a mini mountain retreat. Nate was spending a few extra days with his father.

As the morning news announced a story about a Las Vegas casino, Mitch started to shave. Mandy appeared at the top of his mirror, wearing a pale-pink blouse. A gold cross rested in the nape of her neck. "Good morning, my love. You look beautiful this morning," he said.

"Mandy, do you remember when we used to go to the casinos?" He expected her to answer with an expression that showed she remembered everything about him. He shook his head. “I always seemed to have weird encounters in the bathroom. Remember?”

Blush filled her cheeks; her lips curved up. The amusement in her eyes warmed his heart. He continued shaving the right side of his face. “How about the time a man was selling watches out of a trench coat, in the men’s room? The attendant just stood there.” Mitch stroked his neck. “Ha! Remember the time I had to use the bathroom next to that huge burly guy? He was twice Ti’s size. My watch went off. You’d set it to play “Tender Love” on the hour! Hey, I know, we were young and in love, but can you imagine what he must have thought?” Mitch laughed aloud. “It seemed to last minutes, not seconds! I was so embarrassed.” Thinking about their casino days made him happy.

◆ ◆ ◆ ◆

Jen loaded the car with the usual items. *I’m looking forward to some outdoor adventures on both land and sea: a few hikes, bike rides, and some boating. We’ll need the camera for sure... water bottles and sunglasses.* “Mitch, make sure you grab those refilled prescriptions.”

Jen kept the multitude of little copper-colored jars in a black tin decorated with gold swirls. As he climbed into the car, Mitch handed the pharmacy bag to her. “Thank goodness you fill my dispenser. I’d never figure out all these instructions, what to take with food, without food...”

They drove up to the mountains of Walleycito, eagerly anticipating their special time to recharge.

The weekend weather graced them with two warm sunny days. Saturday, after an early hike and a peaceful ride in the canoe, Ti and Jen went home for lunch.

“Ti, I’ve got big plans for Mitch. No sitting in his recliner today.” Jen packed his favorite potato chips, some bologna sandwiches, sodas, and the rest of the mocha brownies. Finding a flat spot in the yard, she spread out a large yellow-checkered quilt. She brought out napkins and paper plates, arranging the setting. When it was just right, she dragged Mitch outside.

“What are you doing? This isn’t our lunch routine,” he moaned. *Then again, this is kind of exciting.*

He approached the blanket and noticed two garden buckets holding all of the things she'd prepared. He pointed to them. "What are those buckets? And what is this? You can't have a picnic with a yellow-checkered cloth. Who taught you about picnics?"

He laughed.

"She might be quirky, but she's cute." With a twinkle in his eyes, Ti pushed back a long curl and kissed her forehead.

Jen handed a grateful Mitch his sandwich and rested her hand on her knee. The sun caught the angle just right and her ring flashed with color. Mitch looked to the sky, feeling warm and safe. *Thanks Mandy, for being here with us on Jen's silly yellow-checkered picnic blanket.*

Jen didn't keep Mitch out too long, just enough to eat and watch Ti throw the ball for Chip. She escorted him back up the stairs and began to put things away in the kitchen.

Mitch appreciated the distraction. *That felt pretty good. It's nice to forget your worries for a bit.* Despite how much her atypical, girly picnic meant to him, Mitch teased Jen for days. "Buckets," he muttered so she could hear him.

She rolled her eyes.

Sunday morning Jen pulled out their wedding photos. "I can't believe it's been a year already."

"Hey look, the Monopoly man," Ti said with a grin.

"Humph," Mitch replied, but he secretly enjoyed the remark.

The couple huddled together in joyful reminiscence of their best day ever. Jen choked up seeing the four of them hang their special pieces of wood on the wind chime Ti had created.

For a day, they focused on the joy they found in the simple events in their lives. During a long bike ride along the path with the rushing waterfalls, they paused and gave thanks. They took advantage of every celebratory minute.

◆ ◆ ◆ ◆

Back to school time was busy for Jen as she prepared for everyone's return. Teachers would need equipment. Students would need training. Labs would need connecting. After updates, systems would need certifying.

Nate geared up with new notebooks and freshly sharpened pencils. Now in fourth grade, he would participate in the science fair, read more books, and tackle more analytics in math class. He decided not to continue on the basketball team. "I want to spend more time with Mitch. I can come home to help him. I love being old enough to walk home now, especially with Mitch and the dogs waiting for me. It's so cool."

"Cool, huh? You're getting too big, too fast." Jen rubbed his head.

"Mom. Hey." Nate ducked out of her reach.

On the first day of school, Nate ran home eager to see Mitch and proud to have managed his own transportation.

"I'm home," he called out of breath.

"Hi, Nate." Mitch smiled as Nate threw open the door and dropped his knapsack. "What, were you running a race?"

"Sort of." Nate shrugged.

"Want to hear a story?"

"Yeah. Hey guys, chill." Nate sat on the floor while Chip licked his face. Champ and Chase pranced, and Daisy brought him a bone.

"One time, our pickup broke down. A tow truck had to get me, Ti, and one of our workers. The guy arrived pretty quick and told us to get in the wrecker while he attached our truck. We had four men squished in the cab. He pulled onto the road with a screech and, the minute he got on the highway, began going, like, ninety miles an hour."

"Oh boy." Nate sat forward.

"Ti and I looked at each other. We weren't sure we'd make it home in one piece that day. Fortunately, we survived."

"Why was he driving so fast?" Nate asked, just as Mitch had hoped.

"Well, after we got to the garage, we heard the man talking to his partner. The other guy handed our driver a hundred bucks and a case of beer for winning a bet." Mitch shook his head.

"Huh?" Nate looked back from the playful Chip to Mitch.

"We found out that when our long-distance call came in, the men made a bet about how long it would take to get us and return. The driver had made the trip in record time."

"Oh! That was dumb; they should have had a race on a back road, instead of scaring you guys."

Mitch then told Nate about one of his favorite movies, *Bandit and Smokey's Race*, and the two made plans to watch it together.

Two afternoons later, Nate came home with a scraped elbow. "Danny pushed a kid into three other boys, and we all fell on the pavement. Danny got in big trouble." He rubbed his scrape that the nurse had cleaned.

"Let's get a Band-Aid," Mitch said, more to have his grandson feel cared for than because the wound required it. He stuck the brown rectangle on Nate's elbow. "Unfortunately, bumps and scrapes are part of life."

They walked back to the family room. "Yeah, one time Ti fell splat on his face. He was around your age. St. John's, where I worked and Ti went to school, was doing some construction. One of the things on the list was to fix up the large community room. It had a real high ceiling. On the wall around the old fireplace, they were adding stone that would reach up twenty feet to the top. The masons set up scaffolding and rigged it with a pulley to hoist up supplies."

"Cool," Nate said, remembering his first scaffold climb last year.

"Our ingenious little Ti went over to the pulley and stood with one foot in the rope loop for the bucket. Then he reached for the opposite rope, and worked hand over hand to move the pulley system." Mitch moved his hands one on top of the other. "His idea worked for a bit; he got up almost six feet. Then the ropes started pushing apart, and he had no way to keep the one on his foot and the one in his hands close together. The distance increased past his ability to stretch. He lost hold of the rope and fell... flat on his belly."

"Oh man. Ouch!" Nate held his tummy.

"He was okay and just shook it off. He still thinks he had a brilliant idea and with a minor adjustment or two, he would have made it."

Nate agreed with a nod. Intrigued by scaffolding, he understood the appeal to attempt such a stunt.

"Remember, Nate," his grandfather said, "Mistakes train us; they're gifts of humility, wrapped in..."

"Black-and-white newspapers," Nate finished.

"Right... but I still tease him about it."

"Mitch, how come it's okay to tease, but not to make fun?"

"Well, it has to do with intention. Teasing can be a fun way of showing attention and that you care. And I think learning to laugh at yourself is good. But it's important not to cross the line. That's when you aim to make someone feel bad, not good."

"So, you mean, when you tease my mom, or when Ti teases you, it's for fun, but when Danny is mean, it's because he wants us to feel bad."

"Right!"

Chapter 27

Mitch sat with closed eyes as they administered his last chemo treatment. *Mandy, I made it!* The smile he cherished appeared behind his eyelids. He felt warm and safe, confident his health would return. Exiting the familiar building, he ducked from the rain. *Ha! The sky could be spitting nails, and it wouldn't bother me today.* Ti pulled the car around. Mitch got in and clicked the seatbelt. "Done," he said.

Ti nodded. "You did it, Dad."

The next day, Jen took Mitch to the hospital for his post-treatment test. He prayed every prayer he knew by heart and added some off-the-cuff pleading for the right results. His faith was strong. He clung to God's will, expecting it would include a successful outcome.

Filled with optimism, they waited for the appointment with Dr. Leslie. When the time came, three Conners filed into a small exam room feeling anxious and eager, scared and hopeful. They listened and questioned. Like a rubber ball stuck with a tack, their once bouncing hopes deflated—the air that had filled their wishes seeping, hissing out of them with each breath. Mitch and his two crushed kids left Dr. Leslie's office with somber expressions. Although his chemo regimen was complete, his scans were not clear and she could not pronounce a sound bill of health.

Unbelievable. Now what?

Mitch felt numb. His mind raced. He questioned his life, existence, and purpose. He paced, sat, then paced again.

Two days later, Mitch saw his surgeon to ask about further surgery. The doctors deliberated. The oncologists considered alternate plans.

Confusion dominated their minds, and the Conners became scared.

Really scared.

Still, as human nature dictated, Mitch, Ti, and Jen clung to an opportunity for success, or at minimum, to keep things just the way they were. Hectic schedules and continued treatments were preferred to any alternative that might mean losing the indispensable leader of their family.

Amid conflicting emotions, Mitch continued to function. He prayed, forging through a raging sea of dread and dreams. He tried to look forward to the future, and to changes he thought might help him heal.

"Ti, we should build again. Jen what would you think about working in the mountains and Nate going to school there?"

"That'd be great, Mitch. Do you think we could make it happen?"

For years, Mitch yearned to build with his son again. Dreaming about it encouraged his outlook. *This time we have Jen to assist and Nate to learn.*

The bills that accumulated from Mandy's illness and the log home burning down forced them to forfeit their construction business. They got steady jobs to get back on their feet. *All seemed lost then, just like now. It took a big change to overcome that mess, so maybe this time too... Somehow, someway, the right stuff fell into place. Not quickly or easily, but it must have been in God's plan.* Mitch remembered those days of struggle and despair, as well as how they ended in triumph.

Focused on new opportunities, Mitch was ready to conquer his disease. *I'm still young. I have goals. My family needs me... I want to live this life.* He leaned forward to survey the room. Jen sat at the desk filing paperwork. Ti lay on the floor with his feet raised along the arm of the couch. Chase and Chip lounged next to him.

Nate walked in wearing his football pajamas. "Good night, Mom. Night, Ti." He reached to give Mitch a big hug.

Mitch welcomed the embrace, which lingered. When Nate stepped back, he looked at the boy, noticing his hands and feet—still small, yet growing every day. Mitch cherished thoughts of Nate's next few years. *After forty years of adventures with Ti, I'm looking forward to mentoring Nate and creating a sequel to my M-&-m storybook with a volume of M-&-**n**'s.* As he looked around the room, with its simple couch and under-dressed windows, he felt blessed to be with his little family. *Paradise.*

It was pure grace, disguised as normalcy.

Mitch couldn't have been more pleased if he'd been a millionaire in a mansion. Everything he loved and lived for was right next to him.

Hello! First, the important stuff: Mitch completed his six months of chemotherapy. He had a scan, just as they'd done at the halfway point. Regrettably, the scan is not clear; it shows two small, dark patches, which the doctor believes are cancerous bubbles of fluid. We've been seeing and speaking to everyone, including the oncologist and original surgeon. The surgeon said he was surprised Mitch is doing as well as he is. That remark devastated Mitch and gave us a more grim understanding of his condition. We knew some cancer remained after surgery, but we'd believed the chemo would cure it. Tomorrow, Mitch undergoes a procedure to drain the pockets. The pathology report is critical to see how far from a cure he might be and to determine the next course of action. If the results are clear, that's great! If not, his oncologist will offer alternative treatments. I cannot find the words to describe our feelings. Mitch recalls memories and talks about the future, looking both back and forward with eagerness. We really, really want him to be well as soon as possible. Thank you for your love and prayers. We feel them every day.

◆ ◆ ◆ ◆

One chilly afternoon, Nate brought home the rubrics for his first science fair experiment. The Conners welcomed the pleasant and somewhat amusing distraction. Nate read the outline. The four of them spent the evening discussing ideas over dinner.

"Let's do something with wood," carpenter Ti suggested. "How about we see which type of wood burns the hottest?"

"Or the fastest." Nate added.

"We'll look around tomorrow when we get to the cabin." Mitch stood with his empty plate. "I'll bet we can find at least six different kinds of wood on the property."

Following a pleasant Friday drive, Ti and Nate gathered branches. Ti showed Nate how to strip away the bark, measure, and cut each one. "They have to be the same size, or your results won't be accurate."

A week later, they began the experiment. Mitch lay on the couch with a stopwatch. Ti handled the torch in the fireplace. Nate called out the temperature from a creatively rigged thermometer every ten seconds as

Mitch sounded a "beep." Or almost every ten seconds—Nate caught him dozing twice. Jen scribbled the stats. The glow from the burning sticks warmed the family, gluing them together and solidifying their bonds as they relished working, learning, and laughing together.

Nate organized the data and created charts to depict his findings and report conclusions. Designing a poster with six sections, he displayed the details for each wood in a different color. One of the most original experiments submitted to the fair that year, it won second place.

◆ ◆ ◆ ◆

Back at work, Ti pulled the hood of his sweatshirt over his head and walked back and forth with the blower. A windy, rainy night had left a chill in the air. Brown, orange, and yellow leaves flew from the sidewalks and doorways. No matter what season, he ensured the place looked perfect.

By the time the breakfast club arrived, he was ready for a hot cup of coffee. Betty came in with muffins and fruit from a family brunch. "Tomorrow, I'll bring French toast sticks and banana bread."

"Great! Betty, you're an excellent baker." Rick reached for a muffin.

"Yeah, before we know it, she'll be baking up a storm of nut-roll cookies and apricot-filled pastries for the holidays." Cassie scooped a spoonful of cut fruit.

As Ti bit into a blueberry muffin, Deirdre walked in.

"Ti, be a dear and give this to your father." She held out an envelope. "It's a thinking-of-you card. I wasn't sure if get-well would be appropriate at this stage. I want him to know I think about him all the time." She flashed a smile and walked out. Ti blinked.

"Ignore it," Rick said. "She means well but says the oddest things."

"How was your Sunday brunch?" Cassie asked Betty.

"Good, despite the monkeying around. My nephew was complaining about football withdrawal since he got married. So, my brothers tied his wrists and gagged him with their neckties. They teased him about being '*bound and tied*.'" Betty told the story and chuckled. "Men! They missed half the game goofing off about missing games. I'll never figure them out."

Cassie and Betty looked to Ti and Rick, who glanced at each other, uncomfortable with the idea of having to explain the male phenomenon.

Ti changed the subject. "Hey, did my father tell you about the time two kids who worked with us chained themselves together for a bet?"

"Nope." Rick relaxed with the new line of conversation.

"That illusionist, Casey Dulane, did a show on TV. His assistant chained him and dropped him into a tank of water. The next morning, we were talking about his great escape. Frankie found some old chain and three padlocks in the workshop, and Luke wanted to prove it wasn't so hard. Tony bet he could beat him. The stakes were twenty bucks and a chunk of ego to see who could get down the hall to the key and release himself first. Frankie chained them and cinched the padlocks. They rolled and waddled down the hallway as the rest of us watched and cheered. Tony got ahead and was reaching for the key with his half-freed arm." Ti held his elbow and waved his lower arm. "All of a sudden, Luke bit Tony on the thigh. He screamed. The two of them tussled on the ground as the pastor came in, wondering what all the ruckus was about. My father had a tough time explaining that one. He told the pastor, '*Competition is healthy. Failing is how we learn and grow, and succeeding is how we're motivated to try more.*' Then he shrugged while the pastor shook his head at us."

◆ ◆ ◆ ◆

A few nights before Halloween, Ti helped Nate try on his costume. As they fit each part, Mitch cleared his throat. "One year, Ti wore a cowboy costume for a whole week. He had dark snakeskin boots and a tan hat. His favorite part was a brown, studded holster. I should have known that if he didn't become a sheriff, a tool belt would be in his future. Man, he loved having a belt that could hold stuff." Mitch's eyes twinkled. The activity distracted them from worrying over the next day's doctor visit.

That night, everyone lay awake, wondering what would come next. They coveted the miracle of remission. Yet, so far, they'd been denied.

Dear Lord,
Thank you for my wonderful family,
and the gift that was today.
Guide each of us under this roof,
This is what I pray.

He closed his eyes and added, “Lord, You were supposed to help me get through these challenges. Please have some great plan up Your sleeve that allows me more time with my family. I have lots left to do.”

“Mandy, beg God to help me. I’m not ready to leave them.” Mitch thought about the day he brought her home from her second surgery. She’d been frail but full of faith. Brightness had shown on her pale face, and he never forgot the attitude and grace she portrayed as she went through each step in her journey. “I’m scared,” he sighed.

Ti started to doubt whether prayer could really change things—it hadn’t with his mother. Fearful and angry, he pulled his knees up closer to his chest. *This isn’t the time for more bad news; I’m ready for a good report.* He felt his muscles tense as he pondered all the reasons why anything other than restored health was sensible. *God, show some compassion. Please let my father be well.* Ti rationalized the outcome he so desperately wanted from the depths of his being, and finally fell asleep from exhaustion.

The next morning, Dr. Leslie spoke of medical details, blood counts, cancer types, fluids, and masses. Confusion reigned as Mitch felt his body and mind go numb. In the end, she recommended more treatment. She pointed to the dark area on the scan. “Here. We want to treat this area with radiation therapy.” Her voice sounded confident. “Mitch did so well on chemo, this should be easy for him to tolerate.” She explained how it worked, common side effects, and typical durations.

Jen scribbled it all down in her notebook.

“I also recommend an antidepressant,” Dr. Leslie said. “You’re going through a lot of serious physical and emotional stress.”

“Yeah, I think that and a sleep aid is in order. I need to fight this battle with all I have,” Mitch agreed. Ti and Jen supported anything the doctor suggested, glad for Mitch to stay confident while he waited for his body to catch up with his will.

That afternoon, the phone rang. “Howdy, old bugger. How are things?” Millie’s familiar voice greeted Mitch.

He grunted in response. “I’m going to radiation.”

“Stay positive old chap. I’m praying this will work.”

“I start on November first, All Saints Day. I like that.”

"It's a good sign, my friend." They chatted for a few minutes before she wished him well and hung up.

Later, he went to sleep talking to many of his Saint friends, asking and pleading for their intercession.

"Dear Lord," he began tearfully. "Please, don't abandon me now."

He sighed, letting out a long breath.

St. Anthony, find me a cure the way you found Jen for us.

St. Francis, lead the way. Show me the path to get well.

St. Christopher, give me more time with Nate and my future grandchildren. It's wonderful to be mentoring another little one.

St. Joseph, Ti and I could be carpenters again. I want to be with my family, building structures as well as memories.

Oh, St. Jude, don't let me feel hopeless. Turn this around.

St. Michael, fight this devil in me. Help me win...

He paused, listening for a reply from any of them. "Oh Mandy, help me... go to the angels and saints... ask them... I think they forgot me. I'm not done. I have so much more to do."

◆ ◆ ◆ ◆

In their costumes, Jen and Nate walked through the neighborhood, along with Kay and Scott. They caught up to Allie, Travis, and her twin nieces. The moms were able to chat and relax in each other's company, while the kids enjoyed spooky scenes and treat harvesting. Watching Nate skip and laugh, Jen felt more serene.

Happy Halloween! The doctors have recommended a new course of action. Mitch gets his first dose of radiation tomorrow. He's looking forward to it starting, ending, and completing his cure. He complains about pain in his back and abdomen. According to Dr. Leslie, it all makes sense. Honestly, none of it makes sense to us. Nevertheless, he'll be going for a treatment every weekday for several weeks. The appointments last about fifteen minutes. He feels he's in good hands, and we can see he's counting on this. On a brighter note, Nate fulfilled his community service requirement. He will receive Confirmation in the spring! Mitch is sponsoring him, and they're both proud of the idea. We're all praying. Even the doggies have their paws crossed for their best buddy! With so many of us behind him, he'll pull through. Your love and support continues to give him courage.

Mitch began radiation on schedule. He saw the specialist after completing each round, but didn't get a warm, fuzzy feeling from this man, as he had from the compassionate medical oncologist who'd supervised his care throughout the chemo. Required to work with this doctor instead, he felt a little abandoned and longed for Dr. Leslie's gentle demeanor. Still, Mitch remained a good sport for each appointment.

He underwent three weeks of treatments, during which he was tired and weak. His blood counts remained deficient, and he required two sessions of hydration and one transfusion. As he completed his third week, he stopped working and started eating less and resting more. The radiation was not as kind to him as the chemo had been. Ti and Jen clung to hope and looked forward to Thanksgiving.

The four began their holiday with a quiet ride, thankful to be together. Once home, Mitch sat in his favorite spot in the family room, surrounded by his pups. He wore jeans and a striped shirt that was topped off with a red and black insulated flannel. "I'm looking forward to your stuffing, Jen. And that green bean goop of yours."

"Yeah, I'll do the sweet potatoes and cinnamon apples for you this time, but don't get used to it." She smiled at him.

Ti started the turkey early. Nate offered Mitch a hot cup of ginger tea. Mitch breathed in the holiday aroma and drifted off to sleep. The rest of them carried tubs of Christmas decorations out of storage and began setting up the big tree that had brought them so much joy only two years prior. That tree had become symbolic of their new family.

Nate hung decorations as Mitch had taught him, with small tacks that fit between the logs of the cabin so that, after the season ended, there was not a hole or scratch to be seen. Mitch dozed. *I wonder if that silly Jennifer will wrap up a new toothbrush, bath beads, and socks again. Funny how her version of Santa fills stockings with practical things. I wonder what'll be under the tree in Santa paper for us too.* He secretly liked her wacky Santa rituals and rubbed his feet together thinking about the new socks he would soon wear.

Ti, Jen, and Nate watched him sleep, sad for his inability to enjoy the time with them. On the other hand, they smothered him in affection and surrounded him with holiday hope, proving they needed him to be a part of their ever-growing traditions.

Lenny and Camille stopped by Friday morning. Over coffee and crumb cake, they spoke about their trip to Florida, a niece's wedding, and their newly painted paddleboat. "Mitch, you'll have to go for a ride this spring."

Mitch shrugged. *I never understood the reason to work so hard for a boat ride, even when healthy.*

"Mom and me will go." Their little bicycle enthusiast hopped off his chair with powdered sugar on his lips.

Saturday, Mitch called Jen into the room. "Jen, I'm afraid. What if there is no path to victory on this one?"

"We'll do everything we can, and we'll keep our faith. You taught me that, more than anyone." She hugged him.

He leaned on her, crying for a second time over the four days. Yet he also soaked in being at his favorite place, watching his family do all the things that made him secure and proud.

Back home Monday morning, Jen brought Mitch for his quick but intense radiation therapy. She saw the doctor at the counter while she waited. "Is there anything we can do about Mitch's appetite and fatigue?"

The gruff man handed Jen a business card. "Here. The social worker can help you better understand his condition and manage your emotions." He started to leave, then turned. "You do realize this will beat him sooner or later, don't you?" he asked in a callous voice.

Jen just stood there.

"Uh," she gulped. *What?* Her jaw fell; her eyes narrowed. *No, of course not. Absolutely not! I do not know that.*

No one had said the word "terminal." No one had even implied an "end" for Mitch—no one, until this moment.

Mitch was sick and getting sicker, but that was supposed to get him to a point where it would all turn around. *This suffering is not for nothing.*

The doctor departed. Jen stood, her bottom lip quivering. A nurse who had seen the exchange ran around the counter and hugged Jen. Tears tumbled down their cheeks.

"Jen," Shianna said, "Mitch may not beat this, but he's got a lot of life still in him. Appreciate that. Live in each moment of each day. Plus, he has one of the most supportive and loving families I've ever seen. And I've been an oncology nurse for many years. A lot of our patients have to go through this alone."

Even though she'd only known the Conners for a month, she was quite fond of them. Mitch walked in slowly every morning, with his distinctive Mitch-gait and bright smile, waving his cap at her. Anytime he found a willing ear, he volunteered conversation about his family or his mountain home. The nurses knew each dog by name.

"Trust me: both his spirit and family will carry him far still."

Jen composed herself before Mitch came out. He gave his little old-man salute to his cheerful nurse as he shuffled past the counter.

"How was your Thanksgiving in the mountains?" she asked.

"Splendid as usual," he answered, with a smile and a deep breath as he recalled the holiday aroma. Shianna saw him sparkle from his time at home. She winked at Jen to remind her of what they'd spoken about, and to reaffirm her point: Mitch enjoys life, and simple pleasures, even now.

Meanwhile, Ti met with building administrators to discuss a project to add privacy along the right side of the grounds. They spoke about dollars and drainage, tree types, and options for minimizing sound and sight. Jackson pointed to the large lawn area and shrubbery beds. "You really keep our place pristine, Ti."

"It's bred into me. My father fed our yard with all the right fertilizers, at all the right times of year. When I was growing up, we had thick bushes and flowering plants all over our landscape. Our lawn was green into the dry days of summer. Neighbors envied Dad, but in a good way." He took a step off the curb. "In fact, my father taught some of them. Our street got to be known as, well... scenic. Loads of people went for walks down it. I guess it was just nice to look at. I had forgotten about all that."

"I'm sorry Mitch isn't doing better," Jackson said.

"Thanks, Jackson," was all Ti could say in return.

"I like hearing about Mitch's old times."

Ti chuckled. "Actually, I remember something else. When our mailman had gotten older, he started driving his jeep on the edge of the lawns all the way down the block. There were no curbs. My father grumbled for months before he retired. That's my dad."

"I admire how close you and your father are, Ti. You really respect each other." Jackson turned to go inside.

"Thanks, Jackson. I appreciate that... and all your support, especially lately." *He's a compassionate supervisor, who's shown us a lot of understanding through Dad's illness.* Ti was determined to prove how much Jackson's kindness meant to him by working even harder than he always had. His attitude would forever reflect his gratitude.

Jen dropped Mitch home after his treatment and drove back to work feeling hollow. As she pulled through the common lot, she saw Ti surveying the new tree line with Jackson. Just seeing him helped her feel more secure, but her stomach knotted knowing she would have to wait to tell him what the doctor had said. She took a deep breath and focused on seeing him soon, and hugging him for a long, long time.

CHAPTER 28

Jen scurried around preparing breakfast for Nate, coffee for Mitch, and lunch for both of them. She got her earrings put in and her hair tied up before walking Nate down the driveway. Kay was driving the boys to school after a harsh wind joined forces with an unusual drop in temperature. Back in the kitchen, she started to clean the dishes.

Mitch called from the next room. "Jen, you better dial 911. I don't feel right. My chest is tight."

"What?" The dish dropped into the sink with a clatter. She left the water running and ran to him, hoping her ears had deceived her. She blinked. "What do I tell them?" She punched the numbers into the phone, half-dazed and wholly frightened.

"Tell them I have chest pain and need to go to the hospital."

The operator picked up after one ring. She relayed his words. The man dispatched an emergency squad. Jen dialed Ti's number and left a message that balanced on a thread between urgency and calm, hoping he'd call back quickly. She shut the water and sat with Mitch.

The ambulance arrived. A woman took Mitch's vitals, while a man gave him chewable aspirin and questioned him about his medical history. Jen handed them a blue index card listing his many medications.

"He's being treated for kidney cancer..." Her hands shook.

"Dr. Leslie... Yes... No..." Mitch answered each query.

As they prepped him for the ride, Ti called. "What's up?"

"Hi, hun. First, we're okay. Mitch had chest pain. An ambulance is taking him to the hospital. They're almost ready to leave."

Ti swallowed. "I'll meet you there."

They found each other in the familiar waiting area and sat down.

"More waiting." Ti held Jen's arm wrapped in his own, mentally adding up the number of hours they'd spent in hospitals over the last year. "What the heck is going on? How much more can go wrong?"

A middle-aged doctor with dark eyes and green scrubs walked toward them. "The tests show your father had a mild heart attack. We're taking him into surgery." The words stuck in Ti's ears like the echo of a sonic boom. His jaw agape, he attempted to comprehend.

"You'll want to see him before he goes under." The doctor walked beside them, scribbling on his clipboard.

"Hey, you." Jen peeked around the curtain.

"What's the matter? You decided you need even more attention?" Ti half chuckled, wiping the corner of a misty eye.

Yeah, I just want to focus on anything other than cancer for a change. "Hey, I gotta' keep you guys on your toes." Mitch smiled at his kids. "I'm feeling all right now. Don't worry."

"You better be all right. We love you!" Jen hugged him.

They returned to the cold, pale waiting area. After an hour, Ti ran home to check on the dogs and returned before anyone had news.

Jen made some calls. "Hi, Kay. I hate to say this, but we're back in the H-place. I'm sorry... can you pick up the boys today? I'll owe you."

"Of course, don't worry. Tell Mitch I'm praying for him."

"You're a dear." Jen sighed as the arrangements for Nate fell into place. *Thank God for our friends.*

When the nurse brought them back, Mitch seemed okay—groggy, but jovial and relaxed. *I can barely open my eyes; not sure how much more of this I can take.* "What the heck did you guys do all morning?"

Jen forced a wilted smile. Ti gave sarcasm back to the cantankerous but adorable patient. "Us? You got to take a nap for the last four hours."

Mitch got settled in a room. Much too familiar with the hospital routine, Ti and Jen went home for a light dinner and crashed in bed.

"Well, that was unexpected," Ti said with his arm around Jen's shoulder. He fell asleep from sheer exhaustion.

Hello, everyone! As some of you may have heard, Mitch gave us a scare yesterday. He decided that the radiation was too draining and the only way out of it was via heart attack! Actually, he's doing better than we expected. He has two new prescriptions, which brings his total up to twenty. No wonder pharmacists go to medical school. He's weak but in good spirits. We'll be seeing him later, so we'll deliver everyone's greetings. Please keep him in your thoughts and prayers.

◆ ◆ ◆ ◆

The middle of December saw much activity. Between work, hospital visits, chores, and doggie patrols, Jen managed to prepare for the holidays. They'd decorated the house over Thanksgiving, and most of the gifts had been stashed away since the summer.

Mitch seemed stronger, although he'd lost a little more weight. He remained interested in what was going on at work. Each evening from beside the hospital bed, Ti kept him up to date.

Rose, who had originally established the pray-and-feed club, again organized a schedule for those wanting to send a meal. Jen and Ti spent as much time with Mitch as possible. Coming home to a casserole baking in a low oven was a blessing. Grateful for their friends, they learned about God's work, miracles, and the positive aspects that exist amongst grief, despair, and difficult human experience.

Mid-week, Nate visited his beloved pal. His innocence and zest for life encouraged them all. "Hey, Mitch!" Nate smiled holding up his ATV toy.

"Hey, buddy!" *Ah, just by having my grandson around I can feel the Holy Spirit lifting me up. What a breath of fresh air.*

"Mitch, I'm so happy to see you. I was scared you got real sick again."

"I'm sorry. I don't want you to worry. Listen Nate, scary times are gifts of faith wrapped in brown paper bags. They look plain and stiff on the outside, but you still find something way down in there. I want you to remember to have faith when you're scared, okay?"

"Okay."

"So, what have you been up to?"

"Well, today in gym class, I ran around the track the fastest!"

"Wow, that's great!" Mitch delighted in hearing his grandson's voice.

Rose and Brock came by the next evening, insisting Ti and Jen take a break. The week passed slowly, as Mitch remained jailed in the white room, bound by thin plastic tubes. After what felt like weeks on end, the doctor released Mitch into Ti and Jen's care.

Back home, Millie was the first to check in. "Hey, how's that ticker?"

"Good. Believe it or not, I feel better without that radiation crap."

"I believe it. How's the family?" she asked.

"They're amazing. When I feel like a rundown old shack ready to collapse, they haul in the sheetrock, shingles, paint, hammers, and sanders. I gotta say my family and friends are reinforcing me."

"Don't you go getting all mushy on me after fifteen years of ornery."

"I'll never admit I said any of that." With a jovial snort, he hung up.

As the holidays approached, the doctors put all further medical discussion and direction on hold until after the New Year. Mitch would see Dr. Leslie on January fifth. Until then, everyone focused on sharing the season together. Jen convinced her family to celebrate Christmas Eve at the mountain house. Her family members had come to accept her relationship with Ti and supported her commitment to helping Mitch through his illness. They joined the Conner festivities in a not-so-traditional-but-oh-so-lovely place. Jen baked their favorite cookies, even though Ti and Nate ate most of them before their guests arrived.

Mitch had little appetite, but knowing the Christmas baking was occurring as usual was all he needed. He looked around his decorated home, remembering when Mandy took the time to decorate, bake, and add all those touches that make a holiday truly a holiday.

I'm so happy Ti is experiencing all this again. Jen treats the ornaments much like you did, my love. Certain ones had specific places on the tree and if by chance an eager-to-help male in the house placed one in the wrong spot, it was merely adjusted when no one was watching. The two ladies loved holiday decorating and their styles were remarkably similar. Both were excited about the manger scene collectibles, cookie selections, and wrapping each gift in the right-colored paper. With a smile, Mitch reflected upon Jen's influence on Ti, but also on himself. She brought back fond memories of his special wife.

"Mandy, isn't Jen good for us?" he asked, leaning back in his recliner with closed eyes. Mitch heard the commotion in the next room and felt content—extremely fatigued, but content.

Although Mitch slept through half of their holiday, Jen's family enjoyed a festive ambiance along with a scrumptious dinner. Music played, the kids amused themselves with new toys and coloring books, and Nate got to show off his special cabin in the woods. He played with his cousins but stopped to check in on Mitch regularly.

"Mitch do you want a cookie? Should I let the dogs out now?" Each time the clock bonged an hour, Nate visited Mitch. Jen was proud of her son; his thoughtfulness helped her find a silver lining in their atypical holiday.

Nate tugged Ti's sleeve, leading him to the basement. "Ti, we need to get the big sign you made Santa." The spray-painted plywood board read, "SANTA WATCH OUT! Don't burn your butt in the fireplace!"

On Christmas morning, the four of them opened presents. Mitch was tired by the time they finished with the Santa-filled stockings. He ate two chocolate-covered mint patties, placed his toothbrush on the coffee table, pulled on a pair of new socks, and nuzzled down with Chase for a nap. Nate opened his gift from Santa, then he and Ti spent the day assembling his new racetrack.

They were happy, yet sad at the same time. In constant contradiction, they felt lucky but unlucky, blessed but forgotten, joyful but forlorn, optimistic yet scared.

They existed peacefully in their wooded world for a week. Ti beat Jen and Nate in his favorite game, and Mitch declared him "The Master." Jen triumphed in cards, and Nate won another board game.

"Mitch, wanna play?" Nate asked.

"No, thanks," Mitch said.

Nate turned toward him an hour later. "Ti just won again."

"Any amazing word combinations this time?"

"This time 'riverbed' pushed him over my score," Jen scowled.

"Like father, like son," Mitch chuckled.

After much appreciation for the season, their home, their guests and each other, they headed back to face the next phase of their lives.

◆ ◆ ◆ ◆

Back in reality, the family began the New Year with fresh recommendations and plans for healing. The social worker gave the Conners whatever attention they needed anytime they brought Mitch in or called with a question. Dr. Leslie ordered an immediate scan followed by another three weeks later to determine whether the disease was holding steady or getting worse. Mitch continued to fight fatigue as well as intervals of discomfort. Ti remained strong and positive in front of his father, but on the inside, he crumbled like a fistful of breadcrumbs, as he realized what the delay in treatment might mean. The specialists spoke of a new therapy for Mitch as soon as he was strong enough. They sent his records to three facilities offering clinical trials and one seemed promising.

"Hello, Mr. Conner," Dr. Leslie greeted him with a solemn expression. "After reviewing the second scan result, I'm afraid to say that there is a marginal increase in the dark patch on the image. I'm sorry, but even a tiny growth confirms your cancer is thriving."

Three stomachs dropped. *Where's the good part… with a solution?*

Mitch stared at her, convinced she was mistaken.

"So what do we do next? What's the plan?" Jen readied for action.

"The best course of action is outpatient shots and physical therapy. I want Mitch to increase his weight and muscle strength, so he can participate in a clinical trial beginning March first."

Jen went online for nutritional suggestions. "Ti, I read that he can eat anything, especially with lots of calories."

"Yeah. I asked around at work too. Everyone suggests those nutrition shakes. They said he'd do better with small meals more often."

Jen pulled out the blender and filled it with calories: whole milk, ice cream, pudding, protein drinks, and yogurt. She flavored the shakes with blended banana, peanut butter, chocolate, strawberry, blueberries or cinnamon, and topped them off with whipped cream. The shakes maintained his weight, while he ate less and less at suppertime. Meals had to be tempting and easy to chew and swallow. His Friday pizza slices no longer included crusts, pleasing Chase, Champ, Daisy, and Chip, but not Jen. Occasionally, he slipped food off his plate to his drooling pooches when no one was watching. However, he devoured the shakes singlehandedly, so Jen was sure to have two in the refrigerator every day.

They tested his blood levels regularly. Often something was deficient: potassium, calcium, or even hydration. Like a seedling, at times Mitch would sprout with potential. Other times, he was scorched or trampled. Each time, he rooted his stalk in the earth to try again.

As the end of February approached, Mitch was walking daily and consuming his shakes, but he'd not gained quite enough weight. Desperate to heal, he yearned to meet the requirements for the March clinic.

Ti prayed, pleading harder than ever. He begged the saints to help his father beat this disease—just for a while, allowing more time with their family. *I'm not ready to lose him.*

Pulling Jen toward him, Ti said, "We can't let Dad know, but this is not going well. I've seen it all before, and... I don't know what to do if he doesn't make it to that new drug. He's still two pounds shy of his goal. How can he fight this on his own?" Jen cried, feeling helpless to comfort Ti or to find a way to get Mitch ready for the trial.

That night, Mitch stared at the ceiling.

Dear Lord,
Thank you for my wonderful family
  and the gift that was today.
Guide us all under this roof.
  This is what I pray.

Picking at the seam on his blanket, he continued, "Lord, you were supposed to help me. I'm still waiting for You to show me Your divine plan—a plan where I get out of this mess. I have too much to finish here... on earth with Ti, Jen, and Nate... first... before heaven."

He sighed. "I miss you, Mandy. The saints aren't listening. I've been asking all of them... just like I did when you were sick." He inhaled. "Did they forget me? Do you think the new drug will do the trick? I'm scared."

Mitch lay awake. His blanket hem unraveled as he pulled the threads. He closed his eyes. Rainbows swirled inside the blackness. Then he saw Mandy's gentle face. Her mouth curved in a shy smile; her eyes filled with empathy. Wearing a sundress and gold crucifix, her hair was tied behind her head with a pretty orange and yellow bow. The sky was dark and overcast. But after a few moments, it changed to a brighter blue that sparkled like her eyes. She turned her gaze to the green and white field that blossomed behind her. Mandy gathered a handful of daisies and sat on a gray stone near a pond. Two ducks swam in circles. She held the bundle of flowers to her chest, studying the simple beauty in each petal. He watched her strong chin and confident shoulders as she touched the flower tips. He drew on her strength and felt better. Mitch slept.

Jen weighed Mitch the next morning. One more pound and a little less napping would have been best, but he had certainly improved.

She called Dr. Leslie. “What else can we do to get him to qualify for the new treatment?”

“Perhaps Mitch can start the trial in his current condition. We can note and monitor his weight and fatigue. Any improvement would give credit to the new drug. I’ll make some inquiries.”

The doctor’s nurse called that afternoon. “Bring Mitch in for testing. He’s staying on schedule to begin treatment as planned.”

A huge sense of relief swept over them. *Thank goodness! There’s still hope to be had.* Mitch sat tall on the ride to the center.

“Mr. Conner, we’ll call you when the blood work comes back.”

“Sounds good to me.” Mitch popped his cap on his now completely bald head. “Trial, here I come.” *If I had the energy, I’d skip out that door.*

Yet, even as they awaited the results, Mitch developed a fever. Dr. Leslie admitted him to the hospital.

Ti shook his head. “Jen, he’s going to miss the trial.”

Feeling suspended in a freefall, she uttered, “I... I know... I...”

But, stronger and more determined than ever Mitch hung tough, yanking energy from sheer will. *I am going to be in the next round of that trial.*

Ti and Nate traveled north to Walleycito to pick-up mail, vacuum the vacant rooms, and plow the driveway. Although the two enjoyed the time to bond, Ti got an eerie feeling. He was... suddenly... the elder.

One Thursday evening after six weeks of back and forth, up and down, strong and weak moments, Mitch got insistent. “I want all three of you to go home to the mountains tomorrow and stay Saturday.”

“But Dad,” Ti said.

"Listen, I know what needs attending to. It'll be good for you to be there, take care of things, breathe the mountain air, and return to me stronger and better Sunday morning. You are tired too."

"Mitch, no," Jen murmured. But he wanted to give them this gift to show his love and gratitude in return for their constant dedication.

"No, Mitch. I'll stay. Ti can go with Nate and the dogs."

A tenacious Mitch held his ground. "I can manage in this place without you for a day and a half. You'll see how strong I can be."

Ti took Jen's hand and they walked to the lobby. "Jen, it is important to consider his wishes."

"But, Ti, I don't mind staying with him. I want to stay." She pleaded, standing on tiptoes to gaze into his eyes.

"Honey, listen, he's giving us something and it matters to him, just like we feel good to give to him. You saw his conviction; we can't say no." She lowered her heels and glanced to the floor. Ti tipped her head up and tucked a curl behind her ear, exposing more of her worried expression. "We have to do this." He kissed her forehead.

They arranged a line of visitors throughout Saturday—morning, mid-day, afternoon and evening. Betty, Millie, Cassie, and Rose volunteered as the plans fell into place. Jen clicked her phone off.

"You're all set. You won't have time to miss us," Jen said.

They spent time with their patriarch before setting out late Friday night. Filled with doubtful minds and reluctant spirits, the trio left for the mountains and the duties waiting there. Saturday morning, they took the pups for their annual checkup. On the way in, Chip and Daisy tugged on their leashes toward two beagles, and a large tabby.

The knowledgeable Dr. Townsend handled the Conner clan with ease. "Three of the four could stand to lose about five pounds."

They looked to one another. "Mitch!"

Nate put his palms around Champ's ribs and explained, "Mitch gives them all the food he wants my mom to think he ate."

A long-time acquaintance of the Mitches, Dr. Townsend gave Ti a heartfelt glance filled with understanding and sadness. Then he continued, "Teeth, ears, paws, and bellies all check out perfectly."

While at the house, Ti cleaned and stored the snowplow, changed the truck's fluids, cleared the mucky gutters, and fertilized. As apprentice, Nate handed Ti tools and managed to rake both the lawn and driveway.

"What else can I do?" Nate sensed the need to finish a lot in a short amount of time. They cleaned inside and out, ran errands, and serviced the furnace. They fit a lot into one Saturday.

Jen kept her promise to call Mitch. "You're not missing a thing; all work, no fun."

"Nothing new here. But, see? I told you I'd be fine." Mitch spoke in a singsong voice, like a five-year-old proving a point. "Millie just left. She brought a silly balloon and snuck me a piece of cheesecake. Oh, was that good. You'd be proud, I ate every crumb."

"That's fantastic. I think I'll buy a cheesecake tomorrow."

I wish I was with them, but just a few more weeks... I'll be on my new medicine and we'll all be home together.

After dinner, Jen called again. "What's up?"

"I was at therapy this afternoon. There is a new lady."

"Oh?"

"Boy is she mean. This lady didn't just toss the ball; she drove it at me with all her might every time she had the chance."

"Was she really that bad?"

"You don't know the half of it. I can't get over how this old gal got her jollies by throwing it at me. I have a bruise on my arm to prove it. You'll be checking it out when you get back." He chuckled.

"I'm proud of you for sticking it out. How've you been eating?"

"Okay. Not tons, but okay. See you in the morning."

"You bet! I can't wait to give you a big hug and kiss," she pledged.

◆ ◆ ◆ ◆

Jen, Ti, and Nate were up early, preparing to head back. Mitch called before sunrise, very agitated. "Jen, I don't feel right."

She responded to his distressed tone with her own. "What's wrong?"

"I'm not sure. I'm so sad, and so tired. I think... I won't make it. I think... I realize I can't beat this."

"But you're doing so well. You've been eating, going to therapy, talking with the other patients. Your new treatment starts in two weeks." She cried, confused, wanting to make it better, but not knowing how. "Are you unhappy there? What do you need? Rest. Give us time to get there."

"I know. I was doing fine. It's not the place, it's just a *feeling*. I think... I'm overwhelmed... Who am I kidding? I can't heal my body at this point. The cancer is still there and it won't leave."

"Oh, Mitch," she whispered. "Don't say that. We all have faith. We'll keep fighting together."

"What? What's wrong?" Ti opened the truck's rear door. "Tell him we're on our way. Nate, grab that box of donuts. I'll get the cooler. Chase, Champ, come on... in the car."

"Sit tight. We're on our way." Jen tried to encourage him in this strange new mood.

"I'm tired. I feel alone and sad. Even talking with Rose, Brock, and the other visitors—it was just going through the motions." Mitch's voice cracked. "I'm really tired."

Ti drove them back like a drill boring through a log. They were by Mitch's side just as visiting hours started. Jen saw tears in his eyes.

"Oh, am I glad to see you."

They embraced him with kisses and hugs. "What's going on, Dad?"

"I can't tell. Last night I woke up around three o'clock. I missed you guys like never before." He spoke as if surprised. Enveloped in an invisible shadow, he paused, grasping for words that could convey his feelings.

They waited, giving him time to explain.

"I guess I figured out how sick I really am." Mitch appeared weighed down, as if trudging through swamp mud.

After some time, they left Nate and went to the nurse's station. Jen asked to review his chart. She noticed they'd not recorded his antidepressant since Friday.

"That can't be it. It's such a small dose." The nurse tapped her pencil.

"It must have given him some confidence," Jen said.

"I'm sure it was an oversight." The nurse's somber face turned pale.

"How is that possible?" Ti turned around, throwing his arms in the air.

"I'll get it immediately." She waddled down the hall at a fast pace.

Jen took Ti's hand and sighed. He shook his head, cleared his throat, stood tall, and reentered Mitch's room.

Jen watched them. *I wonder if there's more to it. Perhaps Mitch overheard something about his slow progress, or maybe the almost catatonic state of his roommate frightened him.* Something had changed his outlook—suddenly, drastically and definitively.

When her shift began, Ti and Jen went to speak with the nurse they knew well. "Sandy, Dad's not himself. What went on last night?" Ti asked.

"Do you know anything about how Mitch got so lost? What may have caused this... sudden... surrender?" Jen sputtered.

"I'm glad you're back. A woman arrived late last evening after his other visitors had gone. They discussed mortality and death late into the night. She suggested he recognize the peace he'd receive *'on the other side.'*" With raised brows and dropped jaws, they listened. "She advised him to *'understand his situation.'* The woman stayed in the chair beside him half the night. Honestly, it was weird. I've seen her before, but while you were away, she acted... more like a family member. Are they a couple?"

Ti and Jen figured Sandy was referring to Deirdre.

"They're good, longtime friends. That's all." Ti blinked.

"Well, she must be close enough to have influence," Sandy said.

Sullen, Ti felt like a limp balloon, as if the air had been sucked out of him. *It's not fair. Dad was going to hang on, at least for another few years.* Powerless and crushed, he collapsed with his back against the wall.

"But," Jen defended, "Mitch was doing so well. Compared to other patients, he was energetic and strong. As of Thursday, he'd met the weight requirement. He was going to start his new medicine!"

Ti put his arm around her shoulder.

Her furious voice calmed to a whisper. "I just don't understand."

"Maybe you can change his mind." Sandy touched her arm.

"Not so sure about that." Ti knew Mitch better than anyone and understood his conviction to a decision.

The talk with Deirdre only multiplied the melancholy effect from the missed drug. It all led to the call that Jen still heard resounding in her ears. Mitch had had a spark of fight left in him, but as he pondered the inevitable, that spark faded.

Mitch's concern for his family and the difficulties they might endure through his remaining illness smothered his resolve. Recalling Mandy's struggles, he feared for Tiger, Jennifer, and Nathaniel—so much so that he accepted the terminal nature of his condition. Deirdre had offered Mitch something no one else had, reason to surrender this life for the next. *Yes, Mitch, eventually this will overcome your earthly body. Fighting is a tough road on all of you. Don't be afraid of what is next; don't be afraid of God's will.* Loving his family so deeply, Mitch was willing to yield now and spare them more months, possibly years, of this difficult lifestyle.

Not knowing Sandy had overheard his talk with Deirdre or had relayed anything to his kids, Mitch kept his thoughts to himself that dismal Palm Sunday. They respected his need to share his feelings when he was ready. Mitch tucked his emotions away for a while, making small talk about their trip, Nate, and friends' business. He felt safe. *Oh Lord, I'm so glad they are with me.*

Desperate to motivate Mitch to fight and stay with them, Ti prayed their love would allow those embers to reignite once more. *I need him. We need him. God, let him feel how much.*

Neither Jen nor Ti felt burdened by the demands of his illness. Mitch had taught, and proven every day, that family meant most in life. If he was weak, if he needed doctors or attention, it mattered not. Mitch was a treasure greater than the largest pearls, the purest gold, or the richest gemstones. He was a part of the M-&-m duo, and now the Conner 4x4—a family made up of four humans and four canines.

It must stay that way.

CHAPTER 29

Jen and Ti left the care center baffled and desperate to stay grounded in the winds of this new monsoon. Praying she could still throw Mitch a life preserver, Jen called Mitch first thing in the morning. "Hey, Dad, how ya' doing today?"

"Can you come back?" Many times when Mitch had been a hospital hostage, Jen asked if he needed her and he always answered the same way: "Of course I need you, but I'll be fine until I see you later."

This time was different.

This time he sobbed, "I need you."

"Hang on. I'll be right there." Jen called back and spoke to the nurse.

"Mitch declined breakfast and says he'll skip physical therapy."

He usually enjoyed his sessions. For weeks, he'd employed his charms and toyed with the compassionate therapists.

But not today.

Jen pulled her car into the Pastoral Center parking lot and found Ti. They drove to the care center. Entering his room, they did not see the usual sparkle in Mitch's eyes. Instead, they saw a glossy luster that was relief and gratitude for their presence.

The understanding he had come into depressed him. Heartbroken, Ti and Jen sat on either side of his bed as he confessed all the feelings that had consumed him over the past twenty-four hours: his fears, his fatigue, his acceptance. The three sat close together with steady, wet streams on their cheeks as Mitch explained, slowly and meekly. Holding each of his hands, Ti and Jen listened.

Finally, Mitch said, "Take me home."

"Dad, we'd love to take you home. We've been hoping you'd feel strong enough to go to the cabin for Easter vacation," Jen said.

"Ohhh," Mitch sighed.

"Jen's been working with the doctors. She has you scheduled to see Dr. Leslie tomorrow, and a release appointment first thing Wednesday. We wanted to surprise you after all the plans came together."

"And it's still two weeks before your clinical trial starts. Perfect timing." Jen encouraged him to see their logic.

The old charismatic Mitch smiled, before the new despondent Mitch took over, causing his whole body to wilt. "Take me home to be at my favorite place. To be with you. To be with my dogs. To find my peace. I am through fighting. I am finished."

"Finished?" Ti sucked in a breath.

"What do you mean?" Jen swallowed.

"Finished... fighting... this..." Mitch spread his arms.

Ti felt his innards turn to soggy oatmeal. "Oh, Dad." Ti squeezed his hand, hoping to infuse some hope back into Mitch.

"You'll feel better; you'll see. You've been doing so well." *Please, God. Please*. Jen's wet eyes glistened, confessing emotions that swayed between fear and faith.

"We'll see," he said to console her, realizing they needed time to digest the idea. "Take me home."

"Do you mean right now?" Ti asked. "We're supposed to see your doctor tomorrow. We planned to be on the road Wednesday before lunch. Do you want us to change that?"

"We're off the whole next week. I can't wait to spoil you the entire time," Jen said.

"Less than forty-eight hours... hmmm... okay," he said, sitting taller. They each released a long, held breath. Then, as if someone flipped a switch, Mitch lowered his gaze. "I hope I can make it."

"You might not make it?" Jen asked, wide-eyed. Ti stared, silent.

Mitch smiled at them with all the love in his heart. "No, no, I will be fine. That week with you sounds like a wonderful fantasy—one I want very much. It will be special." Relief washed over him.

Once the on-and-off flickers ceased and Mitch brightened steadily, they ran to work to arrange things before their week away.

Dear Friends and Family: We want to share our plans for taking Mitch home to celebrate Easter in his favorite place, surrounded by what he loves. Mitch told us he feels discouraged about his ability to battle his illness much longer. As I struggle with words to say what I cannot comprehend, I want you to know we have cherished each of you, your support, prayers, and love. Please understand we are uncertain about what the next week will bring...

She had no idea how to express all she felt. But she let everyone who followed his journey, who inquired about him, who loved him, who prayed for him know. She had to communicate... something.

That day and the next, Mitch saw a continual flow of beautiful faces come to wish him well, and a few to say goodbye. Some realized what could happen. Others refused to admit any gravity, but needed to see him before he left. No one knew anything for sure. Friends came at all hours to chat, sit by his side, recall fond memories, and remind him how much he was loved. He had over fifty guests in those two days—all people whose lives he'd touched simply, deeply, and profoundly.

Jen collected doctors' orders, hospice research, and drug information. Ti prepared emotionally for their time together.

As planned, Ti and Jen took Mitch to see his oncologist on Tuesday. They spoke about all aspects of his current condition. Dr. Leslie wrote prescriptions for pain, mood, sleep, and stomach ailments. They discussed the importance of keeping him comfortable.

Guiding her elbow, Dr. Leslie walked Jen out of the room. Standing at the familiar counter, she explained, "Mitch could get a fever or his pneumonia could recur. Given his acceptance, you should not treat it. You should not call the local hospital. Do you understand?"

"Yes, barely... but... yes." She choked out the words that were wedged inside her throat.

"Also, and this is important. You should not force him to eat or let him feel badly for not eating."

"Uh, okay." Jen nodded.

"That is the body's way of shutting down," Dr. Leslie explained.

Mitch seemed happy and reassured to have seen his doctor. "Goodbye, Dr. Leslie. And thank you." Mitch waved.

The appointment and the ride took most of his energy. Back at the care facility, they got Mitch settled in his room, then left to tend to Nate and the dogs. A worn-out Mitch slept. When they returned an hour later, they found Millie reading a thin book of prayers by his bedside. She prayed, without drama or need for recognition, secure in their friendship.

Seeing them enter, she stood and offered heartfelt hugs. Ti choked up. "You're a dear. Thank you."

Mitch finished dinner, as more friends stopped by to visit. Speaking casually, they sat in folding chairs around his bedside. Mitch sat up with his head back against a pile of pillows. When desired, he offered commentary, proving he was quite aware of the conversations taking place. His eyes were tired beneath his silver-rimmed glasses, but he thrived on hearing each of those special voices.

Before they left, Ti and Jen kissed his pale cheeks. He grinned, grateful for his kids. As they turned out the light, he prayed.

Dear Lord,
Thank you for my wonderful family
  and the gift of another day.
Guide them as they struggle with my leaving,
  This is what I pray.

"I miss you, Mandy. Soon we will be united again, my love, and we can watch over Ti together. I hope you are ready to help me do this. I need you now more than ever." He took a deep breath and thought about how much he missed her pretty smile.

Ti and Jen left the care center late and in silence.

Jen felt desperate to bring him home. The words she'd heard over the past two days swarmed in her mind like bees around a hive. *I'm through fighting... I hope I can make it... don't treat it... don't force him to eat...* Only one thing was clear—she would do whatever he needed. She planned to sit by his side and offer all the support and love he could take.

Ti craved quality time with his father. He'd experienced illness and death with his mother. He put on a tough exterior, but felt weak and empty. The hurt intensified as he witnessed his father's strength decline each week, and now each day.

Thinking about what would occur in only a few hours, Ti packed the car. Anxious about the trip, the bumpy roads, and his father's pain, as well as what the week ahead would bring, he proceeded on autopilot.

Feeling anxious and frightened, Jen re-checked her lists. She completed the required paperwork and arranged a meeting with hospice. However, nothing seemed clear; nothing made sense.

Once in bed, Ti lay rigid. He stared at the ceiling as tears dripped onto each side of his pillow and questions ran through his mind: *Will these be my final days with my father? Will he change his mind once he's at home and get better? Will the ride be okay? Can we manage his needs on our own? Will he suffer?*

Ti lay with his eyes open and overflowing. His heart seared as if pierced with a branding iron. He knew he would do anything for the man that gave him life and every good trait he possessed. *My father is my idol... The man who mentored me and my friends through our teenage years; who showed me how to live, love, and laugh through the difficult parts of life; who gave me everything he could. The man I teased when he dented the top of his head and when water sprinkled out after he soldered copper pipes. The man who gave me my love of sports; who taught me to drive a stick shift, a snowmobile, a Jet Ski, a tractor, and a boat...*

There was nothing this man did not know, or did not do for his boy.

This was Ti's wonderful, amazing father, who'd taught him about manhood, integrity, enjoying life, appreciating small things, and standing up for what you believe in no matter who said or did what about it.

Now, there was only a little Ti could offer in return.

◆ ◆ ◆ ◆

"Where's Mitch?" a resident asked as she threw the ball.

"He's tired today." The aide checked the attendance on her clipboard.

"Well, I miss him. He's a lot of fun." An elderly woman wearing an embroidered vest tossed the ball across the circle.

"Me too. Mitch is such a gentleman," another said.

"I hear he's getting ready for a vacation at home with his family."

Ti and Jen were up and out early, prepared for their 9:00 a.m. release appointment. With the car packed, Ti stopped at work to pick up a blessed afghan that his friends had special ordered. While Ti passed a few minutes nervously, saying goodbye to his breakfast friends, Jen wanted to visit the chapel in a last-ditch effort to ask—to beg—God for help.

"I'll go with you." Rose followed and sat down beside her.

Jen knelt and bowed her head, but her heart and mind were with Mitch. Without any understanding of what lay ahead, she longed to finish the paperwork and bring Mitch to his favorite place.

Jen had a lump in her throat and a chemistry experiment simmering in her belly. She began to sob. "Oh Rose, how do I take him home to '*be finished*'? He must feel so helpless." A tidal wave of emotions swept her into a sea of despair. "How will I know what to talk about, how to respond, or what to suggest? Why can't he just get well? Just for a while. I'm sorry... I know I need to be strong."

"You have been strong, dear. It's all just catching up with you. Trust me. You'll know what to say and do as Mitch needs you."

Jen wept, heaving as her friend held her. Once she pulled herself together, she went to back to Ti.

"I need to go to him... Even praying isn't helping." Jen touched Ti's arm.

Ti's comrades encouraged him with loving support and memories of things they loved about his father. Pleased he'd stopped, Ti held the afghan folded over his right arm. His eyes watered. He felt angry, deprived, hopeful, and blessed, all within seconds of each other. He accepted their hugs. Then Ti, too, was ready.

Living in a foggy daydream, they progressed through the awkward morning. Jen sat by Mitch, waiting for her release meeting with the nurses, administrators, and physical therapists.

"In here, Mrs. Conner." Sandy showed her to a conference room.

The administrator pushed a pile of papers toward her. "These require signature. This document states you've gathered his belongings and all unused medication..."

"The ride might be very uncomfortable. Are you prepared?"

"We have pillows..." Jen's mind swam.

"If he can't do the road trip..."

"He will. Nothing will stop him from getting home." That was the only fact of which she was certain. Most of their talk blurred into a mist before reaching her ears.

Exiting the meeting room, she saw her parents come in with Nate to say goodbye before their trip. Nate needed to see Mitch, speak with him, and provide testimony of his love for their precious but too-quickly-diminishing relationship. Jen's soul ached as she considered what Nate felt and the loss he too would suffer. *Those two share a remarkable bond.*

"Thanks, Mom, for keeping Nate until we see how this is going to go." Jen's lips were thin as she forced a smile. She turned to her son. Her eyes softened. "Nate, you should tell Mitch how much you love him and talk about the fun you had and how you will always remember everything about him, no matter what."

Nate nodded.

"And you should say goodbye in case Mitch doesn't make it back."

Nate seemed to understand. He approached Mitch, trying to speak with his quiet voice and shy fear but couldn't find the right opportunity amid the crowded room.

Sandy noticed the timid boy vying for Mitch's attention. "Mitch, there's something I forgot to give you." The nurse wheeled him down the corridor. Then, winking at Jen, she retrieved young Nate, who spent a special seventeen minutes alone with his hero in a room down the hall.

Meanwhile, Ti prepared to spend time with his father—uninterrupted, uncensored, sincere, whole, and open.

Just before Mitch got in the car, the Bishop arrived. Over the past two days, Mitch had given each visitor a few minutes of weary eyes and slow speech. However, for this guest he perked up.

"Bishop!" he called. "You came. Oh, I'm so happy to see you! Bishop, you know what?" He paused for one breath. "I am going home. I am going home to be at peace—to depart this life and go to heaven."

Bishop saddened; every muscle in his face fell. He gave his friend the blessing of last rights.

"That's a first-class ticket straight up, coming from a Bishop," Mitch insisted. Then Bishop said a prayer with his hand stretched over his old companion's pale head. His faith brought Mitch a sense of tranquility.

Mitch continued to have one purpose—to see his home in the mountains. After two valuable days of digesting, preparing, arranging, and organizing, they were ready for their expedition.

Ti gently hoisted his frail father into the back seat. Jen handed him the afghan. Mitch wriggled a little and folded himself between the cushions.

They pulled away. The ark, minus one boy, was on the road as in old days, although this was anything but a traditional trip to the mountains.

CHAPTER 30

"Oh, Mitch, it's lovely," Mandy whispered.

"I couldn't resist picking it for you. Look, the color is so unique... special, like you." He leaned in, handing the wildflower to her. He kissed her forehead.

"You take such good care of me." She studied his face from her white-sheeted bed, surrounded by medical equipment. "I thank God for you. Soon, I'll tell Him in person, and I'll watch over you until we meet again. I want you to trust that we will meet again." Mandy's smile was thin yet confident. Her eyelids drooped, but Mitch could see the glitter of their love still sparkling in her eyes.

"I don't want to think about my angel returning to heaven right now. How about I read to you some more?"

"That would be fine. Where did we leave off?" Mandy leaned her head back and listened to the sound of his voice.

◆ ◆ ◆ ◆

Mitch crumpled into a seemingly uncomfortable mound and fell asleep minutes after their voyage began. "I'm glad he's able to rest after all those warnings that the trip might be painful," Jen said, looking back at him.

Ti drove, staring ahead, recalling Mitch's vitality only two years ago: a sturdy, almost two hundred pound, five-foot-eleven pillar of fortitude and confidence, full of enthusiasm and cheerful wit. Seeing the lump of disease that had overtaken the man he cherished as his father, friend, and career partner slashed into his nerves like a thousand sharp blades. He considered his father's perseverance as his mother journeyed through the final stages of her illness. *I hope I can be as strong.*

They forged ahead in silence. At the rest stop, Ti and Jen took turns exiting the car. Mitch partially woke in the commotion, but fell back into his dreamy state in seconds.

Two hearts thumped with vigor and throbbed with sorrow as Mitch's kids brought him to his special place. The log home they'd built together, the beautiful countryside, the peaceful quiet of the trees and wildlife, his favored blue plaid couch, his four legged pals...

Mitch was going home.

Ti's emotions stretched thin amid gratitude for having such a special father, despair over letting him go, and rage at being forced to say goodbye too soon. *It's not fair; it's just not fair.*

Jen envisioned waiting on Mitch hand and foot, making shakes, bringing him medicine and lemonade, sitting with him, and hearing his stories. She'd had the privilege to be nurse, pharmacist, taxi driver, secretary, and nutritionist, and there was much more she wanted to give him to show her love. She was proud to be his daughter-in-law. *Mitch has given me and taught me so much in such a short time. He's loved me unconditionally. Knowing him is an honor.*

The car approached the driveway. Tails pounded all sides of the rear compartment. The dogs panted; the cat mewed. Pulling up to the house, Ti and Jen let out a breath and looked at each other.

"Now what?" Ti said.

"Ummm." She shrugged, realizing they had no strategy for getting Mitch into the house. The mere one hundred and sixty pounds he had disintegrated into still needed to be carried up the stairs.

They woke him, excited to share his homecoming.

"Hey, Dad, do you know where you are?" Jen asked.

"Yeah," he replied with half opened eyes. "We're at the pit stop."

"Nope, we're home!" Ti retorted.

"No we're not." His sleepy head fell back down on his chest.

Ti led the dogs to the yard and carried the cat upstairs. Jen brought in the gear. After ten minutes, they tried again. "Hey, Dad. We're home!"

He opened his weary hazel eyes and surveyed his surroundings. *I am home!* A glimmer of light appeared in those glassy eyes.

"Hey, yeah, we are home." He gazed over the property, the trees, the familiar flagpole, and the shed, slowly steering his head from one side to the other. He looked out the open car door, "Now what?"

Jen giggled at Mitch's comment, identical to his son's. *They are so alike, right down to their thoughts.*

"Ti's getting the wheelchair."

"Here we are." Ti arrived as escort. "Let's get you in."

"Then what?" Mitch wondered aloud.

"Who knows? We're taking it one minute at a time." They'd gotten used to living day to day, hour to hour, and finally, minute to minute.

Drawing Mitch to the edge of the seat, they gently spilled him out of the car and poured him into the wheelchair. They headed for the front porch. Only eight steps to the first landing and seven more to the top. Ti backed the chair to the first step and stood behind it.

"Mitch, smell that mountain air. Take it all in." Jen inhaled. He smiled widely and breathed consciously.

"I'll pull. You push from the bottom once it's lifted." Ti braced his foot on the base of the chair.

Ti and Jen executed their heave-ho plan all the way to the top, excited to reach the crest. Through the doorway and only twenty more feet away, his plaid couch waited.

They scurried into the family room. The joy that spread through Ti would have given the toughest muscle guy goose-bumps. He needed that moment. *We made it.*

Mitch squirmed to get as comfortable as he could. His dogs licked his hands and wagged their tails.

"Would you like some water, a shake, a few crackers... anything?" Jen asked. He accepted tea and warm oatmeal. Mitch looked around like a prisoner released—as if the room was filled with rainbows, halos and other signs of promise from God.

He patted his dogs and spread the afghan over his legs. "It's amazing to be home." He slipped placidly into sleep, and remained that way.

He barely moved. His kids stayed with him, going to the bathroom or kitchen in shifts. They roused him to take his medication. He seemed peaceful, but not aware. He just slept.

Ti and Jen planned to sleep on the opposite couch so they could stay nearby. Despite feeling exhaustion from their emotional homecoming, they could not sleep. When morning dawned, Ti fed the dogs while Jen read by Mitch's side. Later, Jen toasted bagels while Ti watched the news.

Weathering a foggy mist of unease, they awaited the arrival of a woman from hospice. Jen had spoken to Julia on Tuesday before they left. "Tomorrow we're getting him discharged from the care facility. He asked us to bring him home and doesn't expect to go back."

"What will you do after Easter week?" the hospice nurse had asked.

"I..." Jen had no insight.

"We should meet first thing Thursday morning to get Mitch evaluated and into the program," Julia had suggested. "This way he will have support over the holiday weekend. What's the address?"

At 9:15, a white sedan pulled up the driveway. A drizzle of relief rained over the room as a short, stout woman entered, commenting on the beauty of the cabin and the appeal of the surroundings.

"No wonder Mitch asked to come home," Julia said.

Julia began interviewing Ti and Jen. They discussed Mitch's history, his recent lack of activity, medications, and needs. Then she physically evaluated Mitch. As she performed the exam, she introduced herself to him and described what she saw aloud. Drowsy Mitch obliged like the cooperative patient he always was.

"I'll be sure to have a hospital bed delivered this afternoon. You'll want a tank of oxygen on hand." Julia scribbled more notes.

As they spoke, Jen's eyes swelled with giant gumdrop tears. They rolled down her cheeks as she choked on her words. "We didn't get him here soon enough. He's been asleep since two hours after we arrived."

Jen had been muttering something similar all morning. Mitch's last wish had been to spend time at his home with the ones he loved. They had grand plans to visit, talk, help, comfort, and grant his every whim during and beyond Holy Week—an exceptional time. They would share Easter dinner even if it meant only a teaspoon of soft, scalloped potatoes. She'd make his favorite dish anyway.

But that wasn't happening.

There wasn't anything they could offer him. Their hearts ached; their souls burned for contact before there was no more time.

"He's barely conscious." Jen sobbed, her chest heaving as she gasped for air, crying, angry, and confused.

Tears fell on Ti's face as he cupped her hands in his. "Jen..."

Julia beseeched them. "Jen, Ti, listen to me. When a patient is going through the acceptance of their soon-to-be passing, they often need or want one more thing very badly. Have you heard stories about people who hang on until a particular loved one arrives to be with them?"

Jen nodded. Ti sniffed.

"Good. You've heard those stories because it's quite common. Mitch wanted to be home. Once home, his condition would likely have declined at the same pace, regardless of which day you arrived."

"Trust me." Julia looked at Jen and touched her shoulder. "You've done everything you could. You made proper arrangements to ensure his comfort, which is a gift in itself. Comfort is extremely important at this time. You made good decisions about what you thought was best—all from your heart. You should have no regrets."

Ti cleared his throat. "Those two days we ran around organizing his trip, getting important medicine, learning how to treat him, and arranging for Julia's help, was all so we could provide the right care on our own."

"But..." Jen swallowed hard, knowing they hadn't a clue about such delicate care prior. She remembered Dr. Leslie's private counsel.

Ti paused to take a breath and to make his point, "I repeat... the right care... *on our own*... that was critical."

"Yes," Jen acquiesced, her head whirling.

"And Dad got to absorb a steady run of affection from so many loved ones, including last rights from the Bishop. That was important for both him and our friends. I wouldn't have denied either of them that." Beneath his pain, Ti felt secure in their choices.

Jen dried her eyes with the cuff of her sleeve and put her chin up. They continued to discuss Mitch's care and preparation for what might come.

"Mitch has healthy circulation and a strong heart." Julia nodded, suggesting he still had significant time to be with them. She reviewed the importance of the medication schedule. “The best thing you can do now is keep him away from discomfort.”

Julia ordered liquid morphine and other unfamiliar drugs. She handed Jen a folder with brochures and highlighted the contact numbers. “I’ll arrange for an aide to visit. I’ll see if she can start tomorrow.” She gave them all the realistic reassurances she could, and then she left.

Before lunch, Mitch’s sister Colleen stopped in carrying groceries. “Let’s put these in the fridge.”

“Would you like some tea?” Jen filled the teapot. They sat at the table.

“I hate to say this, but you two need to think about funeral preparations. I want you to have time to consider every aspect before you find yourselves in the throes of it.”

“All Dad spoke about was making sure we don’t deny anyone he loves the chance to say goodbye.” Ti picked at his fingernails. “He asked for two services: one for his mountain family and one for his work family.”

Jen sighed. “Otherwise, we’ve hardly considered it. We were counting on having a whole week to understand Mitch’s wishes.”

Ti and Jen thanked her, saw her out and went back to the couch.

“Mitch, remember our picnic? I could get the yellow-checkered quilt and put a shake in the bucket.” Jen’s voice quivered.

“Hey, I’ll go get the scaffold and we can start that roof work you’ve been moaning about,” Ti said.

They stared at Mitch, sleeping.

“Did I tell you about the time I nailed my foot to the roof?” Ti asked.

“Nope.” She looked up at him.

“Yeah, I was laying a new roof. It was pitched, so I was standing at an angle. I’d put the nail gun down between my feet as I placed the next section. Somehow, my depth perception got off. As I went to put the gun down, the tip hit my foot. Since my finger was still on the trigger, it fired. The nail shot through my sneaker and caught my big toe. I was literally nailed to the roof.”

“Oh my!” She cringed. “For real?”

“Yup.”

They smiled at each other as they sat in Mitch’s famous room speaking about the house, building, and what project they might tackle next.

Ti meticulously followed Mitch's medication schedule. Jen encouraged him to sip some tea and have some pudding.

"Where do you want this?" The deliveryman brought the hospital bed into the house. A second man carried oxygen tanks.

"Here in the family room. We want him to be able to see the TV and the yard." Ti led the way.

"Yes, this is good. He'll love being in here with all of us." Jen nudged the wheel and locked it.

The men explained how everything worked. Jen and Ti made the bed. Using the lower blanket, they scooched Mitch up into a good position, then watched him rest. The dogs sniffed at the bed and looked up at their master. Showing their affection, they licked any time a stray limb hung over the side. Not one attempted to climb on the bed. Champ stared from their favorite couch seat, longing to be in Mitch's lap. Chase paced, whining for his human. Daisy kept her head down. Chip did not leave the carpet at the foot of this new furniture.

That evening, Lenny and Camille visited. Lenny sat on the floor. He pet the dogs and called them each by name, confusing the two chocolates as he often did. Chase nudged him over on his back, while Chip and Daisy licked his face. He laughed, prevented from getting up until the dogs had finished their tickle attack.

Ti made coffee. Mitch listened while Lenny spoke to Ti about the latest movie he'd seen, new electronics, and stories about the locals. "Did you hear about the two kids who drove a car out on the lake ice last winter? They got halfway across and fell through!"

"Oh my gosh." Jen waited for more of the story.

"Yeah, they got out okay. Crazy kids." Camille shook her head.

Silently, both Mitch and Ti smiled, knowing that each of them at one point in their youth would have done something just as foolish.

Camille spoke about Mitch and Ti building their log house, reminding Mitch of the many good things he had accomplished.

"Mitch," Camille insisted, "no one can build a home like you. If it were possible, we'd never live in anything but an M-&-m-built house."

"True," Lenny added. "Our cabin's as solid as they come."

They shared memories, including a few Jen hadn't heard before.

"Remember the time we were walking the dogs when those bikers passed? Some gravel got in Daisy's eyes, and she howled. Chase went nuts. He was so protective." Camille forced a grin.

Mitch enjoyed the stories, which touched his spirit like an old favorite melody. They snickered over construction mishaps and Mitch's hot sauce meltdown at the Chinese restaurant. Picturing Mitch's beet-red face, Lenny laughed so hard he cried. The memory was a good outlet for emotions he preferred not to show. As the minutes passed, they basked in the glow of love that shone through their long-standing friendship.

Cherished like family, Lenny and Camille supported Ti and Jen with genuine sympathy and unconditional love. Lenny offered to help break the boat out when the time came. He wanted to be there for Ti, knowing there would be a huge void in his father-son routines each season at the cabin. Lenny was the closest thing Ti would have to a father, and not having children of his own, he considered Ti a son.

Camille hugged them both holding back tears as she darted out the door. Lenny turned to Ti, shook his hand, and patted his arm with compassion. Deeply moved, he left feeling great pain and sadness.

CHAPTER 31

Ti and Jen hugged tightly before assuming positions of careful watch for the night. Jen spread a blanket over the couch cushions. Ti opened the window closest to Mitch. “There you go, Dad. Okay, time for medicine.”

Throughout the night, they kept one eye and one ear on their sleeping father. Finally, around 4:00 a.m., they drifted into a calm slumber, confident their doggie timers would wake them.

Suddenly, the peaceful silence was broken. “So what’s a person gotta do to get a decent cup of coffee around here?” Mitch said in a strong voice, sitting up straight. Ti jumped back to consciousness. The clock read 6:35.

Jen blinked. “Hey, look at you!”

Ti ran into the kitchen, and hit the brewer’s ON button. “Coffee in three,” he said, reentering the room.

Mitch looked around. “Hey, when did we get this gadget?” He swept his hand from left to right across the bed.

“They brought it yesterday. You were pretty out of it,” Ti said.

“I was? Hmm.”

“Yeah, we met a nice nurse who’s helping us with the medical details. She sent this stuff; it should help you,” Jen said.

Ti supported Mitch as he slid off the bed and moved to the couch.

Jen scurried over and sat beside him. “Just look at you,” she repeated with such glee she almost exploded.

“Hey, look at you,” he retorted, not sure what all the fuss was about.

She cleared her throat. “I’m just happy to see you awake, to talk and visit, that’s all.” *The nurse was right; we’re not too late!* A bit confused, she felt a bizarre elation next to him at that moment—so strange, but so good. *How could there be even a hint of joy in any of this?*

"Coffee's ready." Ti came in from the kitchen, holding Mitch's mug. He, too, was pleased and proud to offer something, anything, to his father. Jen beamed as Mitch took the cup and breathed in the coffee-scented steam.

Taking a sip, Mitch's taste buds danced to the flavor's melody. Champ jumped on the couch, laying his head and one paw across his master's thigh. Mitch pet the silky fur and looked around. *I'm so happy to be in my old chair, surrounded by my family, my television, and the countryside.* Taking it in, his eyes settled on his kids. Mitch realized that they needed time with him and needed to know he was okay in whatever way he could be. "What are we doing for Easter, Jen?"

"Colleen came by. She brought groceries and a ham."

"That's nice."

Jen puffed up her chest. "And I'm going to make your scalloped potatoes. You'll even have some because they'll be delicious." She couldn't wait to do that for him. His famous scalloped potato recipe was an Easter essential.

"Jen, would you bring the recipe book to me?"

"Sure." She dashed to the kitchen, opened the drawer, and grabbed the blue binder. Mitch had food-stained scraps of paper stored throughout the cabinets for years. Last winter, Jen had collected and retyped each one to create his very own cookbook. Enthused even more than when he'd opened the box last Christmas, Jen offered it to him.

Mitch accepted the binder. He thumbed through it, not really seeing the contents, just touching it and thinking about the recipes it contained.

She watched him. When he was ready, she helped him find the page.

"Do you have all the ingredients? No substituting or altering like you normally do. I know how you cook, Jennifer." He looked up with a smirk.

"Nope, no changes this time. Promise," she said.

"Bake it covered for an hour, then another fifteen minutes uncovered, you got it?" He spent a few minutes talking about the details. He seemed to want to teach it to her.

Delighted, Jen ate up his attention in ladle-sized portions. She took his advice to heart. "I'm going to cook it exactly as you would."

Ti returned after a shower, consuming his second cup of coffee.

"Hey, can you freshen this up for me?" Mitch held up his mug.

"Certainly."

"Are you hungry?" Jen asked.

"Uh, yes, I am."

"What would you like? How about a nice soft-boiled egg?"

"Mmmm, yeah, that sounds good... so, make it two." Mitch held up a pair of skinny fingers that formed a wilted V-shape.

Jen ran to the kitchen. *The eggs have to be perfect, now more than ever.* As an old dog, there were no new tricks when it came to Mitch's eggs. He'd practiced for years and had perfected his own technique.

Ti called to Jen. "Hey, don't forget, five-fifty."

All three recited it together, "Five-fifty," remembering the first time Mitch accepted egg help. He had sat in his red-and-black-checkered flannel with Champ on his lap, ordering them around.

"Remember Jen," he'd yelled, "it's not a six-minute egg; it's a five-minute-fifty-second egg. Preset the timer. Not a second can be off."

"Okay."

"Don't forget to run them under warm water so they won't crack... And, when they're done, run cool water over them to stop the cooking."

"Uh," Ti had said, "I think we can handle a few soft-boiled eggs."

"And lots of black pepper, please," Mitch had added.

"Got it," Jen said, amused by his devotion to his method.

Ti chuckled about that day, mere months ago. *Where are his pushy comments now?*

As Jen followed his guidelines, opposing feelings coursed through her veins: thrill to help, but sad too. *What would we be annoyed about today, if Mitch were well enough to tease and pester us? He'd probably be elbowing me away from the stove, hogging the kitchen, smirking at me.*

Meanwhile, Ti sat in the family room near Mitch, each of them in their place. When they'd rebuilt the house, the two bachelors had designed every aspect to be just right, including the practical layout of the family room. A coffee table centered the wall, opposite a large television. Mitch's couch was on the right, with easy access to the kitchen. Ti's matching couch was on the left, near the back deck, so he could tend to the dogs.

Ti sat in his seat near his father, sipping coffee. He thought about all they'd done together and how much he wanted this week to be good for them. Instead of chatting, he obeyed their "man-rule" and enjoyed the moment. "Men," Ti would say, "don't need to talk to know what the other thinks or feels. Just like fishing, it's all in the being."

Jen returned and handed Mitch a smooshed, seasoned egg in a bowl.

"Oh boy, that looks delicious," Mitch said, taking it as ardently as Champ when offered a dog biscuit.

"Hey," he frowned. "This doesn't look like two eggs."

"Yeah, yeah," she said. "I have the other one ready for you if you are able to finish. Usually lately, you don't finish the first one."

"Hmm, you're right. How come you're so smart?" He lifted a shaky fork to his quivering lips.

"Do... you... want some... a little... help?" Jen asked, feeling awkward about offering help to what was once such a sturdy and determined man. He did not like needing help, nor accepting it. But lately, he had relinquished to some assistance from Jen. Ti did not dare—that would have been too much for their strained emotions.

"No, I think I can do it myself." It took a little bit longer, but he managed. He held out the bowl with a soft smile and a bit of yolk on his lower lip, ready for egg number two.

Jen brought it over before Mitch could sit a second long enough to decide he might not want it. As he nibbled, they sat quietly for a moment to consider how much these little things would forever mean to them.

"There's a nurse's aide coming to see you this morning," Ti said. "She's going to help you freshen up."

"Oh?" Mitch recalled little of yesterday's interview.

"Yeah, we'll take turns getting ready." Ti turned to Jen, "Your turn."

She stared. She looked to Mitch, and then glanced up the stairs where her shower was waiting. She looked back. As interested in the tub as Toby, the expression on her face was catlike, as if she would dig her nails into the carpet to stay put.

"He'll be fine. Go quickly," Ti coaxed. Grabbing both of her hands in his, he pulled her to her feet and spun her toward the room's archway.

Jen gave Mitch an extra-big hug and ran up the stairs, only to return seven minutes later, showered, with fresh attire, and a wet ponytail. Ti smiled. *This is the girl who needs an hour's notice to go anywhere?*

"If we put the feed out on the large rock, over there behind the shed," Mitch pointed, "the deer will visit but leave Jen's garden alone." He alternated between conversing and looking at the news, the dogs, the yard, and the knots in the wooden log walls, which he knew by heart.

"Ti, does the screen door still squeak? When do you think we can fix it?" He studied his kids when they wouldn't notice. He memorized their expressions, their voices, their movements. He spoke to them about normal everyday stuff. A few hours passed as they visited, shared, appreciated, and loved. The time was incredibly good for them. Mitch smiled. *Ah, this morning is a gift, wrapped in brightly decorated paper and shiny bows. It's everything I'd wanted in coming home.*

As 10:00 approached, Jen peered out the door for Mitch's guest. Not sure exactly why, they looked forward to meeting her. When the doorbell rang, Ti herded the barking quartet into the basement. Jen welcomed the young, petite nurse's aide into their home. She introduced herself as Emily and admired the log cabin. Wearing jeans and a purple hoodie, she was fair and plain, and cute as a button. She walked beside Jen to the family room, where she found Mitch in his recliner. Jen sat next to Mitch, proud to make the introduction. Ti felt pride in showing off his hero too.

"It's very nice to meet you, Mr. Conner." She touched his hand.

"Oh, Mitch, please."

"Who's causing all that yelping and scratching?" Emily asked.

"Those are Mitch's four babies, who are not so shy." Ti raised his brow.

"That's okay. I would love to meet Mitch's family."

Ti opened the door. The dogs dashed into the living quarters to greet Emily. She allowed them to lick her hands and sniff her clothes.

"Animals are little miracles," she said. Evident in the first few minutes, Emily had love and compassion for all living things. They admired her ability to dispense warmth, and the easiness she brought into what otherwise might have been an awkward room.

"What are their names?" She laughed as Daisy nudged her arm. "And how old are you guys?

"That's Daisy, my only girl. She's five," Mitch said in a sound voice. "The black one is Chase; he's my oldest at eight. The yellow one is Champ, who's seven. He's my cuddle buddy and has the biggest appetite you've ever seen. Once, he devoured a twelve-pound bag of dog food before I found him in the pantry. Boy, was his tummy bloated!"

Emily chuckled.

"And this is Chip, my youngest, at four," he finished, pointing with a half-bent, half-raised arm.

Effortlessly, Emily spoke to Mitch about his home and encouraged his bragging about how he and his son had built it together, both times. "It's just beautiful." She looked around. "So, Mitch, what can I help you with this morning? Would you like to clean up? Can I prepare anything for you? What would be good?"

Jen retrieved the basin from the care center containing his personal effects. They discussed a sponge bath and fresh clothes.

Mitch spoke up. "I think I'd like a bath... a... a real bath."

"A bath?" Jen sounded a bit apprehensive.

"If you're up for it, I'll help Emily get you in and out of the tub," Ti said, happy Mitch had an interest.

"Of course, that would be fine." Emily spoke with a reassuring nod. Secure and ready, she knew giving him such simple pleasures would leave Ti and Jen with a lasting sense of tranquility.

Mitch sat for a moment.

He thought about how he appreciated his time soaking in his tub, and how Jen had bought him bath salts, bubbles, and a pillow. He remembered Ti teasing him about his long, warm baths, especially how he came out of the room sighing with ecstasy.

After two minutes he said, "Yes, I'd really like a bath."

Without hesitation, the pint-sized aide helped him into an old favorite activity—one he'd missed over the past six weeks. Emily's skill in maneuvering the weakened Mitch impressed Ti and Jen. Transporting him was like moving a hundred and sixty pounds of floppy cooked noodles.

Mitch went into the tub. The warm water caressed his stiff muscles and the bubbles tickled his skin. Emily conversed pleasantly with Mitch. Ti could hear them talk as he hovered nearby to help just in case.

"That was so great!" he told them in his old blissful tone.

Ti delighted at Mitch enjoying his surroundings and things that were dear to him. He witnessed the simple joy something like a cup of coffee and a bath had given him.

Jen was proud of Mitch for attempting the tub. She recognized how precious these moments together enjoying simple comforts could be. She remembered Mitch's toast that beautiful day in the garage—decorated with pinecones and daisies.

"Royal castles are built from bricks; majestic mansions are constructed with sticks. Everyday moments build a lifetime of love, friendship, and cherished memories. Find value in the little things. Don't forget what matters, what is real, and what is you."

It was never more true than at that moment.

They said goodbye to their new acquaintance. "See you tomorrow."

Mitch enjoyed a fabulous morning. He had pudding, gelatin, and half of a banana shake. Two of his sisters stopped in to see their brother and offer Ti and Jen assistance should they need it. Each visit brought amity and passed what could have been difficult time. The air remained light and more in tune with friendship and support than fear and gloom.

"Ti, each minute today is a blessing," Jen said, "...a memory we'll tuck deep into our hearts forever."

"I know... probably one of my final M-&-m's." Ti sighed. "I can't tell if I'm thrilled or devastated because I'm both."

"I know. I'm so confused." Jen looked upward, as if understanding existed beyond the ceiling.

Ti followed the medicine schedule. Jen offered snacks or hugs and handholding whenever she could without smothering Mitch even though she wanted to smother him under an airtight dome of affection.

Nighttime fell. Everyone relaxed. For two days, Chase had been fighting a stomach flu, but that night he seemed to worsen. Champ joined in, exhibiting the same symptoms. The two Labs kept poor Ti up a bit more than he would have liked. But Ti was determined to care for all the members of his family, in whatever way they needed, throughout this ordeal. *I wonder if the older dogs are not sick from a virus at all. I bet grief's upsetting their tummies.* Ti was certain they just knew.

"It's okay, boy. I'm here," Ti whispered.

With closed eyes, Mitch lay listening as Ti spoke to Champ. In his mind, he saw Ti stroking the yellow fur, caring for his dog. *My pups are in the best hands possible.*

Mitch prayed that night, as always, pleased that he could still rhyme.

> Dear Lord, thank you for giving me the best family anyone could ever ask for, and the gift of time with them, no matter how brief.
> Support my amazing kids; keep their hearts full of love and faith to deal with their grief.
> This is what I pray.

He added, "I miss you, Mandy. I hope you are there to greet me. I'm sad to leave them, but I know I will join you soon. Once we are united, my love, we can guide Ti, Jen and Nate together. I pray you will help me do this with grace."

Mitch swore he saw her eyes, just her eyes, in a bit of pale-yellow light as he drifted out of consciousness.

CHAPTER 32

Ti opened the back door to witness a sunrise, vivid in shades of rose, coral, and lava. As the dogs wandered out, he took a deep breath and, for the first time in a long time, Ti spoke to his mother. "Mom, I hope you're watching over the best man this earth has ever seen. I really don't want to let him go... Now I know how he felt all those years ago. I finally understand what you two went through." As he turned around, Ti thought he noticed a faint streak of light skyrocket across the heavens.

Mitch started his day with a cup of coffee. He sniffed the aroma and savored the rich, familiar scent. Jen sat beside him, sharing a few hints from one of her homemade crossword puzzles. He smiled, enjoying her clever clues, but had a limited attention span. After a few laughs, Jen got up to get Mitch some tapioca from the kitchen.

"Ti," he called in a whisper.

"Yeah, Dad," Ti sat forward to look at Mitch.

"Take care of her and love her like I did your mother. She's another gem," he said in a raspy, sincere voice.

"I know, Dad." A lump formed in Ti's throat.

A short time later, Mitch's aide skipped up the steps. Her ponytail bounced all the way up, still swaying as she rang the doorbell. The dogs greeted her. She visited with Mitch, engaging him in more conversation: talk of his wife, his dogs, his kids, his work, and his home—things for which he was most proud.

Mitch spoke in a soft but excited tone. "Oh, Mandy was beautiful. There is a photo on my dresser. Ti can show you."

"I'll be sure to take a look. I bet she felt lucky to be with you."

“Constructing the log cabin was a great adventure.” Mitch went on to tell a few M-&-m building tales.

“Emily, you should have seen their wedding. The place never looked better. Jen decorated the porch with silk sunflowers and daisies.”

“Oh, I love daisies too.”

Mitch chuckled. “Jen stuck those flowers everywhere. She lined the wall ledge around the entire garage. I remember thinking *‘how simple, but exquisite.’* Perfect to represent them.”

“Sounds wonderful.”

“Yes, everyone enjoyed it—one of my happiest days ever.”

Champ let out a snort. “I remember getting Champ. We drove three hours to the breeder. He was the one that piled on top of all the other puppies in the pen. His father was huge. Champ inherited his appetite.”

Mitch shared his stories one by one, until it was time for Emily to go.

Ti felt good about Mitch’s ability to brag, even now. He got up to take a shower. Jen hugged him as he passed, then reached for her book.

Mitch squirmed; Champ jumped down to the floor. He patted the couch next to him. Jen sat. Mitch took her hand, tapped it softly and sat back. He touched the ring on her finger. The memory of the day he gave it to Mandy flooded his consciousness, as a rolling wave fills a hole in the sand. Light breezes had sailed through the air on that picture-perfect day. They walked along the creek where they’d swum as children. Although he’d purchased the ring two weeks prior, he hadn’t taken custody of it until that morning. Once in his possession, he knew he wouldn’t be able to keep it from her. He smiled at how he’d almost knelt down right in the parking lot.

Jen watched him, his head back and eyes closed, wondering what his mellow smile meant.

Mitch breathed softly as his daydream continued. Happy, young, inspired by a walk in the sunshine, his special girl valued the natural wonders around them. As they strolled along the path by the creek, Mandy pointed to the old oak that had once held the Tarzan rope. Mitch took hold of her outstretched arm and swung her around to face him. Along the scenic path filled with spring blossoms, he knelt down and opened the pretty, velvet box.

"Mandy, you are an angel on earth and I would be honored if you and I could share every day: each morning filled with hope, and each evening filled with reminiscing." Mitch spoke from his heart.

Her lips parted. "Yes! Oh, Mitch, yes forever!"

A spunky Mandy had pulled him to his feet and almost toppled them both to the ground. She kissed him with smiling lips. He could feel her tender presence—perhaps even stronger now. Mitch sat feeling no discomfort, only the soft, warm blanket of her love.

After a few quiet moments, he turned toward Jen. "Jen, take care of Ti. He's a handful, but he's a good man."

"I know. I adore that son of yours. I love him with all my heart." She sucked in a breath. Their eyes met and she grinned at him. "You created him; you know him best."

"Despite all the mischief, he was a good kid. He's grown to be a man of honor, and I couldn't be prouder. Well, he's a little spoiled maybe."

"Part champ, part scamp," she teased, letting out a gurgled giggle. She cleared her throat. "Ti is special. I love all of him. He's my hero."

"Help him with Nate. He's not used to being the adult; he's played the role of son all these years." Mitch paused and then sighed. "Nate is wonderful; you did a good job with him. He's going to make you proud."

Jen swallowed, hanging on each precious word.

Mitch sighed again. "I will miss him too. Having a grandson, even for a short time, was incredible beyond words. I remembered so much about Ti growing up as I relived similar times with Nate. Nate will always be my bike-riding, riddle-telling little buddy." Mitch paused as tears swelled in his eyes. He leaned his head back again.

Jen's tears overflowed, gliding down her cheeks while she held back her urge to sob.

"Jen, you were the daughter I'd always wanted, and I know you will take good care of my son." He stroked the back of her hand.

"I love you all more than I can say," she squeaked.

"I know, sweetheart," he whispered, letting her understand his inner feelings before he left. They sat quietly, holding each other's hands for a few more minutes.

When Ti returned, Mitch reminded him that he should check the furnace and oil tanks regularly. "Never let the tank get below one quarter."

"Right, Dad." Ti nodded.

"The water filters will need to be changed come May."

"Thanks, Dad," Ti said several times, and they both knew he was not referring to Mitch's reminders. They relished their time together.

◆ ◆ ◆ ◆

Another night passed. Dawn glowed upon Easer Sunday—a day which represents glory and spring and resurrection. The Conners barely noticed; it seemed like any Sunday, or any day for that matter.

Mitch did not have the flare he'd possessed only hours prior. Even though it was a holiday, Emily came and spent time helping Mitch freshen up. Emily and Mitch spoke about upcoming town events, her daughter, animals they'd owned over the years and other easy-flowing topics.

Mitch appreciated her visit but was a little sleepier as he began to slip further toward malady. Like thirsty camels, his kids drank up the last few days while his glow reflected his old self. But the time felt unmercifully short. They wanted weeks and months of it.

After lunch, Mitch became lethargic and, by afternoon, he moaned and squirmed uncomfortably. Jen read by his side.

Ti called her to the kitchen to start dinner. He laid the cookbook on the counter and pulled the ham out. "It was nice of my aunt to get this." The Mitches loved dinners that simmered for hours, filling the house with delicious aromas. "Maybe Dad will smell it and find more energy."

"Do you think so?"

"I know you want to make his favorite part, so you peel the potatoes while I chop the onions."

"But..."

"No but. I'll stand here to keep an eye on him."

"Do we have to cook? It's not Easter without all of us," she whined.

"He'd want us to go on as normal. And he still may want some of those potatoes." Ti nudged the sack toward her.

Jen stared at him.

"C'mon," he said.

They put the famed casserole in the oven and set the timer. The scent of heating ham filled the air. They hugged, sad to see Mitch so sleepy. Jen sighed. *God, please, let him want some of those potatoes or even a jellybean—anything that might give him a taste of our family traditions.*

Jen read two pages, and then took a break to sort through photographs. She collected several pictures that included Mitch or something special about him. Although she cried at times, the memories felt good.

Mitch's discomfort increased. He developed a cough, choking on thick fluid, which often needed to be expelled. The two sat steadfast by his side.

In the quiet of one moment, Ti uttered, "I love you, Dad."

"Good, then, don't let me hurt," the senior Mitch responded in a hoarse, shaky voice.

Ti snorted, half laughing, half crying. He knew he and his father had tough exteriors. They had to be rough and tough and hard, and although the reply wasn't what Ti expected in that difficult moment, it was more precious than the standard reply.

It was Mitch.

Between the words, between the years of scrapes and mishaps, there was a lifetime of "I-love-you-too's." All the bricks of their experiences and the sticks of their memories had built them an estate filled with love.

Mitch was still treating Ti "like a man" with all he had left.

As the evening proceeded, Mitch calmed. His breathing changed, becoming more labored, hindered by the phlegm. Ti wished to share an Easter meal with his father one more time. Now symbolic, his favorite ham and those cheesy potatoes, like many Mitch-things, would forever have meaning. Alas, it was not in God's plan that night.

Ti's stomach growled. He coaxed his wife into having some late night dinner. He knew Mitch wanted them to forge ahead.

Or so he thought.

Sitting with an uncomfortable stomach, Jen pushed some green beans around her plate with her fork. Ti had not swallowed two mouthfuls of ham when Mitch needed them. They both rushed to his side. Ti grabbed his hand; Jen grabbed Ti's.

A menacing bolt of fear shot through the room.

Mitch, born at Christmastime, seemed ready to join Christ on Easter through some strange spiritual corollary. He gagged, turned pale, and gasped for breath as his eyes rolled back.

"We love you, Dad."

"You'll always be with us."

Terrified, they wept as he stopped breathing; fear and grief consumed them. Ti nodded to Jen in a telepathic statement. *This could be the end of his long, hard journey.*

Mitch stalled for approximately fifteen seconds, and then a deep breath caught. He breathed, still with them. Jen exhaled. Ti held her. The reality that their time with human-Mitch was escaping like the last grains of sand falling through an hourglass stung them to their cores.

They sat with their patriarch, holding his hands. Mitch began to experience the symptoms again. Jen called the hospice number.

"Julia, I... he... um... Mitch is... gagging... gasping... we... what do we do?"

"Sounds like a seizure. I'll stop by," the kindhearted nurse said.

"No, Julia, you're with family; it's a holiday."

"Really, it's okay. I'll be there shortly."

Jen felt relief. She held Mitch's pale hand. She stroked it as she stared straight at the front door. *The nurse is going to come and make it all right. She will know what to do.* Her heart was breaking. As she glanced toward Ti, it shattered. Ti was sitting on the couch holding his head in his hands.

Almost an hour passed as Jen sat on the wooden stool next to Mitch's bed, looking for signs of light coming up the driveway.

Her mind and emotions swirled. *What does this mean? Is he really leaving us? Already? What should we do?*

They were not supposed to prolong his time with them. He'd made that clear. Dr. Leslie had explained. They had agreed. Yet Jen was frightened.

Ti seemed better able to comprehend what was happening, but he suffered to see his father endure any of it. "God... *please,*" he begged.

Until recently, they'd all believed Mitch could recover on his new drug and enjoy a few more years. Ti knew that possibility had been gone for at least a week, and that his father would soon leave them. He knew Mitch had spent the last few years hoping his son would find someone special to build a life with—especially in the never-to-be-realized, miniscule chance that something happened to him. So Ti would not be alone.

And he wasn't.

Ti remembered joking about Mitch's aging: what it would be like when he was ninety, and what kind of home Ti would put him in so he could go on building and boating without any inconvenience. It had all been in jest, although he wished it were real so they could have more time.

This is not fair; it's way too soon!

Mitch spent his last healthy year in sheer delight that the couple had found each other, and impressed with how they got along. They enjoyed both work and play, similar to what he and Ti experienced as a father-and-son team. Mitch felt grateful for Jen and Nate. Jen made a big difference in their everyday lives and in taking care of their family. Nate looked up to Mitch, mimicked him, and learned from him. Mitch possessed even more vitality since they'd come along. It was a marriage for them all—a dream come true for each of them in their own way.

Ti and Jen waited for Julia. They were not sure how her presence would make it better, but it had to be better. When she drove up and entered the house, Julia went to Mitch, checked his pulse, and then walked to the counter where they kept the medication. She spoke to Ti and Jen, explaining things they could not understand. In a comforting tone, she reviewed how they should handle different symptoms. Sympathetic to their despair, Julia visited that night more for the two of them than for Mitch. By answering their questions, she did all she could. Then Julia left.

Feeling helpless on their own again, they knew their role. The most important thing now was for Mitch to pass on with dignity in his own home, on his own terms, with his own possessions and loved ones all around him. Their responsibility was hard, but it was all they were able to give him. And they wanted to give him anything they could.

Somewhere deep inside they knew they could do it; they could be strong for him, talk to him, keep him calm and comfortable. Ti spoke to Mitch about old times. Jen read her book and told Mitch what was happening with the characters. They prepared for "couch-time," which had replaced "bed-time," and tucked themselves in with the television on and

Jen's book on the table. They rested, keeping one eye and one ear open for any sign of distress.

Easter Monday arrived with pink light and gray skies. Ti made coffee, hoping for another surprise—hoping that his dad might join them, at least more wholly than he had last evening.

Mitch woke, although his experience was only pleasant for a few hours.

"Ti, can you help me rotate?"

"Of course, Dad. How?"

"I don't know. I have pain, but I can't figure out exactly where."

Mitch tried the bed, the couch, and then the wheel chair. He sat by the back door and looked upon his yard as the dogs walked out on the deck. For ten minutes, he soaked in his favorite scenery.

"I'm sorry, Ti. The chair's not working either. I can't seem to avoid this pain." He shifted his weight to one side. "Let's try the bed again." He fussed and wriggled with soft moans.

By lunchtime, Mitch again began sputtering-up dark fluid. Taking turns, they held cups and cleaned him up. Ti longed to see him relax with a reprieve from the difficult process. *Just a few days ago we'd yearned to see him wake up*. Ti exhaled at the utter irony of the whole affair. Nothing was certain. Nothing was clear. He didn't know which way to pray, or what to hope for anymore.

Mitch's constant agitation distressed Ti, who maintained the medication schedule, bringing each remedy to his father as directed. Not so tough now, Ti gently, humbly served his idol, as his father had served him all those years. He dripped the medicine into his mouth. The drug gave relief, carrying Mitch into a deep state of lassitude.

Ti articulated each word. "This one is different, Dad. Lift up your tongue, don't stick it out, okay?"

Frail, adorable, little Mitch listened like a trooper. Ti dropped the liquid under his tongue as tears ran down his face and splashed on Mitch's bed.

"You are the absolute best patient." Jen admired Mitch even more.

He may have been stubborn, precise, proud, and at times prodigal, but the man took every shot, every poke, every ounce of the disastrous experience with poise and cooperation.

He had always been, was still, and forever would be a champion.

While Mitch dozed, drug-dazed, Ti and Jen watched a movie. Often, one or the other would wipe Mitch's face or stroke his hand. Mitch squirmed in his sleep, with intermittent whimpers, groans, and coughs. Jen shared the next chapter of her book with him. Ti and Jen experienced moments of easiness, glad they could give their father his last wish. They also endured hours of gut-wrenching horror observing his painful departure.

Later that afternoon, Ti and Jen expected a visit from Rose and Brock, who had been some of their most valued supporters and two of the kindest people on earth. Brock had brought communion to Mitch every week. Rose had given them a strong shoulder to lean on and pep talks that saturated them with understanding, tenderness, and faith. A gentle, soothing woman, she gave credit to God in the world.

Twice during long hospital weeks, they'd insisted Ti and Jen take a break, volunteering to keep Mitch company. Ti refused to leave Mitch alone after work, and he did not trust just anyone with the care of his father.

After their Easter celebration, Rose and Brock arranged a trip to bring them dress clothes and shoes. The Conners kept no formal clothing at the cabin. Ti and Jen had focused so keenly on getting Mitch home for their week together, they had not prepared for an "end" possibility.

When Brock and Rose arrived, they were not uncomfortable amidst the heartbreaking state of affairs.

"Once Mitch woke up, he really enjoyed his time here," Ti said.

"Yeah, he ate and talked and even had a bath." Jen brightened with a momentary gleam in her eyes.

"But last night, we think he had a seizure," Ti said. Jen noted a little apprehension in his normally masculine tone.

"This afternoon, he was restless." She glanced toward Mitch.

"Yeah, we tried moving him in and out of the bed and his chair."

Mitch coughed and moaned.

"We really want... to... make him feel... better," Jen muttered.

"The nurse advised us to increase the pain meds quite a bit."

"We sit with him, talk, and get him anything he's able to ask for."

"But, as of an hour ago he's barely able to speak, so we're not sure what he wants when he calls out." Ti slumped, as if despair weighed across his broad shoulders. He had a burning desire to do more.

With love and sadness, their friends empathized with their horrifying, difficult, and yet profound situation.

Ti and Jen found comfort in their friends' presence. Rose offered kind words that moved them. "Remember, we have the ability to live on through the people we leave behind, through the impact we have had on their lives. Just think about the lives Mitch touched. So many loved him, needed him, trusted him, and relied on him. I want you to remember that Mitch leaves his legacy in countless minds and hearts."

After sharing memories and reassurance, Brock offered communion.

"I don't think Dad can take it," Ti said.

"Well, we can share it on his behalf. Perhaps it will bring us closer in some way." Brock prayed. "Lord, hold our beloved friend and father in Your gentle arms. Caress away his discomfort. Envelop him in Your profound love and care."

"Would you like to pray a decade of the rosary together?" Rose reached for Jen's hand. Jen accepted it and nodded. Hand in hand, they formed a circle around the bed. Ti and Brock lifted Mitch's bony fingers as they started to recite the well-known prayers. Ti's eyes brewed with waves of tears and Jen sobbed steadily. They prayed... and witnessed.

There lay their incredibly special father—suffering, dying, and only moments ago barely able to communicate—now clearly reciting every word of every prayer in the entire series.

They completed the round and thanked God for the blessings He had bestowed upon them.

Ti stuttered.

D-Dear Lord,

Thank you for this time with my father. I will forever be proud of him, and treasure our life stories. Please, I beg you, take care of this man—one of your finest creations. You know how truly special he is...

This is what I pray.

"Amen," Jen said with her head bowed.

Mitch quieted. His gagging halted. His agitation ceased. His face became less distressed. He slept, seeming to feel a sense of peace—the peace they had so desperately wanted for him.

His calm was a little miracle—the only one allowed, as Mitch's mortal health would not be restored. Yet it was a miracle nonetheless.

Relief consumed Ti. Observing his father's suffering was a grueling and severe task. Devoted to staying by his father's side, he would see him through whatever was next, for as long as it took. But he had a terrible time understanding and accepting the anguish Mitch experienced.

Their guests offered final words of guidance and support. Rose and Brock said farewell to their esteemed comrade, wrapped Ti and Jen in deep, loving hugs and left.

Each dog took a spot in the room close to Mitch's bed. Mitch's breathing, no longer labored, turned hoarse, and after an hour, became startlingly loud. Jen had never heard such sounds, despite all the snoring she'd experienced between Ti, Mitch, Nate, and worst of all, Champ.

She sat by Mitch's side with her book but could not focus on the print. She pulled the laptop closer. Photos engulfed her attention, while her heart swelled over the memories each contained. The images captured what Mitch's life was all about. She looked through the pictures of the wedding and wind chime ceremony, of Ti and Mitch putting up the chimney, of the dogs and Mitch lounging on the boat, of Mitch towing Nate on the broken tractor, and one of her and Mitch dancing at a cousin's wedding. As she reviewed them, she felt proud of the stories they told.

What a man.

Those photographs provided a grand testimony to all he believed: hard work, good fun, making the best of each day, and most of all—family. Family was everything to Mitch. There was nothing he wouldn't do for his family. Jen felt his love even then, next to his frail, thin frame. She saw Mitch as she touched his fingers. She saw him with strength and cheerfulness. It was good to reminisce, and she hoped they'd always recall those things when times got tough. She listened to the chilling noise, wondering why it was so different from his other sleeps.

Ti sat beside Chase on the couch. He looked over to his cherished father. He didn't know what to think. He was supposed to be strong, yet he felt vulnerable. He was supposed to carry on, yet he yearned to be a kid again. He wanted his father to bail him out of this trouble too—just like the time he'd left the truck running and it rolled through the neighbor's fence, or the time they broke all those windows with Luke's moped, or the time Frankie's lips got glued together, or the time he got spray paint in every pore on his hands and face. Yes, Ti wanted his father to come to the rescue and make everything okay... one more time.

Ti had good memories, and he knew that each and every good time came to him because of his father. He also knew that each and every difficult time he'd known, his father had seen him through. Although Ti was now a fully-grown thirty-six-year-old, six-foot-one, intelligent, strong definition of a man, he didn't want to be without his beloved Dad.

Ti tried to distract himself. "Jen, you hungry?"

"Nah, but I'm sure you are. How about I warm some leftovers? There's plenty since we never really ate last night." She went to the kitchen.

After only a minute, she reentered the room with her head hung low. "Never mind. Somehow during our eerie evening, we forgot to put most of the food away."

"No!" Ti breathed. He had nothing to look forward to but a decent snack. The days were dark and dismal; the hours passed; they gave service; they assisted; they waited. For Ti, a meal was a time indicator, proving it moved forward. Unfortunately, half of the food was still in the oven. Only the portions visible on the counter had been put away.

He sighed, his nerves shot.

"How about a sandwich? We have ham and rolls." Jen forced a grin.

Keeping the mood light, Ti said, "Well, I guess if my father couldn't have those darned scalloped potatoes, he wouldn't let either of us have them either."

Not sure how to plug along, they half-giggled at the idea. Jen brought two small sandwich plates into the family room. They sat on the couch together. Ti munched on his first roll filled with fresh ham and cheese. Jen left her sandwich on the plate and watched Mitch.

She stared. So much had happened in so few days—so many emotions and tests of will.

She tapped Ti's arm.

"Look... I mean... listen." Her voice was barely a whisper.

"Hmm?" Ti mumbled, wiping the corner of his mouth.

"His breathing is softer... and slower," Jen said.

Mitch's loud wheezing diminished.

Once again, the two rushed to Mitch. They grabbed his hands. They stood side by side, their rapid heartbeats drumming a rhythm that seemed to grow louder and louder from fear, sadness, and wonder.

Another seizure?

More choking?

The female dog, Daisy, turned her back on the room and faced away from Mitch. The air was still.

"We love you!" they instinctively said at the same time.

"Don't worry about us. We promise to take care of each other."

"We want you to be at peace... and be happy..."

Mitch's breathing slowed further.

"It's okay," Ti said, with ceaseless tears that contained both utter sorrow and desire for his father to be well as he moved on to what was next. "We have each other. Go be with Mom now." Ti bravely encouraged Mitch's spirit to be free, as one releases a dove into the open sky. He understood his father's only desire for almost four decades was that his son be well taken care of to live a good, happy life. Mitch had achieved all of his dreams.

With closed eyelids, Mitch saw clearly. He saw his angel in a bright, white glow. Mandy's hair flowed over her shoulders; her eyes sparkled. She smiled, with outstretched arms that looked and felt inviting.

"It's time, my love." She spoke joyfully to the man she'd cherished all these years. He could feel her embrace drawing him from this life to the next. He was confident, content, and free of all physical ailments.

"We love you so much." Jen sobbed loudly.

Mitch grunted a reply and released his last bit of air. His breathing stopped. There were no lines of struggle on his thin face. They sat still, holding his hands as they wept. The sentiment lingered. "We love you so much!" And his groaned reply echoed in their ears.

Dear Mitch was on his way to heaven.

CHAPTER 33

After a few silent, still moments, Ti stood up. “We have to call people,” he said and began the process of his father’s physical exodus. Mitch’s spiritual departure had been the most amazing, emotional, devastating, horrific, treasured, transcendent moment either of them had ever witnessed.

With many decisions ahead of them, Ti and Jen felt unprepared. After succeeding in giving Mitch all they could in his last few days, they now stumbled, as if lost in a menacing cave filled with darkness. However, heaven sent a few angels to light the way. Family and friends called to offer support and assistance. Aunt Colleen stepped in the next morning to guide their meeting with the funeral director.

“Have you considered songs, prayers, or readings?” he asked.

“Do you have a list of readings they could take home and go over? That might help.” Colleen walked beside them as they entered the casket room.

“Good idea. We’ll want to consider what fits Mitch best,” Jen said.

“Yeah, that and my father was the quick decision maker in the family. Jen and I tend to mull things over before choosing anything,” Ti said.

“Yeah, that’s true. See, we need you already.” Jen assumed Mitch was watching, smiling, ready to tease them, even about this.

“Do you have clothes you’d like him dressed in?” the suited man asked.

“We’ll get something and bring it back,” Jen replied.

“We’re putting him in everyday jeans. That’d be more him,” Ti said.

Ti and Jen gave the entire process all their energies. They slept little. They cared for sick dogs. They struggled with grief, but somehow found a sliver of contentment through arranging the best, most meaningful final celebration of Mitch’s life possible.

They recalled the advice Mitch gave them often, starting with his toast at their wedding. "*Don't forget the simple things. Find beauty in normal events... bricks and sticks, kids. It's all in the bricks and sticks...*"

After meeting with the funeral director, they started considering parts of the service. Sentiment ruled as they selected every piece with care. They pondered prayers, readings, and music. They chose the songs Mitch had used at Mandy's funeral.

With Brock's help, Jen typed everything out, composing a wonderful memorial booklet. They designated participants to represent friends and family members who were significant in Mitch's life. Jen arranged printed photos on posters, creating a tangible testimony to the man and their many special memories of him.

Selecting the prayer card proved more of a challenge. The verses had Ti in tears no matter how many times he read them. After a day of consideration, Ti felt good about the verse chosen to represent his father. However, he debated the image for the other side. "Would Dad prefer his favorite saint, Francis? Or St. Anthony, who helped us find each other?"

"Do you think they can print some of both?" Jen asked, following Ti to the closet. She pulled forward the white shirt with maroon pinstripes. "How about this one?"

"Yeah, definitely. That was mom's favorite."

"Here's a nice pair of shoes." Jen held up a pair of brown shoes with dark ties. "Oh, wait, I didn't see this." She fingered a missing chunk in the heel of the right shoe.

"They are perfect." Ti chuckled. "As a puppy, Chip got a hold of these the day after my father got them. That's one of his more famous chews. Dad still wore them. His jeans covered the hole, but he showed it off most of the time anyway."

"He might like to have a dog memento with him," Jen said. "Actually, I'll ask my father to stop at the cottage. Maybe he can get the little photo album we made before Mitch's first surgery."

"Dad would like that," Ti said. "He brought that thing with him to every hospital stay since his illness began. It'd be nice for him to have it forever. He's probably already bragging about his dogs up there."

In his father's wallet, Ti found a prayer card that had belonged to his mother. He tucked it into Mitch's shirt pocket.

"I put a tattered piece of paper in his pocket. I want it close to his heart. Please be sure no one removes it," Ti told the undertaker, handing him the stack of clothes.

The whirlwind week of service preparations culminated in the most beautiful send-off they could have imagined. Healing through their efforts, they hosted two incredible celebrations of Mitch's life, one in the mountains and another in the suburbs. Both churches were full to the brim. A group of friends and priests traveled the distance to attend the funeral in Walleycito. A few days later, Mitch's memorial service in the suburbs boasted no fewer than twelve celebrants on the seemingly small altar.

The Bishop presided over both services. He bragged about his friend, attesting to Mitch's generosity, faith, and dedication. "Mitch valued the important aspects in life: God, family, and home. Home meant a lot to Mitch. He built houses for people to reside in and share their lives, which transformed the structure from a house to a home. Mitch also ensured that we were comfortable at the Good Shepherd Pastoral Center as if working with his extended family, making it a home away from home for all of us."

Everything the eulogists said echoed Mitch's special spirit. Colleen spoke of their growing up and offered stories about her one and only brother. Jen proudly read a meaningful Bible passage. One Monsignor spoke easily, praising his friend's character, integrity, and loyalty.

"Mitch treated us with care and kindness. In his paternal way, he nourished and raised us up. Like the center of an intricate spider web, he connected us together, into deeper relationships than we would otherwise have had. We relied on him to take care of our building and our people. We are fortunate, knowing Mitch will remain a part of us, as his legacy lives on through our memories." He nodded toward Ti. "God has provided for our community by leaving Little m to carry on, with the same love and dedication his father had." He prayed God would find a way to fill young Mitchell, Jennifer, and Nathaniel's void.

Exiting the church, Deirdre approached. "I know your father is at peace. He loved you... all of you, very much. I will miss him."

"Thanks Deirdre. I know how much you cared about Mitch." Ti smiled, understanding her sincerity.

Life would be different going forward, but they had much love and many wonderful memories to hold in their hearts.

Ti and Jen hugged every morning and every evening, clinging to each other as they carried on. Ti's first day back at work was hard, but serene in a mystical way. He unlocked doors, changed two light bulbs, and prepared a supply order. Sticking the legendary green and yellow screwdriver in his back pocket, he went to the cafeteria, where Ernesto asked him to taste the sauce. He attended a smaller breakfast club.

"Brad got a promotion at the electronics store," Betty said.

Easygoing conversation filled the room. They ate their bagels, noting the hollow cavity left in Mitch's chair but looking forward to sharing more stories as the hurt diminished.

Afterward, Ti got a cup of coffee with two creams and two sugars and went to Claire's desk. As she entered the big foyer, she tilted her head. Her face looked sad and confused.

Ti offered her the cup and reached for the key to unlock the top drawer that held her bracelets. A tear ran down her face as she held out her wrist. Ti hooked the clasp with a smile, and then walked down the hall.

"You, little m, complete your father's life and are a living testimony to all he was," she whispered under her breath.

Nate prepared for Confirmation, praying often to his favorite angel in heaven. "Mitch, I sure do miss you, but I'm gonna make you proud."

"Mitch misses you too, Nate. I'm glad Ti is here to sponsor you."

"Mommy, Mitch is my sponsor. No matter where he is and no matter what happens, he will always inspire my faith and guide me."

"That's right, Nate," his mother said, supporting his astounding conviction. *Huh, Mitch is already shepherding Nate.*

Mitch's grandson insisted, "I'm the luckiest kid at Confirmation."

"How's that?" Jen zipped up his robe.

"Because I'm the only kid with two sponsors: Mitch in heaven and Ti who will walk with me here." Nate kissed her cheek.

In awe, Jen's heart swelled with love for Mitch, Nate, and the Holy Spirit. *Thank God for Nurse Sandy who made sure Nate got some alone time with Mitch the last time they were together. That must have been some special talk.*

They went on—living, loving, appreciating. Whenever Nate was confused or upset, they would talk about the issue. Afterward Nate would refer to the problem as "spitting wood" and picture Mitch's polka-dot shins.

Often Jen would ask, "What do you think Mitch would do?"

The answers they presumed sometimes gave them strength and sometimes made them laugh, but always made them feel better.

Jen owned a new confidence that she could endure greater challenges. She spoke to Mitch often. She managed the family, dogs, and homes as carefully as he had. Jen felt Mitch in every sunset. She marveled at flowers, deer and eagles, and continued to appreciate her father-in-law in the nature around her. She remembered her old "triumph-philosophy," now influenced by the man she admired. *I can grow from this too. Mitch can still inspire me and fortify my faith. I miss him so much, but I will be strong and well again. I've got a family to take care of.*

Ti walked proudly in and out of the maintenance office. He cared for his building. He cared for his wife and family, his dogs, and his home. He saw his father in things he did—normal, simple things. He felt him in dreams and noticed him in signs, advertising slogans, and even in himself—during moments when he observed his own rugged hands or thinning hair. He found an even greater respect for the man who made him, and who he aspired to make proud, even from afar.

Jen's stomach flipped and flopped frequently. Lately though, it flopped more often. *Mitch, is that you? Did you send Ti and me a gift?*

A NOTE FROM THE AUTHOR

I truly hope you enjoyed this biographical novel. I pray the story of Mitch's life will inspire you in some small way, perhaps as you reflect on a loss you've experienced or a challenge in front of you.

Please consider posting a book review on www.Amazon.com. For an exclusive peek into Mitch's life, via private webpage, go to www.bricksandsticksnovel.com. On the contact page, fill out the form. You'll receive a personalized response and a password for access to photos mentioned in the story.

The publishing company has created a line of greeting cards, featuring mountain scenes from Mitch's favorite place, his pets, and pets within Mitch's extended family. Please visit www.FourPawPrintsPress.com for more information.

Thank you and God bless,
Lillian

Every day we purchase, gather, find, or experience bricks and sticks that build our lives. Each is a gift. Some come wrapped in pretty packages; others seem boring and plain, while some appear downright ugly. But each one—joyous, sorrowful, frustrating, frightening, glorious or challenging—helps us grow. Delight in the colorful packages. Don't pass up those plain ones. And realize the ones wrapped in old dirty newspapers still contain value. It's hard to see past the exterior. It hurts to go through adversity or loss. But if we dare, we might also find courage and understanding that may otherwise have stayed hidden. Perhaps we're reminded to cherish loved ones, have faith in our higher power, or believe in ourselves.